60 Going on 50

Other books by Ed Poole

Lessons from the Porch: A Gathering Place for Telling Our Stories, STEC Publishing, 2003.

Lessons from the Crossroads: Finding My Authentic Path, More Heart than Talent Publishing, 2007.

Ed Poole and Kathi (Robinson) Poole

Lessons from Empowering Leaders: Real Life Stories to Inspire Your Organization Toward Greater Success, Morgan James Publishing, 2009.

60 Going on 50

The Baby Boomers' Memory Book

ED AND KATHI POOLE

New York

60 Going on 50
The Baby Boomers' Memory Book

Cover Design by: Rachel Lopez
　　　　　　Rachel@r2cdesign.com

ISBN 978-1-60037-738-9

Library of Congress Control Number: 2009941946

Morgan James Publishing
1225 Franklin Ave., STE 325
Garden City, NY 11530-1693
Toll Free 800-485-4943
www.MorganJamesPublishing.com

To Jack...

The quality of a person's life is in direct proportion of their commitment to excellence, regardless of their field of endeavor.
Author Unknown

This book is dedicated to Jack Hinkle—The Story Guy, Number 82, The Toe, Mr. Automatic. "Why all these titles for this guy?" you may be asking. Well, Kathi and I figure the only way you'll answer your question is to read the book.

For those of us who know and care about Jack, he is the epitome of the above quote. Like most of us, Jack has been to the highest of peaks and the deepest of valleys, as you'll discover when you read his stories. When he felt excellence slipping away, Jack grabbed onto it, held it tightly, and defined it in terms of the current stop along his journey. One of the many reasons I have always admired Jack is because he accepts his life as he finds it at any given point in time.

There have been many times Jack could have chucked "excellence" out the nearest window, but he didn't. Jack is a survivor. Jack's stories are his and his alone. He shares his stories for two reasons: (1) He has the innate desire to remember and then record those events in his life that hold special meaning. (2) Jack remembers and records those events in order to share them with you. His ultimate dream is that by sharing his stories, you will be encouraged to do the same: remember and then record those points in your life that—above all else—you do not want to forget. Having said that, most of you will be able to identify with the stories Jack shares. His peaks won't be yours, nor will his valleys. However, you'll find **much** of yourself in Jack's life. You'll laugh and you'll cry. But, after all, doesn't the combination of those two extreme emotions define a good story?

Jack and I were classmates in the 1960 graduating class from Columbus (Indiana) High School. As is often the case, Jack and I lost touch for forty-nine years—from the day after we graduated until just recently.

In September, 2008, Jack took it upon himself to track down the email addresses of twenty friends and classmates from 1960, some who were members of the 1959 Columbus High School football Bull Dogs. Our senior year, the Bull Dogs had the second undefeated season (10-0) in the history of the school, which dates back to the late 1800's. As the years have passed by, this team has realized what a feat that was and the accomplishment has made a dramatic handprint on all who were there to participate and observe.

Had it not been for Jack's initiative, our group very likely would never have come together in the fall of 2008, and this book you're reading would never have been written. Jack put his creative mind to work and suggested the main title for our book, *60 Going on 50*. The story of that "technology reunion" beginning in September, 2008, is described in the book. On August 21, 2009, that 1950 undefeated football team was recognized at halftime of the high school game, which took place on the same field the "Dogs" played on during that unforgettable season. For three or four months Jack worked hard and almost daily, communicating with the athletic department at what is now Columbus North High School, to take the dream of a fifty-year reunion of the team and turn that dream into a reality. Again, without Jack's initiative and tenacity, the 50th Reunion may have remained only a dream. Jack Hinkle is a very special human being. After reading the book, we are certain, without a doubt, you will agree with us and see why Kathi and I have dedicated our book to him.

Thank you, Jack, from all of us for bringing and keeping us together during a time of memories, stories—funny and sad—and a shared joy in our all having spent time together in a great community and a wonderful high school. The Columbus Crew shall always be grateful for all you've done to encourage us and provide us one more glimpse of a very special time in our lives. And finally, thank you for getting us ready for a wonderful fiftieth class reunion on June 19, 2010.

**Jack in March, 2009. The van behind him was dramatically adapted
to meet Jack's requirements for hospital and doctors' visits.**

...With Gratitude...

Kathi and I sincerely want to thank The Columbus Crew for providing us the opportunity of working together on what has been the most enjoyable writing experience we've ever had—and there have been several. Thank you: George Abel, Jim Battin, Cal Brand, Jeff Crump, Dan FitzGibbon, Steve Everroad, Jack Hinkle, Skip Lindeman, Larry Long, Rob Schafstall, Charlie Schuette, Jay Shumaker, Bill Spicer, Dave Steenbarger, and Tom Taylor.

In September, 2008, *60 Going on 50* wasn't even a dream. The dream began with Kathi and me, was then shared by The Columbus Crew, and finally became the reality you are reading today. It took a bit of courage for my 1960 high school classmates to first of all share their stories with Kathi and me, and then—WHOA!—to have them appear in this book. To the person, every contributor supported this project from the get- go and did whatever Kathi and I asked of them in terms of meeting the deadlines of Morgan James Publishing.

What a joy it has been for all of us to reconnect, share our stories, and discover the journeys we've been on, taking us from where and who we were to who we're still becoming along this wonderful trip called life. All of us know for certain you have had many similar experiences in your own life. Aren't those experiences such gifts?

Thanks again, guys. As we would say in southern Indiana, "Ya dun good!"

Ed and Kathi Poole
October 1, 2009
Boone, North Carolina

Contents

Chapter 1   Introduction

And even if you were in some prison, the walls of which let none of the
sounds of the world come to your senses—would you not still have
your childhood, that precious, kingly possession,
that treasure-house of memories?

Ranier Marie Rilke

People enjoy stories that rekindle memories of their early years.

Ed Poole

Sometimes our light goes out but is blown again into flame by an
encounter with another human being. Each of us owes the deepest
thanks to those who have rekindled the inner light.

Albert Schweitzer

Has your inner light been rekindled from time to time as you've reconnected with high school friends? Do you find your own treasure house of childhood memories returning from time to time—especially as you get a bit older? Do you ever think about your years growing up—your hometown, your friends, your family, your cuts and bruises, the day you learned to ride a two-wheeler with no one holding onto the seat? Do you remember your first car? What were the top ten songs during your teenage years? What was happening in your hometown, the nation, and the world? Do you remember your high school experiences—senior prom, first girlfriend or boyfriend, first job, the times you got into trouble and (sometimes) found ways to get out of those tough (but probably normal) high school experiences?

Kathi and I know the answer to all these questions is **yes**. The new friends you are about to meet as you read *60 Going on 50* will help those memories resurface. We make this statement with ultimate certainty because of a thought we began sharing five years ago: **The story of any one of us is, in part, the story of all of us.**

In 2005, there were approximately seventy-three million Baby Boomers. Every day over eight thousand individuals celebrate their sixtieth birthday. Imagine how many Baby Boomers would like to rekindle the memories of their early years, high school experiences, and the paths chosen after graduating from high school. Wouldn't you value a way to help you recall these, and other, memories?

60 Going on 50 is a book of stories about growing up in the '40s, '50s, and '60s. The Columbus Crew (as I've come to call them) share their stories about growing up in Columbus, Indiana—stories of their youth, athletic and academic experiences, as well as the stories about their post-high school years.

The stories in this book are about sixteen **men**—stories of the memories we created throughout our high school years and stories of the separate roads we have traveled since May, 1960. **"Men"** is the operative word here. After all, "macho guys" aren't supposed to share our feelings and emotions. We're "fixers" not "feelers." We know how to solve problems and "get things done." How many men, especially from the Baby Boomer era, will openly share the emotional—joyful and hurtful—stories of their lives? Some men are transparent with their thoughts and feelings; however the stories they share are often reserved for a small group of drinking buddies down at the neighborhood pub, where "we've been gathering for, gosh, I can't remember how many years."

Remembering the stories along our journey is impossible without also recalling the many transitions and changes we've experienced. In her book *Broken Open*, author Elizabeth Lesser wrote, "I marvel at what we all do in times of transition—how we resist, and how we surrender; how we stay stuck, and how we grow…But perhaps the most profound of the tools we have at our disposal is the simple act of telling our stories to other human travelers—in circles around the fire, at the back fence with a neighbor, or at a kitchen table with family and friends." Lesser states, "When I am on a bad stretch of the journey, I am comforted most by the stories of other travelers who have made it past the bumps and potholes…"

In my book *Lessons from the Porch: A Gathering Place for Telling our Stories*, I wrote about both storytelling and the transitions in my life. Transmitting our oral traditions was an important part of our culture until technology brought onto the scene TV, computers, cell phones, and other examples that often have replaced those times we shared stories around our campfires.

For thousands of years, our culture was shaped by storytelling. We had no other way to ensure that younger generations would learn about the traditions of our family and our country. We did not have those technological luxuries that became available to us in the latter part of the 20th Century. Many Baby Boomers can remember friends and relatives gathering on your front porch or in your homes sharing stories about their lives. We laughed, cried, played, and worked. Being together with our families and friends and sharing our experiences with them was important.

You may be wondering, "Why is storytelling **the** approach to use in helping us remember our past?" We're glad you asked. There are several reasons. When we tell about our lives, we give shape to the events we've lived. The events take on a pattern and new dimensions of meaning. Experiences change in the telling. Telling stories is an act of healing—the beginning of all forms of change in our lives. A story stands at the core of our being, and more than any other form of discourse, speaks to our hearts. Telling about our life allows us to have feelings we may not have had, or didn't know we had, at the time the event occurred. Our entire life overflows with stories. Each life is unique; therefore, each story is a one-of-a-kind story—a story no one ever lived before and no one will ever live again. If we don't share our unique stories, the world will never know how we lived our life—with all its blessings and struggles.

The experiences and stories of The Columbus Crew are not unlike the experiences of almost all members of our generation, from Anytown, U.S.A. Remember what we shared earlier, "The story of any one of us is, in part, the story of all of us." One of our ultimate goals is that **our** stories will enable **you** to make connections and recall **your** stories.

While entertaining and insightful in and of themselves, the stories shared by The Columbus Crew will help you begin remembering your own experiences during this era. We are all shaped by our environment. Often we forget what influenced us and led us on our journey to where we are today. The stories in *60 Going on 50* will jar those memories.

Both triumphs and struggles will be shared. Life hasn't been a bowl of cherries for any member of The Columbus Crew. Personally, I've had many (what I've come to call) wilderness journeys. When I've been smack dab in the wilderness, frantically searching for an oasis in the middle of the desert, I often wonder how I got there and how I'm going to find my way to the other side. After several of those experiences, I realized one of two outcomes will result from my wilderness times: I'll either survive, or I'll perish. I am a survivor. Each member of The Columbus Crew is a survivor, as is each of you.

At the end of several chapters you'll find questions, memory prompts and blank pages. If you **really** want to bring to the surface your own memories, take a few minutes and jot down your own thoughts. You'll be glad you did. Sure, it will take a little time, but the pay-offs are well worth the time.

Now, hop into your '57 Chevy ragtop and take a ride down memory lane with The Columbus Crew.

Chapter 2   Well, Here's How This all Got Started

The following story about "friends" captures my thoughts about The Columbus Crew. Without a doubt this crew has returned for a lifetime, for which I am very grateful.

Friends
Friends come into our lives for a Reason, a Season, or a Lifetime.
When we know which one it is for a friend, we will know what to do
for that person.

When someone is in our lives for a <u>REASON</u>, it is usually to meet
a need we have expressed. They have come to assist us through
difficulty, to provide us with guidance and support, to aid us
physically, emotionally, and/or spiritually. They seem like a
Godsend, and they are! They are there for the reasons you need them to be.

Then, without any wrongdoing on our part, or at an inconvenient time,
we or our friend will say or do something to bring the relationship to an
end. Sometimes he or she dies. Sometimes he or she just walks away.
Sometimes the friend, or we, act up and force us to take a stand.

What we must realize is that our need has been met, our desire fulfilled,
and our friend's work is done. The prayer we sent up has been answered,
and now it is time to move on.

Some friends come into our lives for a <u>SEASON</u>, because our turn has come
to share, grow, or learn. They bring us an experience of peace, or make us laugh. They may
teach us something we have never known or done. They
usually give us an unbelievable amount of joy. Believe it! It is real!
But, only for a season.

<u>LIFETIME</u> relationships teach us lifetime lessons: things we must build
upon in order to have a solid emotional foundation. Our job is to accept
the lesson, love the friend, and put what we have learned to use in all
other relationships and areas of our lives. It is said that love is blind
but friendship is clairvoyant.

Anonymous

Thank you, Columbus Crew, for being friends for a lifetime!

Along with 432 other individuals, I graduated from Columbus High School in May, 19**60**. On June 19, 2010, our class will be celebrating our **50**th high school reunion, hence the title of this book, *60 Going on 50*.

Jack Hinkle was able to track down twenty of our high school classmates. On November 20, 2008, the inbox on my email account saw a flurry of activity.

The first message I read (going to everyone on The Columbus Crew email list) was from classmate Cal Brand. Cal wrote, "I just sent Ed an email inviting him in, but didn't send Jack's address. I used "thelessonguy" link provided by Tom. I hope it works. Ed and I shared a room our first year at Hanover College. Hope we hear from him."

Jack wrote:, "Ed, I have a group of former classmates wondering where you are and what you're doing. Give us a shout when you get a minute. We are talking memories and stuff."

Later that day, I heard from Jack again. "Ed, I started this email group and now, including you, there are twenty of us. I first thought to get football guys and then it got to all friends. Basically, we started rolling along with the upcoming election and now we're just doing some remembering… Our biggest topic was the 25th Street versus Wilson basketball game back in 1956. Jeff Crump says Clifty beat both Wilson and 25th Street. We're still looking for proof. Welcome aboard."

Larry Bray, my friend, classmate, and next door neighbor for our first thirteen years wrote, "A bunch of guys from the class of '60 have been sharing memories with emails, and it is fun hearing from everyone. I think you might enjoy it as well. The current topic is who won the 8th grade basketball tournament in 1956. Jack, Dan, Jay, and I remember it as a close game won by Wilson. Jeff says Clifty won."

Many of those early emails were about our eighth grade basketball teams—Wilson, 25th Street, and Clifty. By the way, I played for Wilson, and we **did** win the tournament. Remember, we're talking about southern Indiana, where every baby is born with a basketball in his or her crib. During the first week of life, southern Indiana babies learn how to dribble the basketball. The second week finds those babies learning the art and skill of making crisp, clean passes. Upon reaching their third week, they begin taking shots at the hoops, and in the fourth week of life, the babies actually begin to **make** some of those shots. Okay, okay, okay—I may be a week or two off one way or the other, but not by much.

That very evening, I crafted my first email to The Columbus Crew, filling them in a bit on the life and times of Ed Poole. "WOW!!! Am I ever glad you found me. I cannot tell you how your notes have made my day. I don't think the day will get much better, so I may just go to bed after I write this.☺ You have no idea how many times I replay in my mind the tapes of our high school years and reflect on all of you. As is often the case in my life, I don't recognize blessings until sometime on down the road. Each of you was a true blessing in my life. I thank you for that…I so hope you all will get in touch and catch me up. I still miss Columbus and count my high school years as some of the best I've had."

The memories of my earlier years came flooding back. As they did so, I remembered a story Richard Bode told in his book *First You Have to Learn to Row a Little Boat*. Bode wrote about moving to California from New York as an adult. He arranged a luncheon meeting with a boyhood friend from Long Island, someone he hadn't seen in years. At this luncheon, Bode shared about their years growing up on Long Island. Bode talked about what he remembered and what he missed and how, as a man, he had come to terms with what losses he had suffered as a boy. His friend was surprised that Bode was "still struggling" with events that happened so long ago. In answering his friend, Bode said he wasn't struggling but "savoring" what he was remembering about his childhood. He said, "The desire to forget the past is a form of suicide…What should truly frighten us is the possibility that we might lose the power to recall the life we have lived, which gives us our connection to ourselves." The Columbus Crew didn't realize it at the time, but *60 Going on 50* is our way of savoring our memories so we can maintain our connection to ourselves, and now with you.

Over the next few days, the emails came fast and furious, like an out-of-control wildfire spreading through a dry, brown forest. Once the memories started surfacing, nothing could stop the emails. There wasn't a topic left unturned. Talk about a trip down memory lane! The names and places will be different for you, but we bet as you read snippets of what the guys wrote in some of those early emails, similar memories of your earlier years will begin to surface.

"Did I read a reply by Jeff Crump that he thought Clifty won this tournament? I think Wilson played 25th Street in the final game. Clifty won the consolation game."

"I'll stick to my story, at least until I see some proof that I am wrong. My recollection is that our eighth grade year, Wilson and 25th Street beat us in an early (city?) tourney and quite possibly Wilson beat us in the regular season game. But by the end-of-season county tourney, we ended up winning it…(Remember, Eddie Poole was six feet tall in the seventh grade and dominated the basketball court until later in the eighth grade year when we caught up with him?)"

"Steve the class clown was a trip even when we were stationed together at Myrtle Beach AFB, SC for a couple of years."

"Speaking of rides…can't remember if it was Jay or Bob that was driving when we had a wreck in Greenwood on Hwy. 31. Rear-ended someone…thank god we were all semi-sober at the time…which was amazing…huh guys?"

"Yeah, I had Mrs. Ayers at the old barracks 25th Street School, too. Two things I remember the most about her is that she would read to us *The Bears of Blue River* and when the Pink Eye was going around, she put hand soap all over the door knob…Weird what we remember sometimes…"

"Eddie, I recently posted that back in the day you were the best junior high trumpet player in the county. Was that right or have I gotten confused over the years?"

"I think you have some facts slightly incorrect concerning Lake Lemon. You had way too many beers. Janice and I drove you back to Columbus, as you were sound asleep in the back seat."

"Came back home to cold and snow showers which reminded me of the many wonderful days ice skating on The Lagoons. Back then there were a lot of open lots so we had easy access…Someone often made a fire in an old oil barrel and we would get great gangs together for hockey. If we didn't have a proper puck, I recall using an empty can that would end up being pounded into a fairly dangerous metal pellet…I also recall a car load of upperclassmen testing the ice at the canal and all going through…And there was the great slope down from Washington Street in the south Lagoon where we shot down on our sleds and flew out over the ice. Great Fun! But BRRRRR!"

"Larry and I were known to break the ice on Flatrock River and scuba dive under it."

"Yes we still owe for the cigarettes, many of them."

"I bought my first pack in the 9th grade for 18¢. They were a quarter in the machines but some of the cheap stores had them for less."

"My mom still laughs at least once every six months with the story of watching you painting our cottage on Driftwood River. She pulled in and you tossed your cigarette to the ground with a sly smile and a nod."

"I remember learning to do the twist over Christmas break in some of our 'basement parties'."

"Richard and Larry were my next-door neighbors for thirteen years there on Gladstone Ave. We played together every day. Our dads were both volunteer firemen with the East Columbus Volunteer Fire Department. Their dad owned an appliance store on State Street and we bought our first TV from him. I remember the day so well. It was a Saturday and I was so happy because I could watch the Indiana University basketball game AT HOME that night."

"Here we are fifty years later…which high school teacher had the most impact on your life and why? I will start out…Webb Solomon…rougher than nails and how we need him now! He had piercing eyes and a stature that demanded excellence! He saw something in *Lord Jim* that I still haven't seen???"

"My favorite class was Mr. (coach) Stearman's because he called everyone Mister or Miss and Patricia Robinson sat behind me and we talked a lot."

"WOW!!! So nice to see your name again. I remember a few good times when you played with the illustrious Modernaires—our little dance band. In fact, I've got a picture of the band and you're in it."

"One of the smartest things my parents did for me and all three brothers was making us take piano lessons…What a rich part of life music is."

"I do remember the third grade when I followed Mary Jane home from McKinley and treed her up a slide on the playground at Donner Park with a demand for a kiss to let her down. She was a lady and refused. I had a moment of remorse and let her down without my tribute. I was embarrassed when around her ever after, until our 40th reunion when I learned that she had no recollection at all of the event."

"And I thought slipping out of church downtown on Sunday nights to go see a movie at the Crump Theater was an adventure."

"I wasn't a trouble maker kid, just a kid that enjoyed life and had a lot of great friends. The word party…well where is it and I am there."

"Those were the good old days, as you say. We did not need any TV's or computers to entertain ourselves. We were free to roam around a pretty wide area without much adult supervision or protection. Life was much slower then…"

"I remember the '57 Olds Holiday. My dad was so proud to have paid $5,000 for it."

"We got together over at George's house many afternoons to shoot basketball in his driveway. His mother usually had some kind of snack and I remember a lot of fuss being made about the Vernor's Ginger Ale they brought down from Canada."

"I remember that when I was in the barbershop, it was an unwritten rule that if an athlete came in to get a haircut, the rest of us gave up our spot in line to the athlete, especially if he was a basketball player."

"My first job was delivering papers for the old *Indianapolis News*. Afternoon delivery everyday but Sunday. Sunday delivery was early in the morning. I remember the manager would come back to my bedroom window and shine a light until I was out of bed."

"Hot dogs were 15¢ and I had to learn multiples of fifteen up to fifteen before I could get hired. Mugs were 5¢ and 10¢."

"Patrol boys got in the skating rink free on Friday nights, and we got into basketball and football games for free too."

"Do you remember how the river behind your house would freeze? It seems impossible today, but we did skate on that river."

"One day Mr. Elliott was out of the room. I left my seat to go sharpen the pencil at Mr. Elliott's desk. Norman had his legs blocking the aisle. I asked him nicely twice to move his legs. The third time I proceeded with force. Guess who walked in? Mr. Elliott had an arm grabbing technique that stopped circulation. He proceeded to assist me into the hall. He released me out there and my head hit the wall with a loud clunk…You will all probably believe me that when I went home that day and told mom, she said I probably deserved it. End of story."

"I think all of us were scared to death of him…I know I was. I can also remember being spanked by Mr. Reese with the paddle that had holes in it. Man that hurt. Maybe all of those times made us better people…that can be debated forever I guess."

"I don't know if you McKinley guys remember but I was the assistant recess bell ringer due to the several recesses I had to stay in the room. I also may have held the record for trips to the principal's office for a BOARDMEETING."

"Yes, I threw snowballs also…and got whacked for that too. Think I hit one of the teachers."

"I remember getting called to Mr. Reese's office once with a warning not to pull Mara's pigtails anymore."

"You were so funny. You had a hand-carved wooden gun that you hid in your desk, and when the teacher's back was turned, you'd bring that out and pretend to shoot it in the air! We'd laugh, the teacher would turn around, and you'd put the piece of wood back in your desk, all the while maintaining a straight face. You were hilarious!"

"Ms. Fiegel was my English teacher and she walked with a sway in her get-along that I would mimic behind her back until I got caught, not a good experience."

"What is very interesting are the career paths everyone has taken after graduating from CHS. We've got lawyers, preachers, engineers, managers, presidents and vice presidents of companies, union leaders, arbitrators, and many other professions. It has been a trip for all of us and a great life in this wonderful land of America. So it took Jack to get us all talking, forty-nine years after departing the Maple Street Gym for the last time. Hats off to Jack!"

Ed to Jack, "I know there is a reason you brought us all back together, and I know we all will forever be grateful to you for that. I don't yet know all the reasons, and perhaps never will, but I feel something special is going on here, and my belief system says it's all part of what God wants us to be doing right now."

Being authors, a light went on early that December for Kathi and me. We realized the stories The Columbus Crew were sharing were not much different than the stories that could be shared by anyone who graduated from high school in the late '50s, early '60s. Remember, **the story of any one of us is, in part, the story of all of us.** So, on December 4, 2008, I sent an email to the guys.

"Hey to The Columbus Crew… I want to share a quote with you. 'What you need to know about the past is that no matter what has happened, it has all worked together to bring you to this very moment. And this is the moment you can choose to make everything new. Right now.' (Author unknown) I've mentioned before how very much I'm enjoying all the wonderful memories and stories from our years growing up in Columbus. All this got me to doing a 'one person brainstorm'…I happen to think we all grew up in a very special time, one that I've reflected back on a lot, especially now with this group reconnecting. So what about pulling together some wonderful stories and putting them into a book? That's right, I said a book!!!

"I do think there are lots of wonderful stories to share; however, I now believe there is much more to the story, and my thoughts take us beyond 1960. Some ideas:

- All of us got a good grounding from both our common community and Columbus High School.

- After May, 1960, we all made decisions to follow different, wonderfully diverse paths. Why did we choose the particular path we walked after high school? Some have stayed on that initial path. Why did you keep moving down the same road? Others have found different paths that brought more meaning to their lives. Why did you decide to take a turn in the road? What lessons have you learned from the decisions we made that have helped shape who we are today?

"I now realize that our time in Columbus and CHS is only the beginning of our stories. You all have such rich stories to tell. I've been thinking about the fact that the group is all male, and I think that's a benefit. 'Macho Guys' are most always less willing to share their ups and downs, feelings and emotions, about their lives.

"Having shared this idea with some of The Columbus Crew, several of you have said, 'Let's do it.' I'm grateful for those responses. You need to know, I absolutely love collecting stories, organizing them, showing the connections, and putting them in book format. So, that's my story and I'm stickin' to it."

As the days went by, sixteen of the original group of twenty decided to join together in this adventure. We hope the stories we share—about growing up in Columbus, Indiana, in the '40s and '50s, about our high school and college years, about where we ended up and how and why we got there—will help you start your own journey down memory lane. Who knows, maybe our stories will encourage you to rekindle those friendships from long ago.

Let me give you a brief introduction to The Columbus Crew from the *Log*, our high school yearbook (1960). The activities we were involved in during our high school years were listed alongside our senior pictures, no doubt just as in your high school yearbook. A more complete description of the crew is in the Appendix.

Abel, George: College Preparatory; Football, 4; Baseball, 2,3; Intramurals, 1,2,3,4; Chess Club, 2, 3, 4; Track, 1,4.

Battin, James: College Preparatory; *Triangle* Staff Editor 4; Golf Team, 3,4; Recreation Club, 2,3,4; Quill and Scroll, 4; Intramurals, 4.

Brand, Calvert: College Preparatory; Debate Team, 4; Senior Dramatics, 4; Concert Choir, 2,3,4; Golf, 2,3,4; Junior Achievement, 3,4.

Crump, Jeff: College Preparatory; Sports; C Club, 4; *Log* Staff, 3,4; Chess Club, 4; Projectionist.

Everroad, Stephen: Academic; Hi-Y C, 2,3,4; Football, 2,3,4; Basketball, 2,3; Junior Red Cross Council, 3,4; Class Vice President, 4.

FitzGibbon, Daniel: College Preparatory; Football, 3,4; Baseball, 2,3,4; Hi-Y A, 2,3,4; National Honor Society, 3,4; Student Council, 3.

Hinkle, Jack: College Preparatory; Football, 2,3,4; Baseball, 3,4; Hi-Y A, 2,3,4; Sophomore Class President; C Club, 2,3,4; Boys' Chorus.

Lindeman, Clifford: College Preparatory; Senior Class President; Baseball, 2,3,4; Football, 2,3,4; National Honor Society, 3,4.

Long, Larry: College Preparatory; Football, 2,3,4; Track, 2,3,4; Student Council, 3; Hi-Y B, 2,3,4; Junior Prom Court.

Poole, Edward: College Preparatory; Junior Class Vice President; Basketball, 2; Hi-Y B, 2,3,4; National Honor Society, 3,4; Concert Choir, 2,3,4; Senior Dramatics.

Schafstall, Robert: Academic Course; Hi-Y, 2,3,4; *Triangle* Sports Editor, 2,3; Student Assembly, 3; Concert Choir, 4; Intramurals, 2,3,4.

Schuette, Charles: College Preparatory; Swimming, 2,3,4; Student Council, 3; Cheerleader, 2,3; Hi-Y B, 2,3,4; Student Assembly, 3.

Shumaker, Jay: College Preparatory; Basketball, 2,3,4; Baseball, 2,4; Concert Choir, 3,4; C Club, 3,4; Hi-Y B, 2,3,4.

Spicer, William: College Preparatory; Varsity Football, 3,4; Varsity Basketball, 3; C Club, 3; Drama Workshop, 3,4; Entered from Shortridge High School.

Steenbarger, David: College Preparatory; Hi-Y A, 2,3,4; Baseball, 2,3,4; *Triangle* Staff, 4; Drama Workshop, 3; Intramurals, 3,4.

Taylor, Thomas: College Preparatory; Band, 2,3,4; *Log* Staff, 3; Astronomy Club, 3; Chess Club, 3,4.

Are you remembering some of your long-forgotten high school classmates? Do you wonder whatever happened to some of them?

"I saw Eddie Poole listed for Wilson. He was a good trumpet player but didn't have time to work band into his rather full high school schedule. I wonder where he ended up." (Tommy Taylor)

Chapter 3   Columbus, Indiana: A Great Place to Grow Up

Everyone has memories and stories about the place they grew up. Since you'll be reading stories from The Columbus Crew, let me tell you a little bit about the town we called home.

Columbus, Indiana, was organized in 1820 by John Tipton. The first lots were sold in 1821. At that time, the population consisted of the families living in three or four cabins. In 1830, Bartholomew County—of which Columbus is the county seat—had 5,480 settlers. Columbus is located forty miles south of Indianapolis. Today the population of Columbus is around 40,000 and the county population is approximately 70,000.

In 1994, Columbus was one of ten cities in the United States awarded "All American City" status. According to a February, 2002, Biz Demographics ranking of 496 small cities in the United States, Columbus ranked thirtieth. In a 1997 article, "Life in America's Small Cities," Kevin Heubush ranked Columbus the 8th best small city in the United States in which to live.

Columbus had a wide range of activities and programs for its inhabitants. Back in the '50s there were parks and playgrounds operated by the city. In fact, one of those playgrounds was right across the street from where I grew up. Each playground had a supervisor, paid by the city. Many of those supervisors were college students, home for summer break.

Almost every day, I could find a group of friends at the playground across the street. We'd get a game of basketball going. I also enjoyed playing tetherball. For the younger kids, there were swings and slides. When I got thirsty, I walked next door to one of the city's fire departments and bought a coke out of their machine, for a nickel.

Donner Park was huge! It had a wonderful swimming pool, countless slides and swings, two basketball courts, and a big shelter house. Many families had their reunions in the shelter house. I remember getting up early on the Sunday of the Jolly reunion (my maternal grandmother's family), going to Donner Park with Dad, and reserving a bunch of long picnic tables for the reunion. We always had wonderful, homemade food. There was a shuffleboard close by, and we enjoyed pushing the pucks up and down the shuffleboard lanes. Several summer evenings each year, the shelter house played host to a wonderful variety of entertainers.

Columbus was surrounded by farmland where wheat, hay, corn, and beans grew in acre upon acre of rich, southern Indiana black dirt. In the '40s and '50s Columbus matched, or even exceeded, the percentage of the United States population who made their living in agriculture. My cousin had a big farm about fifty miles away. I loved to go there and ride his horses. One year my family visited at harvest time. What a noon feed we all had!

Columbus had a little league baseball program, in which I participated for several years. I rotated between playing first base and pitching. I'm a lefty, but in those days mitts weren't available for left-handed baseball players. I learned to field the ball with my left hand and throw right-handed. My side-arm pitches always threw the batters for a loop and had them scurrying back away from the plate. Many young boys, including me, spent many Saturdays at the local Boys Club. The club had a wonderful indoor gymnasium. There was always a basketball game in progress, and I especially liked joining in those games.

Columbus was a quiet place to grow up in the '40s and '50s, much like your hometown. We all knew our neighbors and often came together on someone's front porch in the evenings to share stories about our day. By and large, people were very friendly and parents looked out for each other's kids. No one worried too much about where their kids were.

Going to the Bartholomew County Fair was the highlight of every summer. There were several events that involved judging food—pies, cakes, bread, jams, and jellies. There was also a racetrack at the fairgrounds, where my family enjoyed watching the harness racing. My Uncle Warren and his family most often came from Indianapolis to enjoy the racing with us.

I remember a variety store right across the street from my elementary school. I would usually park my bike in front of the store after school, go in, and get some penny candy.

A special event each fall was "Pioneer Days." The activities were held in downtown Columbus. Streets were blocked off for three days. There was a wide variety of booths, where people sold food—much of which had been grown on their farms, knick-knacks, pictures, dried flowers, and wood carvings. The rides added to the carnival-like atmosphere.

Downtown Columbus was home to three movie theaters, within four blocks of each other—the Crump, Mode, and Rio. Each theater had only one movie screen. They all had a big stage, often used for concerts and plays. Prior to the movie, we saw some of the world news on "News of the Day," a cartoon—such as Tom and Jerry or Sylvester and Tweetie, and finally the main feature.

Mom sold tickets at all three theaters when I was young. Because she worked there, I always got in free, and my popcorn was free too. Some of your favorite '50s movies may be the same as mine—"Cinderella," "An American in Paris," "A Streetcar Named Desire," "High Noon," "Old Yeller," "The King and I," "Around the World in 80 Days," "Ben Hur," and the list goes on and on.

The three largest manufacturing companies in town were Arvin Industries, Hamilton Cosco, and Cummins Engine Company—the largest employer in town. Arvin's manufactured heaters and casual furniture. Cosco manufactured baby furniture, stools, and other small household items. Cummins manufactured diesel engines. In fact, the rockets that powered John Glenn into space were Cummins' diesel engines. All three companies still exist today.

Columbus was a small town; however even during the time I was growing up there, the impact of this small town was already felt around the country and world.

In 1950, *Life Magazine* sent a team of photographers to Columbus. For eight days they photographed our town—an average, Midwest community. After coming from New York and spending eight days in Columbus, the article was never published in the magazine. Fortunately, the pictures were archived.

©Time/Life, Inc. Washington Street in the heart of downtown
Columbus, showing a typical, bustling winter day.

A Little Story about a <u>Very</u> Big Man

On August 19, 2004, J. Irwin Miller died at the age of 96. Right about now you're asking yourself, "So---who is this J. Irwin Miller and why is he so important?" Well, it just so happens Kathi and I have the answer to both questions.

Mr. Miller was born in Columbus on May 26, 1909. He graduated from Yale University in 1931. From 1931 to 1933, Mr. Miller studied philosophy, politics, and economics at Balliol College at Oxford. In 1934, he joined the family business, Cummins Engine Company. He was executive vice-president of the company from 1944-1947, president from 1947-1951, and chairman from 1951-1977.

In 1950, Mr. Miller helped establish the National Council of Churches and later served as the council's first lay president. He met with Presidents Kennedy and Johnson to push for the legislation that became the Civil Rights Act of 1964. Mr. Miller's friends around the world were both the common and the elite. His personal friends included Queen Elizabeth and Prince Phillip. Later in the book, you'll read a humorous story Larry Long tells about one of the times Mr. Miller and his wife Xenia visited England. You may still be saying, "Okay. That's fine, but I can make similar statements about people I've known over the years. I still don't know what makes this Mr. Miller so special." Just hold on, I'm getting to that part.

J. Irwin Miller was one of the biggest benefactors and philanthropists any city of **any** size could have known—most especially a small Midwestern town in the '50s and '60s with a population of around 25,000. He left a wonderful legacy to the city of Columbus, a legacy that will be ever-present for all citizens and visitors. In 1954, Mr. Miller established the Cummins Foundation. One function of the Foundation was to award college scholarships to children of employees who met the requirements. On a personal note, Dad worked at Cummins, I met the requirements and was awarded a Cummins Foundation scholarship for each of my four years of undergraduate education. Many other Columbus residents can say the same.

The Cummins Foundation maintains a list of the eight to ten exceptional architects in the world. The list is periodically updated. In 1957, Mr. Miller made an offer to the city. He said the Foundation would pay all architect fees for new public buildings in Columbus, if the organization would select their architect from the current list the Foundation maintained—a savings of millions of dollars for those organizations. Our hometown currently has over sixty buildings constructed with the assistance of the Cummins Foundation. The world-renowned architects for these buildings include Eero Saarinen, Eliel Saarinen, I.M. Pei, Kevin Roche, Richard Meier, Harry Weese, Cesar Pelli, John Dinkeloo, Gunnar Birkerts, Ronaldo Guirgola, Norman Fletcher, Dan Kiley, Robert Venturi, Kenneth Carruthers, John Carl Warnecke, Alexander Girard, and Skidmore, Owings, and Merrill. The buildings erected include schools, churches, various government buildings, the public library, the post office, and others.

Columbus is world-renowned as an architectural Mecca—having been given the title "Athens of the Prairie." The community is ranked sixth in the United States by the American Institute of Architects. The top five cities are Chicago, New York, San Francisco, Boston, and Washington, D.C. Paul Goldbergeer, the *New York Times* architect critic wrote, "As a group of buildings by distinguished architects go, there is no place in the United States like Columbus, Indiana."

Six of the buildings designed by internationally known architects and built between 1942 and 1965 are National Historic Landmarks. The other sixty buildings affirm Columbus' reputation as a showcase of modern architecture. Thus, Mr. Miller left a lasting legacy for Columbus, to be enjoyed by many generations to come.

Jeff Crump
Changes in Columbus Over the Last Forty Years

Jeff: I returned to Columbus and have been practicing law here since 1970.

Ed: What are some of the changes you've seen in Columbus over the last forty years?

Jeff: The downtown has changed a lot. If you look at those pictures from *Life* magazine and look at the downtown now, there have been a lot of changes. A lot of the old buildings are still there, but many are gone. Interestingly, when Jerry Angermeier and I went into practice, we were up in the First National Bank Building. I could look down and watch them build the Commons Mall.

Ed: Is that the one that was on Fourth and Washington?

Jeff: Yeah, on the corner there.

Ed: What's at the mall now?

Jeff: They tore part of the Commons down. It was interesting. For a while I was on the Downtown Council. The council did a study and the lady in charge of the study publicly asked, "What is that down there, Darth Vader's castle?" It was ugly. The mall was brown and orange, which was the vogue when it was built. I thought it was ugly then and I still feel that way. A hotel is being built where the mall was. It's going to serve Cummins' offices, which are right there. Cummins is erecting a five hundred person building on that block. Then, the Commons is supposed to be rebuilt.

Ed: When I was living in Columbus, in the late sixties and then again in the mid-to-late seventies, the Commons was thriving. There were so many great stores in there. As I'd go back and visit Columbus from time to time, and go to the Commons, I realized it was losing its stores. Sears must have kept it going for a while. I don't know what happened. Maybe building that new mall out there on Twenty-Fifth Street took too many customers away from downtown.

Jeff: The downtown kind of went south a little bit. The Osco Drug Store and Sears were there. I think the Millers may have paid Sears some big money to stay and it's still there.

Ed: I know the Greeks have closed.

Jeff: Actually, someone is spending about two million bucks to restore the Greeks. It's going to open sometime this summer.

Ed: I'm tickled to death to hear that. I was a soda jerk there for a while. My junior and senior years I worked part-time at the old Major T. Jester Department Store, a couple doors down from Dave Brumfield's dad's barber shop. Of course all that went when the Commons was put in.

Jeff: Brummie's?

Ed: Yeah, Brummie's. Dalton's clothing store and Dell's department store were in the next block. Is Dell's still there?

Jeff: Dell's is still there. You know, Ed, when we were growing up we would go out in the morning and play in the neighborhood all day. We'd come home for lunch, then go back out and play until dark. We didn't have any concerns about somebody hurting us or kidnapping us. I don't think you'd let your kids do that anymore.

Ed: No. Has that issue hit Columbus in different ways or is the town still pretty protected from stuff like that?

Jeff: We're still pretty protected, but Nancy didn't let our kids run. The kids ran in the neighborhood, but she knew where they were all the time. She stayed at home and a lot of the kids were over at our house.

Ed: That's different than just letting them run wild.

Jeff: Yeah, but when we were kids my mom knew pretty much where we were. It wasn't like she wasn't taking care of us.

Ed: When we were growing up, people didn't spend a second worrying about stuff like that and that's a major, major difference today. I spent my entire professional life in public education and much of that time as a high school principal working with teenagers. I would not want to be a teenager today. It's just so much different, with so many pressures. When we were in high school, the biggest thing for some people was sneaking out back in the parking lot and smoking a cigarette. As I look back over the last five to six decades, I think growing up in the 40's and 50's was one of the best times to be growing up. It was just a great time to be a kid.

Jeff: We didn't have a whole lot of money, but we had enough. We lived in a little house that my dad bought for five thousand dollars before he shipped out overseas during WWII.

Ed: Isn't that amazing? When I was in the seventh grade, Dad went to an auction for a foreclosure on a piece of property at 22nd and Pennsylvania. He bid on a small parcel of land. I think he got it for two thousand dollars. My parents built a modest Bedford limestone house there. We moved at some point, probably between my seventh and eighth grade years.

... Savoring *Your* Memories...

1. What was it like growing up in your hometown?

2. How has your hometown changed over the years?

3. Who were the people in your town that left a legacy?

Chapter 4   Let the Memories Begin

Think back to the city or town in which you were raised. What was it like? Do you remember your childhood home? Who were your neighbors? Did your relatives live close by? What did you do for fun? Did you ever get in trouble with your parents? Was the population fairly diverse or mostly homogeneous? Where did you call home?

Dan FitzGibbon
Thoughts about Growing Up in Columbus

Dan: Columbus was a great place for a kid to grow up. It was safe. We had decent schools and good, in some cases outstanding, teachers. There were lots of activities for kids. Many interested adults helped out with those activities. We were a pretty well-off community in a lot of ways and those resources supported a lot of different activities.

Ed: In some ways I think Columbus was ahead of its time. For example the idea of the high school sponsoring an after-prom party to keep kids from going out, getting drunk, and getting killed or experiencing other awful things. In those days, not very many communities provided that kind of activity.

Dan: No, I think you're right. One of the aspects I especially liked about Columbus, which I guess is probably true of almost any small town, is the diversity you have in socio-economics. When we were growing up, within any given neighborhood there were families that were poor, middle class, and wealthy. That mixture ended up in the schools, on the athletic teams, and in the circles of friends we associated with. We got a real exposure to socio-economic diversity that you don't find today in a lot of other places where neighborhoods tend to be pretty secluded, isolated, and you see a lot of "sameness" in terms of socio-economic status. The experience we obviously missed growing up in Columbus was any real diversity in the areas of race and religion. There were as I recall no blacks, no Hispanics, no Asians, or other ethnic minorities in our class. There were a couple of black students a few years ahead of us.

Ed: You're right. We didn't have the racial and ethnic diversity that I feel is important. Unfortunately, because of the lack of a diverse population, when I went off to college I had some quick catching up to do with people who were from other parts of the country and brought those kinds of experiences with them.

Dan: Right. I'm not sure if I personally knew anyone who was Jewish, or anything else other than Christian, when I grew up. I got a little diversity education when I went off to West Point. Of course, there you have people from all over the U.S., plus some foreign countries, and a pretty good range of ethnic, socio-economic, and religious diversity. The best way to learn about diversity, at least among most males in America, is to be a rifle platoon leader in an infantry company. Back in the days of the draft, as I experienced, you saw everyone from just barely high school graduates to college graduates, from farm boys to small-town kids to street-wise big city guys, and every race, geographic region, religion, ethnic group, etc. That was a great lesson for me and a great preparation for everything I've done since.

One of the things I look back on in Columbus that surprises me is the fact that there wasn't a whole lot of political diversity there either. When you and I were growing up in Columbus, we had Republicans and Democrats, but they weren't really that far apart in what they stood for. Also, there was no hint of the fault lines that would later divide us in the '60s and '70s on issues such as civil rights, the war, gay rights, women's rights, and environmental issues. I guess part of it was the function of our era, the 1950s, which were pretty quiet. Another part of the lack of diversity may have been my own isolation, my own ignorance, or the fact that I spent most of my post- high-school time off in other places and therefore didn't see Columbus people evolve in the years after high school.

Ed: Your experience was the same as mine, Dan. The differences just weren't there. I think your point about people who identified themselves with either of the two political parties not necessarily being on either end of the continuum of beliefs of those parties is so true. They tended to be more centrists and the differences were more in degree rather than kind, which is not what we're seeing today.

Dan: Right. At subsequent high school reunions I've been somewhat surprised by a few of the comments coming out of the mouths of people I thought I knew pretty well in high school. Obviously, they've grown in different directions than I. Columbus was a great place to grow up but I'm not sure I would have been satisfied to have stayed there and as a result, missed out on some of the great experiences I've had. A lot of opportunities arose and doors opened once I moved away.

Ed: You're right about some of that sheltered experience. I went off to Hanover College after high school. There were a thousand students then and there are probably twelve hundred today. Unlike your experience at West Point, Hanover was only slightly more diverse than Columbus High School and our hometown. The students were mostly white Anglo-Saxon Protestants, like me. So the issue of diversity didn't really hit me until after I got out of college and started teaching.

Jack Hinkle
My Baseball Fantasy

Growing up in south central Indiana, we didn't live close to any big league baseball towns. Cincinnati was the closest, Chicago next, then St. Louis and Detroit. The baseball I knew growing up was on the radio and later on television. The first live game I went to was in St. Louis to watch the St. Louis Browns. When I got older and could drive, Cincinnati was the place to go. At that time the Reds still played at Crosley Field. I got to watch some great baseball.

I watched Pete Rose and Frank Robinson come into the league. A lot of people don't know that Frank started out at second base before moving to third. I watched some of the greats at Crosley, such as Lew Burdette and Warren Spahn of the Milwaukee Braves before they eventually ended up in Atlanta. One time, the pitcher tried to fool Hank Aaron on a pitch, but Aaron hit it over the centerfield wall, hitting the building across the street.

At one game I sat down the right field line in the upper deck stands. Willie McCovey hit a liner in our direction and, stupid me, without a glove I put up my hands to catch it. The ball separated my hands and almost killed a guy behind me.

If you remember, Crosley Field had pretty high walls, sort of like Boston's Green Monster. Crosley Field was a strange shape. I can still remember the left-field line was 320 feet. The right-field line was 347 feet, and center field was 388—not very far, but with a pretty high wall. Today there is a ball park that has a rise in centerfield. Well, Crosley Field had one back in the '50s.

One night Orlando Cepeda hit a ball that I thought was going to be a pop up to the shortstop, but the ball kept rising. It was still going up when it cleared the light standard on top of the scoreboard—talk about putting it in orbit. Another memory was at Cincinnati's Riverfront Stadium. My wife and I went to the last game of the season. During the game, Willie Mays who was playing for the Mets hit his 660th home run.

The beer salesmen were also an interesting part of the game. When the guys went to a game, we went with the idea we would drink a beer each inning. The vendors usually stopped coming around about the 7th inning. The problem came when there was a bench-clearing fight. Those were the days of Weideman's and Hudepohl. When the fight broke out, our beer guy stopped by and said, "We got the fightin' beer here." I also remember him saying, "Get moody with Hudy."

I moved my family to Kansas City in 1980. We got to see George Brett do his stuff. You could sit in the right or left field stand, first-come first-served, for one dollar and fifty cents.

The last of my ball park visits was in the '80s. I was working on a project and was staying across the river from Three Rivers Stadium in Pittsburgh. For five dollars I rode a boat across the river to the ball park. There was an entrance to centerfield and for three dollars I watched the game. This was around the time Barry Bonds was just starting to play.

Just to summarize my thoughts:

My favorite players were Willie Mays and Ted Williams. My favorite pitchers were Juan Marichal and Robin Roberts, with a little Don Larsen. I thought I was deceptive like Juan, a control pitcher like Roberts, and used the Larsen no windup.

The best right-fielder I saw in person was Felipe Alou. My favorite teams were the Giants and the Red Sox. My favorite announcers were Dizzy Dean and Peewee Reese.

Rob Schafstall
When We Were Growing Up: A Safer, More Trusting Time

Rob: Ed, do you remember when we were growing up? We'd come home from school and our mom would be there?

Ed: Yep. I sure do.

Rob: And she'd probably have something for us to eat. For the most part that's gone in our society.

Ed: It surely is. A lot of things are different today. The fifties and sixties were a helluva good time to be growing up.

Rob: I remember in the summertime I'd leave the house and I might go over to Lincoln Park or Donner Park, but I'd go and do something. I was nine or ten years old and I knew to be home at noon for lunch. After lunch, I went back out. I knew to be home at five, or whatever, and nobody worried about me. I was absolutely safe. Now, we can't let our kids out of our yards.

When I was eleven or twelve years old, I could get on a Leopard Bus Lines bus at 17th and Caldwell. As I recall, the ride cost a nickel, or I could get six tokens for a quarter. I would ride down to Jackson and 8th Street by myself and walk down to the 8th Street ballpark. I had maybe fifty cents, which might get me a hot dog and a coke. My only responsibility was to get home before the last bus ran. Can you imagine having an eleven, twelve-year-old kid doing that today?

Ed: Absolutely not. And by the way, this theme has been discussed by other guys, which tells me it's something we remember very well. I remember going out the back door of our house, walking down the alley, going about a block further, and standing on the corner waiting for the bus. The ride cost me a dime. I'd get on the bus at the corner and get off somewhere up around Wilson Junior High School. After school, I'd get back on a bus and ride home. I always thought that was fun.

Rob: Ed, I remember we didn't often lock the door of the house.

Ed: No we didn't either. You're right about that too.

Rob: And I remember my parents leaving the keys in the damn car out in front.

Ed: Like you said, I think about all the bad things going on in this country and around the world today and all of the precautions parents have to take with their kids. My son's forty and my daughter's thirty-seven. I have four granddaughters and you've got your grandkids. We both know our children have to worry about stuff with their kids that never entered our parents' minds.

Jack Hinkle
The Hinkle Mansion
I grew up in Columbus. We moved to 1727 California Street in 1947. Through historical searching, I was able to determine our house was one of the first ones built in the neighborhood. I don't know exactly how old it is, but it was there in 1906, making it over one hundred years old.

11/27/2008

The mansion was a two bedroom, one bathroom house. My memory tells me the rooms were fairly good size. There was a master bedroom with a bay window that stuck out in front. There were two front entrances—one into the master bedroom, the other went into the living room.

The basement was originally just a small canning and storage area. My oldest brother and my grandfather dug the rest of the basement, which was under the living room and the bathroom. My grandfather also installed a coal furnace to heat the entire house, except for the back dorm room. I still remember the coal truck backing up to the side of the house and unloading the coal into the basement. During the early '50s we had lumpy coal. Later on, Grandpa added a stoker to automatically move coal into the furnace. One of the chores shared by the boys was to empty ashes and clinkers. I don't know about your home in East Columbus, but the house I lived in didn't even have a tub.

Ed: We didn't have indoor plumbing. I remember using our outhouse until I was probably six or seven.

Jack: Well, we had an outhouse too. My grandfather ended up modifying one of our bedrooms and made a bathroom out of it.

Ed: My folks put an addition on the house and we finally had our bathroom. Every Saturday night, I got in there and took a bath. I remember our outhouse used to get tipped over every Halloween.

Jack: Just a one holer?

Ed: Oh yeah, it was just a one holer. I don't remember how I ever survived going out there in the wintertime, but obviously I did. I'm glad we don't have an outhouse now. Heck, at my age, I'd be out there every fifteen minutes.

Jack: You survived by being quick.

Ed: That's right. You did your business…

Jack: You had to mean it.

Ed: You got it. Don't go until you're sure you can get done what you needed to and run back inside.

Jack: The mansion was home for Mom and us three boys from 1947 until 1971. Our house was centrally located about a mile to everywhere—the grade school, church, junior high, city swimming pool and park. The walk to Lincoln Park for baseball and downtown for movies took longer. The biggest challenge was getting to the 8th Street ballpark, a little over fifteen blocks away.

Since we didn't have a car until 1955, walking was the mode of transportation. We had a bicycle or two, but I don't think we ever had three at the same time. I remember Schwinn and Shelby were two types of bicycles back then, as well as a thing called an English bike with more than one gear and skinny wheels.

At that point in time, garages were very seldom attached to the house. If people had a garage it was back on the alley behind the house. We had a shed but no garage.

The backyard was a sports haven, after we destroyed the strawberry patch that took half of the yard. We had a cherry tree until lightning took it down and that became home plate. When I wanted to climb the fence and escape, my run-away tree was over near the street. Our neighbor behind us had a tin-roof garage that had lots of baseball dents in it. I'm sure it was noisy, but Mr. Baxter never complained. When we played football, the goal line bushes were out back, just before the alley.

My brother Jerry and I played a game we called pass over. You could pass, punt, or drop-kick over the ends of the yard for scores. You scored if it went over without getting caught. Where you caught it was where you kicked or threw from. I'm amazed the back window, right behind home plate, never got broken. Another game we played was called three misses. Mom, my brothers, and I would stand in a circle and throw a football to each other. You had to catch it with one hand. Three drops and you were out. Try to catch a spinning football one-handed. Mom was pretty good "for a girl." We didn't have a basketball goal outside, but we were close to the grade school playground and Donner Park was a few blocks away.

One novelty about our house was we were able to set up a goal in both the bathroom and living room, and shoot baskets. The other entertainment was our Arvin's TV console. It had one of those screens that was flat across the top and bottom. The antenna was right out the front door and was turned with a pipe wrench.

The year after I graduated from high school Mom moved to a new house out by the city golf course, which ended our entertainment and fun at the Hinkle Mansion.

Larry Long
Growing Up In Columbus

Larry: There are a few things I learned the most, and felt I walked away with, from living in Columbus. First, there were no limitations. Whether it was the school, our coaches, or our parents, there were no limitations. You could do anything you wanted. Later on I'll tell you that the lack of limitations has been my Achilles' heel. One time it cost me six million dollars and another time eight million dollars, on things where I almost felt I was bulletproof and things would work out. They didn't, and I learned the hard way. Second was the education I received in Columbus. We really did have some great educators.

Ed: Oh my gosh, it's just unbelievable. The whole atmosphere of our high school was great. Setting that atmosphere probably started with Jud Erne. Because I've been a high school principal I know the principal's usually the one who helps to establish the climate and culture. Columbus High School was just a special place and somebody did a heck of a job with hiring people there.

Larry: Living out at Harrison Lakes was interesting. We didn't have much money and I didn't have a car. I had to borrow Mom's car when it was available. So I mainly double-dated with Paul Pringle. If he was going out, I'd get a date too. It was interesting. But also, there wasn't much pressure to date.

Ed: There really wasn't. There were enough fun folks to run around with. When we were growing up, kids did things more in groups, rather than a guy and a gal going out together. I always thought that was probably a pretty healthy thing to do.

Larry: I think it was for all of us. We were pretty lucky when you think back.

Ed: During my conversations with The Columbus Crew, a few people have talked about how we were out much of the day. Our parents usually knew where we were, but even if they didn't, they knew everything was going to be all right.

Larry: I used to hitchhike all over because I didn't have a car. I can remember getting picked up by some gay guys and I was unafraid. It was very different when we were growing up.

Jack Hinkle
My Indy 500

Growing up in a town not too far from Indianapolis, I was somewhat influenced by the annual celebration of Memorial Day. I'm a faithful follower of the Indianapolis 500 mile race. Over the years I have attended, listened to, and watched many of the races on television.

For three reasons, in the early 1950's my favorite driver was Jack McGrath. One was my name is Jack. Another was he drove the Hinkle Special, which is my last name. Finally, Jack Hinkle was the owner of Jack McGrath's car. McGrath was a driver that went mostly unnoticed, because he was usually in the back running for the lead. The more famous Bill Vukovich was usually ahead of him. Other favorites were Larry Crockett, from my hometown and Pat O'Conner who was from nearby North Vernon. Pat was killed on a first lap crash, and I can still picture the rerun of that crash. Over the years it was a normal process to get ready for the month of May. Pole position day was the biggest part of the race—to see who would go the fastest for a four-lap trip, and to hear Tom Carnegie sound off with those famous words, "It's a new track record."

In today's Indy competition, the two hundred mile-per-hour barrier has been shattered. I can remember when the one hundred fifty mile-per-hour barrier was thought to be impossible. A big thrill for my hometown was in 1952 when the Cummins Diesel car won the pole position. We got to see the car at the 8th Street ballpark, along with the driver Freddie Agabashian—quite a thrill for a ten-year-old.

There are several memories of note, such as Tom Sneva breaking the two hundred MPH qualifying mark the first time. I remember the first time a car with a turbine engine was in the race. Parnelli Jones led the whole race and was more than a lap ahead when his car quit. A five dollar part failed. Because of the rain, that year's race was run over two days. I sat in the bleachers on the inside, overlooking the pits. On the first lap, Parnelli crossed in front of me and the second car was just coming out of turn four. It was amazing to see him go by with very little noise—kind of a whoosh noise. By the way, the winner of that race was a fellow you've probably heard of, A.J. Foyt.

Another interesting race was when Gordon Johncock won a shortened race due to rain. The race was postponed a couple of times. On the day the race was finally run, I was working in downtown Indy and listening to the broadcast. I heard the Purdue Band playing the National Anthem. I excused myself, got into my car, and drove to the track. I found a nice spot on the backstretch. After a few laps, I decided to go down to the third turn and watch from that vantage point for awhile. By the time the race was past half-way, I decided to go over to the fourth turn to finish watching from there. The afternoon was well worth the free ticket I got.

I also remember the race in 1961. Some of us bachelors decided to head up to the race the night before and investigate the fun of lining up on 16th Street to compete in the "get the best spot in the infield" game. When we arrived, around ten o'clock at night, 16th Street was lined up from the track entrance back toward downtown. The westbound side was packed. Those people had been there all day.

Needless to say, there was a party happening that lasted until six the next morning, when the gates opened. I found one of my high school buddies sitting in a lawn chair on a platform built in a pick-up truck. He had a tub of beverages, which I was glad to help him consume. The moral of this story is moderation. We partied all night and got to a great spot on the backstretch fence. The problem was, I took a little nap in the back seat of a convertible and woke up on the hundred and first lap. Did I mention it was a sunny, hot day?

One sad memory I had was in 1955. Bill Vukovich was killed during the race. I remember I was cutting the grass for Grandma Fulp who lived down the street from us. In those days, I could mow and listen to the radio without earplugs.

Qualification days were fun. Pole position day was as exciting as the final day, when drivers who hadn't qualified could "bump" other drivers out of the race if they ran faster for their four lap qualifying speed. I liked the in-between day, because I could sit anywhere. The seats weren't reserved on qualification days. I used to sit in one area, and then move to another section just to get a different perspective. The company I worked for sponsored a car one year and had a suite at the track. I was able to go up into the suite built behind the grandstands. I'll have to say that's a nice way to enjoy the track.

The Indy 500 track and race were a big part of my life. Just going to the practice during the week was a great way to spend the afternoon. And being there those days only cost five dollars.

I took my kids when they were young and they enjoyed getting up close to the cars in the pits and standing close to legends like the Unser brothers, Mario Andretti, and A.J. Foyt.

Today, the track is not the same to me because the drivers have changed. The speed took some of the nostalgia away for me. But the event is still spectacular. The Indy 500 is one of those experiences you should put on your "to do once" list.

Tom Taylor
The Culture in a Southern Indiana Town in the '50s and '60s: One Man's Perspective

Tom: The culture of my family is Columbus culture. I didn't realize it was and I didn't realize how important it was to me, until I was past the age of fifty-five. Fortunately, my father didn't die for another twelve years. We talked about everything from Grandpa Taylor's horse, to what Dad did in the war, and situations that I thought had gone wrong or that I didn't like. I would ask, "Well, why did you never…?"

We bought a lot down on Flat Rock River, next to where Cal Brand's family built. We owned another five acres of riverbank on up into the woods. Dad bought it because he wanted to build down there. I was ten at the time. I learned to water ski on that river which was in front of Cal's house. I asked, "Why did we never build a house there?" Dad said, "Oh, it wasn't your mother." I kind of thought maybe it was. He said, "It was me. Before we got married, I built this house on the corner of 23rd and Washington Street and gave it to your mother for her wedding present. We got married and I brought her home to our house that I had already built. Once push came to shove, I couldn't figure out any reason to leave it." So, I finally found out why we didn't build there.

Ed: They lived in that house on 23rd and Washington their whole life, right?

Tom: Absolutely. They traveled for a couple of years in '43 and '44 going around from air force base to air force base in the United States. But that place in Columbus was always their home. During the war when they were gone, Mom and Dad rented their home to a jazz trumpet player who was known as the Blue Baron. Do you know the Blue Baron?

Ed: No. But I'm thinking, what an interesting name.

Tom: Yeah. The Blue Baron was an enlisted man who apparently was guaranteed permanent assignment at Atterbury Military Base. He was over draft age, enlisted, was working at Atterbury and living at our house. He would not speak to my father, because my father was an officer. So this guy, Chicago-based big band leader of the swing era, wouldn't talk to my father about anything. He only communicated through my mother. That must have hurt my father.

Ed: Tom, that's interesting.

Tom: There was a black and white difference in Columbus and that is something I didn't pick up. In first grade, there was one black guy named Billy Pennybaker. I was having my sixth birthday party. I made out the list and Billy was invited. There was one kid that wasn't invited. I remember one of my parents asking, "Why are you not inviting him and you're inviting Pennybaker?" I said, "Well, because he's dirty." My parents felt a need to ask the question, "Why are you inviting Billy?"

In Columbus, the concrete finisher's union was all black. They were very innovative. They went around to all the union contractors, like Dunlap's and Taylor Brothers and said, "Here's the contract we want. Our contract says that you tell us what the job description is and we'll decide how many men to send over. We have a bonding company that will guarantee our work. If we send too few men and the job gets away from us, our bonding company will make good." My father respected that and he respected the concrete finishers, but I don't think he ever hired a black carpenter.

Ed: Did that group get a lot of work in Columbus?

Tom: Oh yeah. All the big jobs in Columbus were union. All the construction work at Cummins was union; otherwise Cummins' union would have struck. All of the stuff that was done for Miller, the bank, and his house was all union.

Family History in the Columbus Area

Tom: This ties back to Columbus, because after talking to you and getting into this book idea, I started thinking about Columbus. It was really Columbus that made my family. It was that Midwest farmer's background that goes back through my grandpa Luke Taylor and his father, Alfred English Taylor who was a farmer out toward Brown County. They were self-sufficient farmers. If you don't do it right, you may starve. They started a construction company that had their name on it. That's where Dad came from. I recognize now, that in spite of the fact I turned my back on Columbus and didn't particularly enjoy my time there, Columbus made my dad and that's made me. I'm a Columbus son, whether I like it or not.

Ed: Did your folks grow up in Columbus?

Tom: Dad did. Grandpa Taylor was born halfway between Columbus and Grandview Lake, right across the road from the Mount Zion Church. That's the old Taylor farm. Grandma Taylor was born out there also, of a German farming family named Swank. Great-Grandpa Swank was a farmer and a carpenter. Apparently my grandpa did some work with him, carpentering out in that part of the county. That's how he met Grandma. Dad was born in Columbus. My Uncle Dean was born in Bemidji, Minnesota where they went to try and establish a lumber business, but it didn't work. So, they came back to Columbus. Aunt Bee was born in Columbus, Bee Zaharako. My mother was born in Rushville, daughter of a railroad man. Her family moved to Columbus during the Depression. The railroad relocated her father. He came down and lived on Franklin Street, right where the railroad crossed Franklin. I knew that side of the family less, because most of the people were from Rushville.

Ed: Didn't your grandma live to be a hundred?

Tom: Yeah, her hundredth birthday was held at her house, where she lived alone. A woman came in every day, fixed her lunch and her supper, and helped clean up. But my grandmother was alone every night and took care of her own breakfast. Eighty people came through the house on her hundredth birthday. She stood up and greeted every one of them, asked about their great-great grandchildren by name, and made it through the whole day.

Ed: Tom that is an unbelievable story. What a wonderful story.

Tom: It is. My Uncle Norman, her oldest son, was up in Rushville, dying of diabetes when my grandmother was about ninety. He was seventy-one or seventy-two and she was in her nineties. One day in December, my cousin went in and asked the doctor, "How's he doing?" The doctor said, "Well, physically there's just no change. He's stable. He's never going to get better. He's had his feet cut off and is on tubes that flush out his system. He has terminal diabetes. He's stable and he doesn't seem to be in any pain. But we believe his mind's going." My cousin said, "Oh dear, that's too bad. He's just been sharp as could be through all of this. I understand. I guess that's going to happen. What's going on?"

The doctor said, "Well the last week he's been talking about going home to mother's for Christmas. It's the kind of throw-back to childhood we see." My cousin said, "Oh, it would be so nice if he could. But she lives clear down in Columbus. Oh gosh, it's too bad that he can't go." The doctor said, "Wait a minute. You mean this man's mother is alive?" My cousin said,

"Oh yeah. She's alive and doing fine." The doctor asked, "And she's going to have the whole family over for Christmas at her house?" My cousin replied, "Oh yeah, we do that every year." The doctor said, "This is this man's last Christmas. There's no question about it. There is no way he is not going to go to his mother's for Christmas." The hospital and the doctor ordered up an ambulance, life-support, and drove him from Rushville to Columbus, for Christmas with his mother.

Ed: That is wonderful. When we were growing up, doctors had a different kind of relationship with their patients. I remember my doctor making house calls. Times sure have changed.

Jack Hinkle
My Friend Forever

Jack: This story is about two boys growing up together in a small town in Indiana. One guy's name is Jack and the other one is Graham. We both grew up in Columbus. The first time we met was during the eighth grade. We were on the same touch football team. One guy was a little bitty guy, didn't weigh very much, and he was the center on the team. The other guy was bigger and a little chubby. He was the quarterback. We played together on that team and had a good time. The next year in ninth grade we came together at the same school. As it turns out, that was first year I didn't make the basketball team. But Graham did.

Graham's house was on my way home. Most days after school when we weren't playing sports, we ended up going home together. We came to his house first. Most of the time, we would stop at his house and play games. We had our own little tournament. We would sit around and play Monopoly or Canasta. Right across the street was Jefferson School. Sometimes we went over there and played one-on-one basketball. That's how our lifelong friendship began.

When we went to Graham's house his mom would always get after us because she was a real clean housekeeper, and she liked her house just a certain way. She had these little white throw rugs that she put in front of the chairs. When we'd go in there she was always telling us not to step on them, but of course I went out of my way to step on them. I always had my footprints on them. She was always getting after me for that.

Graham's dad was usually home because he worked the second shift. We all hung out together. His dad was really nice to me, to both of us for that matter. Graham was an only child, so he ended up picking up a brother in me. We spent so many years just going places.

His family would take me fishing. I was a lousy fisherman because I was afraid to take the fish off the hook. I said, "I don't mind the fishing. I'm afraid I'll catch a fish."

Ed: It took me awhile to be able to put the worm on the hook.

Jack: I got pretty good with the worm. I finally lived through that. But whenever I caught a fish, I ran over to Pop and he would take the fish off the hook for me. I finally figured out I could stand on the fish and pull it off the hook without touching it.

Our ninth grade year, we both played football and then in the summer, Graham was in military school at Culver Military Academy. During the summer, he was away for six weeks. His mom and dad would go up and visit him on weekends. I'd go up with them. Culver Military is both navy and army. I don't know if you remember Walter Hathaway but he was in the other group, the army group. They were called the woodchucks and rode horses. Of course the naval group sailed boats. Graham was in the navy part and took us out on a boat one day. As Graham got older, his mother went to work at Goodman Jester's.

Ed: Major T. Jester's?

Jack: Major T. when it was just that one little store. One time we went down there and the store manager called her Dorothy. Her name was Ruth. But for some reason he always called her Dorothy. Ever since then, I called her Dorothy.

Ed: I worked in the men's department at Jester's part-time when I was in high school. I remember someone named Ruth.

Jack: That's her. I don't know if you ever met Graham's dad. He was kind of a gruff little guy, but he would do anything for Graham. During the summertime when Graham wasn't at Culver, they would take a week or two week vacation to Indiana Beach at Lake Schafer. They invited me to go with them. They rented a boat and we went skiing. One of the highlights of our trip that I always like to mention is, when we were up there, The Four Freshmen were performing in a beer garden there. We sat out in a boat and listened to them perform. After they were done, I took Graham backstage. Ross Barbour and his wife were good friends of my aunt, so I went back there and said, "I'm Patty's nephew." Ross said, "Oh yeah." They were really great. We met them two or three times over the fifty years or so and it was like they just met you yesterday and still remembered you.

...Savoring *Your* Memories...

1. What were some of your experiences growing up at home?

2. Do you remember the house you grew up in?

3. Are all your memories good ones, or do you recall some incidents you wish you could over?

Chapter 5 Our First Eighteen Years: Early Jobs, Fun, and Our Education through May 25, 1960

These stories will continue to acquaint you with The Columbus Crew and how we lived the first eighteen years of our lives. Everyone's life was full of excitement, surprises, learning experiences, and disappointments from as far back as we can remember, up through our senior year in high school.

What was it like growing up in your home? How did you get along with your parents? What did you and your friends like to do? What happened when you got into trouble, either at home or somewhere else? Did you work while you went to school? Stories about these topics, and many more, are told in this chapter.

George Abel
Living Many Places with a Strict Father, and Finding Peace Within

George: This is about my early years and what my home situation was like. I grew up in a very strict environment. My father had been a marine who took his basic training on Paris Island. He was honorably discharged without ever having been shipped overseas, and he had that marine mentality. When he got discharged, he took a job as a machinist working nights for Reeves Pulley Company in Columbus. We bought an eighty-acre farm out in Ogleville. It was just beautiful. Dad and Mom raised chickens on the farm and he worked many, many hours. Dad retired after twenty years with Reeves.

In 1948, I was six years old. My dad announced we were selling the farm and moving. I didn't like that. It turned out we moved to a two-acre tract of land. The land was a flood plain and next to an open dump. I was devastated. All the kids on the school bus and others at school would say, "Oh, you're the guy that lives next to the dump, aren't you?" Dad continued to work at the pulley company. My mother went to work in about 1953 or '54 at Roviar. The company was originally Reliance manufacturers in Columbus. The building's now turned into something completely different. As a matter of fact that building is where the two high schools had their combined prom this year.

Ed: I can't remember. What did they manufacture?

George: Roviar was a clothing manufacturer, mostly coats. My mother actually worked her way up to production manager before they closed the doors on the place. She didn't get any retirement or anything because they just went out of business. This was back before there were any retirement savings guarantees by the federal government. So we had a pretty rough childhood. My mom and dad started a greenhouse business in 1958. They turned it into a fairly profitable business by about 1965. I had two brothers. We were all born in the early forties. We grew up pretty much poor, with hand-me-down clothes and shoes with holes in them.

Ed: I can sure identify with that.

George: Then we had two sisters who came along in the early fifties. My parents were fortunate enough to be relatively prosperous then, compared to when my brothers and I were born. My younger brother had an awful time dealing with that, because our sisters got new clothes. He didn't get new clothes when he was little. My older brother and I were just happy my parents were able to do better than they had been doing.

Ed: How'd you get along with your folks?

George: Well, it was in spurts.

Ed: Yeah, me to.

George: I was a very headstrong person and was not going to tolerate anybody.

Ed: I was going to say, you and your dad may have butted heads a few times.

George: We did. When I was a senior in high school, seventeen years old, I left home. I moved in with another guy and stayed there until the summer.

Ed: You were living there during our senior year?

George: Yes. I stayed there until I graduated from high school. I worked at the A&P grocery store there on Washington Street. The only reason I went back home was because dad came into the store one day. The transmission had gone out on his car. My older brother was going to Purdue, and my parents were struggling to keep him there. Dad said if I would give him three hundred dollars, come back home and save all the money that I could before fall, he would see that I got at least one year at Purdue. I did and he kept his word. He got me one year at Purdue.

I think from that time on, we had a different relationship. But he was a hands-on type father. He would knock us around pretty good. When I got older I realized I probably had it coming. I pretty much kept the hours I wanted to and he wasn't going to have that. Finally, I said, "Dad you're not going to be beating on me anymore. He said, "Okay, you can't live in my house. I run it the way I see fit." I could never remember him spanking one of the girls, but he was sure rough on us boys. All in all, he was quite a man. He only had a tenth grade education and he ended up putting together quite a business and did quite well for himself over the years. Most of it was hard work, determination, having an idea, setting goals, and making it work.

Ed: My dad had to drop out of school at the end of sixth grade. Mom and Dad both worked very hard to provide for my sister and me. They also protected us and they did those two jobs better than any other. I'm sure providing and protecting is what they saw growing up. Dad didn't hit me ever, neither did Mom—but a lot of the other things you're talking about, I can sure identify with.

Jack Hinkle
My Girlfriends
Sandy, Melinda, Jill, Carol Sue, Mary Jane, Janey, Marietsa, Sharon, Julia, Judy, Leslie, Linda, Barbara, Annette, Pat, Jessica, Eva, and Natalie. Growing up in Columbus and having spent my first thirty years there, I had a fair number of girlfriends. Back then, there was a thing called "going steady." Do you remember how the girl wore the guy's class ring and put all kinds of tape, gum, whatever, under it so it would fit on her finger? My situation was a little different from others, because if you look at this list of names, those were **all** my girlfriends, but I never went steady with any of them.

When I was growing up, I was terrified of girls. I was afraid if I said something to them they might say something back. That thought scared me more than you can imagine. That may be a surprise to some people because I disguised my fear with my ability to be funny. I remember going to sock hops, other dances, and parties. I was one of those guys standing over at the side watching. The first girl I danced with, I was terrified I might touch her.

Except for a couple of scary games of truth or dare and spin the bottle, I never came close to kissing anyone except Mom and Grandma. One day after being harassed by a colleague to ask another co-worker out for a date, I finally worked up the courage. The date was set and I was to pick her up at her house. We had planned to go to a movie. The problem was I didn't know where she lived. She told me she lived in the park at Brown County State Park, about fifteen miles from Columbus. When it came time to go, it dawned on me that I didn't know she lived in a house **in** the park. I had been to the park several times, but not to the park superintendent's house. Gulp! On the good side of that, on our future dates I didn't have to pay to get in the park. My first perk.

I don't know if you ever watched the movie *Hitch*. In the movie, Will Smith trained guys like me about the ways to handle dates. I watched this movie to the part where the guy gets her home after the movie. They're getting around to saying good night and deciding if a kiss is in the mix or not. In my case, my date took the initiative while I was thinking about it. She kissed me good night. I was always told you would know when you meet "the one." That night, I was sure I had met her. Who says you can't drive home in a daze?

Approximately eight months later, my girlfriend became my wife. On our honeymoon, we went to a movie called *The Odd Couple*. As of this writing, my girlfriend and I are going on forty-one years of marriage. Throughout this time, except for some time off for making babies, she has been a working mother at every stop we made during my career. We have lived in four different places since leaving my hometown. Along with being a dependable employee for the last twenty years, she has been a nurse to me. When it comes to the term "for better or worse," there is no argument about who got the better and who got the worse. My girlfriend just retired after nursing me for over twenty years and working for over forty-five. She's going to get a chance to do some of the things she couldn't do before.

To end this story, I want to say I made a lot of choices and made lots of mistakes, but this girlfriend was the best right choice I ever made.

Cal Brand
Growing Up With My Parents, My Foster Grandparents, and Being the Oldest Child

Cal: I was born in Seymour, Indiana, about twenty miles from Columbus. The earliest memories I have begin about age two. We lived in a house that had been turned into apartments, right across the street from Dunlap's Lumber Company where Dad was working. That's where he met Mom, who was a secretary there. Mom was a Seymour girl. I have memories of going over to the store with Dad and sometimes Mom taking me over there to see him. I will generally refer to Dunlap's as "the store." I just got in the habit of doing that. When I made visits to the store, I got to be a mascot for a lot of the employees there—a couple of the mill hands, truck drivers, and people who worked in the yard.

Ed: What do you mean mascot?

Cal: They called me Little Beaver, Red Rider's Indian sidekick. I'd just hang out. I'm sure I was curious and just playing. I imagine I got to go to the store because Mom was pregnant with Joan. She was glad to have me out from under her feet. In the course of that time, I got acquainted with one of the truck drivers whose name was Jonie Christopher, short for Jonas. Jonie lived about seven miles south of Seymour, in the little town of Dudleytown. I just took quite a fancy to him. I don't remember exactly how it happened the first time, but the summer after I was two I decided to spend a Saturday night with them. Jonie took me home and I spent time with his family. Jonie thought he would have to turn around and bring me right back. That didn't happen. In fact, I had a great time down there and didn't feel homesick at all. Mom and Dad came down on Sunday and picked me up. That one overnight visit began a foster grandparent experience.

My mother's parents lived there in Seymour, but her dad was a drunk. My grandfather was a fairly good painter. He painted houses. Most of the time when I saw my grandpa, in his later years, he'd be more or less passed out on the couch. The house always smelled of booze. I didn't really feel that close to him. Grandma was all right. Dad's mother had died and his dad was a drunk hanging out in Columbus. So I didn't have any connection with him either.

Jonie and his wife Lena were welcoming to me. They had two kids of their own, June and Marvin. Marvin was probably four or five years older than me. He was enough older that I wasn't a good playmate for him, but he tolerated me. I went down there and spent a weekend with some regularity.

When my brother John was two, he got polio. I have memories of my folks getting an old metal frame army cot set up for him. With that bed, Mom and Dad could tie his arms back and his leg down with weights to stretch him, to keep the polio from causing deformity. During the acute period with John, when I was five, I spent the whole summer at Dudleytown. Mom and Dad would come out on Sunday to see me and spend some time together. But basically, the Christophers took care of me.

Ed: Your sister Joan was born by then wasn't she?

Cal: She was already born. My folks wanted to get Joan and me out of the house as much as possible because they were worried about us catching polio from John. Joan stayed quite a bit with my Aunt Carolyn and Uncle Garnett who lived just a few blocks away. But she was also home a lot. That relationship with the Christophers remained important enough for me that when my son was born we named him Christopher.

Ed: That relationship was most definitely long-term.

Cal: I learned so much there. Their ways were quite a bit different than what mine were at home. In Dudleytown, there was a community of people that still spoke German. In fact, they even had High German and Low German. Of course they were loyal, active members of the German Lutheran Church there, which happened to be Missouri Synod.

Ed: That's pretty conservative.

Cal: Conservative. I have wonderful memories of passing the holiday seasons down there. On New Year's Eve they had games going on in the Luther League Building, the social hall. Us kids would always break away and play tag in the graveyard. Invariably, we'd manage to get in the bell tower and turn the bell over. The people were great. They let us know that wasn't a good thing to do, but they were never angry about it.

The Christophers didn't have a big place. They probably had a couple of acres and they did some farming there. They kept four to six hogs. When I was down there in the wintertime, I often helped in butchering the hogs. It was an interesting experience for a first, second, and third grade kid to watch them slaughter those hogs. Of course we'd do awful things, like kids do. They gave us the eyeballs and we'd put them between two boards and see if we could smash them. The morning after butchering was like Mardi Gras or Cinco de Mayo. We had fresh pork tenderloin that was just, it was impossible to compare it to anything.

The back of the Christophers' washhouse was a smokehouse and it was always a delight to go there. The hams and sausages were hanging in there curing. They kept a little fire in the stove, which was vented out through the smokehouse. They also had the better part of an acre in potatoes. I always had fun there when they dug the potatoes. The Christophers plowed with a mule. We would follow that mule down the furrow and it was just magic to watch those big nuggets pop up out of the ground and fill the bags.

Lena also lived by the days, so Monday was wash day and on to Friday which was baking day. Jonie would often bring me home on a Thursday night. Friday mornings were wonderful because the house smelled of all the things Lena was baking—pies, sweet rolls, cookies, and other good stuff to eat. That was quite a delight. With the cabbage they grew, she made kraut. In the basement, there were crocks of kraut seasoning. The heat was an old fashioned coal stove in the basement with no duct work. They just had floor registers and whatever heat was upstairs is what managed to get up the stairway.

Ed: For the first few years of my life we had a coal bin down in the basement. I remember going down there and helping Dad shovel coal in the furnace.

Cal: There's a world of fun memories with the Christophers. The Krumees lived across the street. They had a daughter who was mentally challenged. She was kept in the house in an upstairs room all day, every day. I suspect today the parents would be taken to court. At that time, it was just accepted as the best way to care for her. The few times I did see her she always looked well and cleaned up, but she never came out to play.

Ed: So she never saw the light of day.

Cal: Not really. Then just north of them, on the corner, was where the Lamberts lived. They kept six or eight dairy cows. One of my activities, when I'd visit, was to go see Edna around four in the afternoon. We'd go out and call the cows.

Ed: Did you help with the milking?

Cal: I tried. I wasn't much good.

Ed: I tried milking cows at my Uncle Willard's farm a couple times and I wasn't very good either. More milk hit the ground than went into the pail.

Cal: I did get to help feed the cows. After the milking was done, we set the milk in the springhouse to keep it chilled. At that time, everybody down there had outhouses. That was another learning experience, especially in the wintertime.

Jonie and Lena also kept chickens, which is how I must have gotten my love for chickens. I enjoyed chickens. My family kept chickens where we lived there in Seymour. My mom took care of the chickens, but not nearly on the scale that Jonie and Lena did. The Christophers had a regular business with their chickens. At least once a week, we'd take a crate of eggs down to the corner market, and the money was part of their family income. I had some exciting adventures in the chicken yard, when the roosters didn't think I should be there. Some of those experiences "got under my nails" and stuck with me.

There are a couple of other stories from Seymour that stand out for me. I remember Dad carrying me down to the Colonial Café. I actually remember sitting on his shoulders. The Café was a typical small-town meeting place. All the regulars had their own coffee cups on the rack.

Ed: And that's where they solved all the problems.

Cal: Solved all the problems of the world. But I don't have a very distinct memory of our visits there. I think that's where I probably began to have some sense Dad was proud of me. I got in enough trouble though, and he and I fought like cats and dogs most of my life.

Ed: Knowing your dad as I did, I can imagine.

Cal: I think there was some kind of foundation laid there in my early childhood that stuck with me. I can remember two whippings I got. One time when I was five, I took Joan and John—who were just three and two—on a hike without telling Mother. We had heard stories that the river close to our house had a whirlpool in it. We'd been listening to Jungle Jim or stuff like that on the radio in the mornings. I was curious to see what a whirlpool was. We got down there and never did find the whirlpool. We were eventually found by our neighbor who lived across the street. He'd been down there with some other folks looking for mushrooms. He gathered us up, put us in his pickup truck, and took us home. When he let us out of the truck and started to bring us up to the house, Mother looked out the window. At that time she was pregnant with Jesse and she was pretty big. She came down out of the back door and grabbed a switch. She had tears running down her face because on the one hand, she was so glad to see us and other the other hand, she was so worried because she couldn't find us anywhere. She told me I'd better never do anything like that again and switched the backs of my legs. I can still remember that whipping to this day.

Ed: You had short pants on?

Cal: You're not kidding!

Ed: I think what's interesting is, wherever you guys had been, she knew you probably needed a whipping.

Cal: That's a key because, as the oldest, what I learned pretty early on was that if either Joan or John got into trouble or were crying, the first assumption was that it was something I'd done.

Ed: All right. How many times was she right about that?

Cal: Well, sometimes. But whether she was right or wrong, I figured I didn't need it. I didn't figure this out in a very articulate way, but I think that was part of my staying in Dudleytown. What I began to discover was that I could get the attention and the affection outside of home that I wasn't getting at home.

Ed: I can identify with that so much. I never saw my mom and dad hug each other. I never saw them kiss each other. They were very private people. I never heard the three words, "I love you" said between the two of them, or to my sister and me. I know the love was there and, in part, that was the way their generation was raised. I also now know that's the role model they saw growing up. But I can really understand what you're saying, because it wasn't in my house from the day I was born until the day I left home.

Cal: I actually did see affection between Mom and Dad, but I also saw a lot of quarreling. Dad was very demanding about a lot of things. Mother seemed to be as determined to be lax, as he was to be demanding. This difference was kind of their dance. She would persistently not do things that she had time to do and knew needed to be done. He'd be persistent in discovering it and giving her grief about it. As a child back there in Seymour, I had fantasies of rescuing her from him.

Ed: Was your mom pretty docile at those times or did she stand up to your dad?

Cal: She didn't really argue back much. I think she just basically let it go. The situation left me with bad feelings toward Dad and because Mother was like me, a small person, his behavior strengthened my identification with her. I think my identifying with Mom made it even more difficult for me, because I didn't feel like I got the attention from her I would have liked.

Ed: I felt exactly the same way you did. Our whole household was non-communicative. I didn't identify with Dad. Some of the jobs he had took him away from home for extended periods of time. Mom was always the one that I felt was the stronger in the family, perhaps as opposed to what you're saying. I always identified with her and never really made that break from her.

Cal: Yep. Well, there's some similarity there, that's for sure. I found I felt better most of the time when I was away from home. I don't think I was particularly mistreated.

Ed: Unless you count the emotional part.

Cal: Fortunately I had lots of friends in the neighborhood, other kids I played with. We spent lots of hours up in the apple and cherry trees. Let me tell you about the next licking I got. I was in the first grade. Workers had dug up the road beside our home to put in a sewer system. There were these great mounds of dirt along each side of the road. There were about a half dozen of us that walked home from school together.

On this particular day, with the inviting piles of dirt, we got into a dirt clod throwing fight. A kid across the way happened to stick his head up at the wrong time and I hit him right in the eye. Of course he went running the three blocks to his house, crying all the way. The next thing I knew, I was in the bedroom with my drawers down. Dad had a belt and wanted to know what had happened. I kept telling him what we did. He kept whipping me. Finally, after this had gone on for what seemed like forever, but maybe ten minutes, he asked, "Who else was with you?" I told him Dean and Chalkie were with me. He asked, "Why didn't you tell me that in the first place?" Well, I didn't know. But later in my life, whenever it came time for me to tell a story, I found myself just pushed to put every possible detail in the story and not leave anything out.

Because Dad was supplying materials for Freeman Field, while it was under construction during the war, he kept getting deferments because he was in a critical industry. Finally, he did get called up. He was gone six or eight weeks to boot camp while Mom was pregnant with John. When John was born in October of 1945, the war had pretty well quieted down and Dad was discharged. During that period of time he was gone I was the man of the house, at the age of three. I have this recollection of Mom being pregnant. We had three or four big cherry trees in the yard. The birds were always in the trees eating the cherries. Mom went out there on this particular day with Dad's old 22 rifle, leveled it at a bird on a fencepost, and fired. The next thing I knew we had people at the house. That bullet carried across the field and went through the window at the concrete plant down the block. That incident inspired me. When the folks at Dudleytown gave me an old single-shot Benjamin BB gun, and I got back home in the early summer, I'd just live up in the tree with that BB gun. Every time a bird would fly in there, I'd try to shoot it. I hit quite a few. It was something. I had to carry the BBs in my mouth and spit them down the barrel. It was a relic, that old BB gun.

The Move to Columbus When I was Seven and Some Early Jobs

Cal: The time came to move up to Columbus. When Dad bought the first house, he bought ten acres and subdivided it. He sold the lots, sold the house, and had enough money to build us a house in Mead Village, on Westenedge Drive. I didn't mention that in first grade I actually had a girlfriend in Seymour. Her name was Marilyn Ebert. We'd walk home from school holding hands. I was a patrol guard on the corner.

Ed: That gave you a certain amount of respect from the girls, I'll bet.

Cal: Well, yeah. Being a patrol guard also got me into a fight. Some guy was not behaving right toward Marilyn one day and we got into a quarrel. We ended up getting scolded for it. I have a very clear recollection of having my first date in Seymour. Dad drove us down to the movie theater and we saw "So Dear to My Heart." I was terribly embarrassed when it was over. I don't know if you recall that film, but the ending is pretty sad and I was crying. At that point in my life, I didn't think it was a good thing for a boy to be crying.

Ed: When we were young, our elders told us boys weren't supposed to cry. After all "real" men don't cry.

Cal: Especially if I was going to be getting in the car with Marilyn and her dad. I hated to leave Marilyn when we moved to Columbus. However when we moved in 1949, I had great people in the neighborhood to play with.

When I was old enough, I started cutting the grass. Dad bought an old Reo gasoline lawn mower and I mowed that big lot for my pay. Then I got into 4H and we tilled up a big chunk of the backyard. I took care of the garden, with a little help, but not really that much. When I was nine I got an afternoon paper route and I carried the *Indianapolis News*.

Ed: That's the same paper I started carrying.

Cal: It was a long route when it was windy, rainy, or cold. It wasn't any fun, but I did enjoy having the money. I got a small allowance. I also did quite a bit of door-to-door sales and solicitation work. The newspaper gave us a reward for selling magazine subscriptions. Then we had The March of Dimes and other kinds of fundraisers. For one of those programs, I sold enough to be king for a day at the sports car races at the airport. I also got a new bicycle out of it, which was a wonderful thing. I just hated going door to door and trying to get people to buy something or give me something.

About that same time, Mom and Dad joined the Harrison Lake Country Club. The club was offering free golf lessons to kids, so I started taking lessons. Then I started caddying. I was one of the small group of caddies at the country club that hung out at the course. We came from all walks of life. There was a pop cooler where we hung out. We figured out if we brought a church key and a straw, we could pop the caps off the bottles and drink the pop right out of the cooler.

Ed: Now that's a new one. You guys were very creative.

Cal: I suspect, like most of us, I spent an awful lot of summertime days at Donner Center in the swimming pool.

Ed: Yep. When we moved from East Columbus to 22nd and Pennsylvania, I did the same thing. One summer I was a "soda jerk" at the soda fountain. I loved it.

Cal: We'd ride our bikes to the pool, swim, and carry on. Chase the girls. I was a little devil.

Ed: Well **that** surprises me.

Cal: No it doesn't.

Ed: You're right there.

Some of My Teachers

Cal: I felt like my teachers in Columbus were pretty great. In the second grade I started out at McKinley with Mrs. Hubbard. She was just terrific. It happened her husband was Cecil Hubbard, who I would see every now and then at Dunlap's. Then in the third grade, I went to "the Barracks."

Ed: On 25th Street?

Cal: Yeah, on 25th and Central. I had Mrs. Ayers. Remember Brad Ayers?

Ed: Sure. He was in our class. I forgot his mother was a teacher.

Cal: She was a great teacher. She liked nature and she brought critters into the classroom. I remember going home with Brad a few times and catching the lizards in the railroad ties behind his house on 2nd Street. Fourth grade was a nightmare. I got Mrs. Swartwood and I was in trouble with her all the time. The school district put in two overflow classrooms, and Mrs. Swartwood had one of those. I remember a windstorm that blew down some TV antennae. Four of us grabbed some of those broken antennae. We got hacksaws from our parents' tools and cut the antennae into tubes. We carried them to school and whenever Mrs. Swartwood went to the board to write something, we'd chew up a wad of paper and slam it on the chalkboard. That made her mad.

There was a space behind the school, kind of in the corner between the school and the furniture store. This space was level dirt. We'd draw a big circle and shoot marbles for keeps. We weren't supposed to shoot for keeps, because that was against the rules. We got caught.

I think the second time I got caught, another guy and I had to go up in the front of the classroom and get some licks from her board. That was exciting. But we had quite a time. I was really glad when that year was over.

Then I was back to McKinley for the fifth grade. I had Mr. Jones and he was just terrific. I remember there were windows all down one side of his classroom. On the front of the classroom and down along the other side, he wrote multiplication tables and we had multiplication races. He put a kid at each end and we worked toward the middle. Whoever got the farthest around the middle won. Whenever we got in trouble for passing notes or talking when we shouldn't, we had to stay in for recess and write multiplication tables.

Ed: Well I'm sure that didn't ever happen to you.

Cal: Oh, I got a lot of practice on multiplication. And I was a patrol boy. In the sixth grade I got to be captain. But in the fifth grade I was a patrol boy.

Ed: When you were a captain, didn't you have a little shield that you could put on the cross strap? Or maybe I'm thinking about something else.

Cal: We had a shield even before we were captain. That's where I was going with this story. When we had that belt and the shield, we could get into sporting events free and we could roller skate free on Friday nights. I got a thing going with Ladonna Whittaker. She and I would go down to the roller rink and skate Friday night after Friday night. Dad would take us down there, because it was just a block or so from Dunlap's.

Ed: I remember I was in love with a girl in junior high who lived right next door to the roller rink, and we'd walk next door and skate.

Cal: My first love, when I got to Columbus in the second grade, was Jill Baker. And I thought I'd die for her. Her mother was the den mother for the Cub Scout group. I used to go there every week for meetings, but mostly just to have a chance to see Jill.

Ed: I was going to say, you probably didn't miss too many meetings did you?

Cal: No. First time I got in trouble for passing a note was in the second grade with Jill. She was my heartthrob. I cannot remember what happened between Ladonna and me. I started taking Sandy Welch down to the skating rink. We were doing some dating then. I also remember from that particular time—and you may well connect with this too—I played Boys Club basketball.

Ed: Yeah, I spent a lot of time at the Boys Club.

Cal: I got my growth spurt early, so all the way up through the seventh grade I was playing under the basket, usually forward. We had a couple of those Boys Club teams play down at the church. We played back and forth between the church and the Boys Club. Dad did some coaching. He used to drive me nuts trying to make me learn how to dribble with my left hand. We had a really fine gymnasium at the church, so that was a big deal. Jeff Crump and Skip Lindeman played too. There was quite a gang of us. That was a great bonding at the time.

My Junior and High School Experiences

Cal: I got started in seventh grade at Northside. Most days I rode my bicycle and would usually pick up Larry Davis, Bill Ryan, and George Hamilton. We were the four musketeers. We did a lot of stuff together. I remember having Mrs. Feigle for homeroom. One time she managed to get herself locked out in the hallway.

Ed: And you guys were in the classroom?

Cal: We were in the classroom. I remember going to the door when she knocked. I looked out and saw who it was. I looked back at the class like, "Should I let her in?" Everybody just roared. We had a lot of fun in that class and played a lot of games. She was a fun person.

I played basketball and football in the seventh and eighth grades. But by the time we got down to Central for the ninth grade, everybody else had been catching up in their growth, and I discovered I was not tall enough any longer to play under the basket. By that time, if you were going to be a guard, you had to have a jump shot. I didn't have a jump shot. I tried some shots but decided I wasn't going to get it, so I gave that up. That's when I started being more interested in golf. I went out for football my sophomore year. The coach set me up as a linebacker in one of those scrimmages. And doggone it, but some big guy came around my end carrying the ball and I tackled him, but I thought it was going to kill me. It wasn't good and I thought to myself, "What in the world are you doing? You can get a letter on the golf team and you don't have to worry about getting beat up." So I let football go.

Going back to Central, I did pretty well in the ninth grade. We formed a student council and the students elected me president. I also got in an advanced social studies class. We had to do a special project. I did mine on Germany, Nazism. I read all the books, the Third Reich stuff.

Ed: I wrote my senior research paper on that topic.

Cal: For some reason, the whole Nuremberg Trial process stuck in my mind. It ended up having a pretty strong ethical impact on me, particularly in terms of relationship to authority. It also instilled in me an apprehension about the church and the state getting too cozy, having studied what came out of that.

Ed: It's amazing you were able to focus in on that topic at a reasonably young age and doing so made such a lasting impression on you.

Cal: I'm sure I got some help from my teacher and I got a lot from what I was reading. I think at that age a lot of us were pretty interested in what the hell had gone on over there. I had uncles in the war and they told stories about it. It did get an intellectual curiosity going for me that turned out to be important. I also wanted to mention how, during that time, we used to hang out over at the Olympia Dairy. It was almost like there was a status thing around who sat together in the booths.

Ed: Yep, I can remember that, as well as the great greasy burgers, fries, and shakes we got there.

Cal: That was the context in which I first heard the rumor that Janie and Marietsa might be interested in having a date with me. It went right to my head and of course it was pretty exciting too. They were knock outs. That's when I broke up with Carol. Carol lived in the Questover-Roth subdivision. That was walking distance from where I lived in Mead Village. I just spent a lot of time with Carol. We never had sex, but we sure did a lot of heavy making out. We spent a lot of time alone in her recreation room. It was early teenage deep love. I just thought I needed to see about Janie and Marietsa. I had my date with Janie first. We just couldn't seem to carry on a conversation. Then I went out with Marietsa. She seemed about two or three years more mature than I was.

Ed: That's interesting. She and I went to State Street Elementary School together.

Cal: Well, she was gorgeous and so smart. I remember meeting her a couple of times at Pasquale's to have pizza. After I got my license and was trusted to be on the road, I took her up to Indianapolis to hear the Dave Brubeck Quartet. After a month or two, it was pretty clear we might be friends, but I wasn't in her league. At least I didn't feel like I was in her league. I went back and asked Carol if she would take me back and she said, "No." I turned sixteen that summer and went up to Culver Naval Academy with George Hamilton, Larry Davis, and Bill Ryan. I spent eight weeks up there.

Ed: Was that a good experience?

Cal: Yes it was, in a lot of ways. I found I really enjoyed the close order drill work. I learned to take care of my clothes and my room for inspections and put a spit shine on my shoes. Because I was sixteen, I was allowed to smoke. There were a couple of smoking areas where I used to hang out with some of the other guys that smoked. That was big stuff. A couple of us decided the Culver Inn had a very vulnerable way of displaying their merchandise and we could fairly easily liberate a carton of cigarettes. I think we liberated three or four cartons.

The Inn noticed the shortage in their inventory. They talked to the Culver Academy people and the next thing I knew, we had a room check. Low and behold if they didn't find six or eight packages of Old Gold cigarettes in my desk drawer. So, I was found guilty of stealing, confined to quarters for pretty much the remainder of camp—a little over a week. I could still do the drills and the required activities, but when everybody else had free time, I had to be in that room. I think calling home and telling Mom and Dad that I'd stolen the cigarettes was probably one of the hardest things I'd ever had to do up to that point.

Ed: I can imagine. Was that something you felt compelled to do or did you have any choice about it?

Cal: I don't really think I had any choice. I was told I needed to call my parents, although I didn't do it from the office. I called from a payphone. My parents were embarrassed and ashamed of me. Actually, they decided the punishment I got from Culver was enough, so I didn't have any more. When I got home I still had my driving privileges. I jumped right in the car, drove to Carol's house, and asked her again to take me back. She still said, "No." So I started trying to figure out who was I going to go out with.

I went out a couple of times with Julia Reece, Senator J.R. Reece's daughter. She was a year ahead of us. I think I got hooked up with her because I helped with the class play. And this is one of my favorite stories. After one of the evening rehearsals I took her home. At that time we had an old Plymouth station wagon. We found a back road not too far from her house. They lived on Hwy. 31, north of town. We were sitting there making out. It was colder than hell, so I was running the engine on idle to keep the car warm. After a half hour, it got warm enough I turned the engine off. When I went to turn it back on, the battery was dead. I'm out there in the middle of nowhere. So I walked back to a farmhouse, maybe a half a mile away, and left Julia in the car. I couldn't think of who in the world could help me out of this mess. I called Tommy Marshall. You remember him?

Ed: I do remember Tommy.

Cal: I got him out of bed, told him my situation, and asked if he would mind to come and get me. He helped me get my car started. I took Julia home. I kept the engine running, drove the car home, put it in the garage, and went to bed. After I got home from school the next day, Mother wanted to know what was wrong with the car. She went out to go to the store and the car wouldn't start. I said, "Well I don't have an idea. It was driving fine when I brought it home last night."

Ed: Yeah, that's exactly what I would have said.

Cal: Well it was true. Then I met Betsy. She moved here from Shelbyville and we fell in love. That relationship lasted four years and it was wonderful.

Ed: Yep. I remember as we left high school and began our freshman year as roommates at Hanover College, we both had a tough year because of…

Cal: …Yeah, separation anxiety.

Ed: That's right.

Cal: After she left for Butler University, I used to go and pick her up from school and we'd go into Indianapolis and spend the night. We found a restaurant that we liked that would serve us alcohol, even though we were underage.

One of the themes I remember about high school is that I was continuing the business I mentioned in my childhood—about staying away from home. I got involved with the golf team, debate team, the school choir, school theater, church, and Junior Achievement. Most of the time, I worked at Dunlap's. When Mal McMullen opened the driving range out on Hwy. 31 above the river I worked for him. Most weeks, if I was home one night, that was a lot. I was just out, out, out. That meant sometimes I had a problem getting my school work done. But I was caught emotionally about grades. I set myself up somehow that if I did as well as I could, I would put myself in a group I didn't want to be a part of. I had a lot of friends who thought getting straight A's reflected brown-nosing teachers, and I wanted to stay friends with them.

Ed: What do you mean by that?

Cal: There was a little group at school we thought of as goody-goodies and brains. I didn't view them as regular kids. I wanted to be a part of the other groups and I used that in some way to rationalize being an underachiever. I still graduated thirty-fifth in the class. If I'd just paid attention and done my homework, I would have graduated something more like tenth or fifteenth. But I was so involved. I had about six different peer groups that I was a part of.

I had this neighborhood gang. Then there was a group I referred to as cruisers. We spent a lot of time just cruising in the car. We cruised through Fritch's Big Boy. We spent a lot of time in the car smoking cigarettes and just being a nuisance. I had a group of friends from church. And then there was this party crowd that had a fluid membership. When somebody had one of those basement parties, you knew who was going to be there. I also had buddies I hung out with from the golf team, debate team, and from DeMolay.

Ed: You did have several social groups with whom you could interact. That's very interesting.

Cal: And I was a different person with each group. Part of the reason I treasured being with Betsy so much was, even at that time in my life—between the music, the literature, and all my other interests—I had a romantic side, a poetic side. I didn't really feel like that was too welcome among the guys, but I could be at ease with Betsy. I could write her a poem or be sweet and affectionate and it was all great.

Do you remember the gang wars here? I haven't read anything in our emails about these.

Ed: Gang wars?

Cal: Between the Rebes and the Sucks.

Ed: Oh gosh, I do remember those names now. I always tell people that we didn't know anything about gangs when I was in high school, but by golly, you're right.

Cal: Get a grip, Ed. You didn't have very many close encounters.

Ed: No I didn't.

Cal: I was identified among the Sucks. The Rebes dressed after the fashion of Elvis Presley, with their collars turned up and their shirts unbuttoned.

Ed: Do you remember anybody in the Rebes?

Cal: I remember some faces. I couldn't put names with them. But I remember some encounters. I remember a fight after a football game where one of our guys got his collarbone broken. I also remember the encounter at the Crump Theater when I was sitting with several other Sucks. Half a dozen of those Rebes came in and sat in the row behind us. One of them dug his thumb and fingers into the back of my neck. I thought my head was going to be pinched off. We made arrangements to get out in the alley and settle the score behind the youth center. Fortunately that never happened. But they were known to carry switchblade knives and most of us had some forms of defense in our cars. I know some of the guys had a piece of garden hose with chain laced through it.

Ed: Then there was the tire iron.

Cal: Or the cutoff baseball bat that we kept under the driver's seat in case of a confrontation.

Ed: See, I missed out on all that. I remember those two names but that was just an experience that was out of my frame of reference.

Cal: Well, I think you were lucky.

Ed: Probably, yeah. Although not remembering the gang wars allowed me to have at least this one mythical image of my high school.

Cal: The geographical assumption was the kids that were in the Rebes were from East Columbus.

Ed: I grew up in East Columbus. I moved my eighth grade year to a little house at 22nd and Pennsylvania. I remember having this really embarrassing image of having grown up in East Columbus. That's where I went to the Church of Christ on Indiana Avenue. I had a lot of friends there from Sunday School and Youth Group. I just totally left all those friends behind because I thought when we moved into that house at 22nd and Pennsylvania I'd hit the big time. I pretended I didn't know them, even when we passed in the halls at high school. I guess by moving to the north side of town before high school, I escaped my identification with the Rebes.

Cal: Well Marietsa lived in East Columbus and that made me a little nervous when I was going to see her. I always looked over my shoulder because I didn't know what was going on.

I was in the college prep track in high school. By that time, I was pretty impressed with what J. Irwin Miller had done here. I thought the thing I wanted to do was become a corporate lawyer and get hooked up with a big company like Cummins. I wanted to be in a position to help that company be a responsible citizen in some community. It was that thought I carried to Hanover with me. I was looking mostly at law schools and Hanover had a pretty good rating as a pre-law school.

Jim Battin
A Problem with Education

Jim: This story is about when I was a junior in high school. I was in geometry class. Mr. Morris was our teacher. I was sitting there and he was talking. I didn't understand anything he was saying. I kept going from class to class and I noticed he was building one concept upon another. Therefore, it was extremely frustrating because I never got the first one. In fact, it was one of the most frustrating experiences of my high school career. I remember looking around the classroom. I don't remember the specific people, but everyone else seemed to know what was going on. I became terrified. I thought, "I just don't understand this. And I don't know what to do." One day I decided I couldn't do this anymore. I raised my hand and said to Mr. Morris, "I don't understand any of this, and I'm not sure what to do." There was a chuckle in the class. Raising my hand and openly admitting I didn't know what was going on was a huge step for me.

Ed: I guess so, Jim. Raising your hand and saying what you did is something many students are terrified to do—especially appearing "not to know" in front of your peers.

Jim: I remember my comment stunned Mr. Morris and was awkward for him. Basically, he just passed it off and moved on. But I remember thinking to myself, "I simply have to take responsibility for my own learning, because I have to figure out strategies. It isn't fair to count on someone else to read my mind and know what I need." In retrospect, I could have done things differently that day in geometry class, but the fact is I felt helpless and didn't have the mental capacity at that time to deal with it. For example, I could have met with Mr. Morris separately for help. I could have asked classmates who seemed to understand, but I was too embarrassed. My mom and dad didn't know how to help. Dad went to the eighth grade. He didn't know geometry. Mom didn't know either. To this day I remember I just thought, "Everybody else seems to know this." Later, I found out they didn't. I thought, "I've got to develop a different approach because I don't like this feeling."

In my current work, I see a lot of kids. Today when I see kids who seem to be lost in education or their lives, I think back to that geometry class. Doing so gives me empathy towards their situations and makes me realize the importance of preserving each student's personal self-worth in the learning process. Today this means offering key concepts in a variety of ways, so that students with different learning styles can have an opportunity to grasp concepts "in their way." Addressing different learning styles is one of the challenges of educators, given their teaching time is being reduced, class sizes are growing, etc. I think the current trends toward team learning, project-based, and hands-on learning are helping and should be continued.

Ed Poole[1]

Columbus was a great place to spend my first eighteen years. Of course I didn't know any other community, but I can't imagine any other place could have had the same enchantment, fun activities, and quality of schools as did my hometown.

I grew up in East Columbus, an unincorporated part of the city of Columbus—later to be annexed so there is one Columbus. By many, including myself as I grew older, East Columbus was considered living on the "other side of the tracks" from the city itself. Cal Brand just shared a story about the gangs when we were in high school. The Rebes were from East Columbus.

As I later discovered, the range of socio-economic status in East Columbus was lower to middle class. Most of the adults, like my parents, were blue-collar workers. When Dad and his brother were four and three respectively, their biological parents placed them in an orphanage in Attica, Indiana. At some point, both boys were adopted by a family who lived in Indianapolis. Sometime later, the family decided two boys were just too much for them to handle. My dad was placed back into that same orphanage and stayed until Grandpa Poole adopted him. Dad finally had a permanent home.

I wish I could tell you that I know about what must have been an unbelievably difficult time in Dad's life, but I can't. Dad never talked to anyone about that period in his life. A few weeks after Dad died in 1989, I spent two days in Columbus just talking with Mom. I generated a list of twenty-six questions I wanted to ask Mom, hoping I could fill in some of the holes in Dad's early life.

To my amazement, Mom didn't really know much more about Dad's early years than I did. With every one of those twenty-six questions that dealt with those years in the orphanage and his two adoptions, Mom's response was the same: "I just figured your dad didn't want to talk about it, so I never asked him." I do know Dad had to leave school after the sixth grade to work with Grandpa Poole in the construction business. According to Mom, both Dad and Grandpa worked very hard, and I have no reason at all to doubt her. She did tell me that one time after living in St. Louis and working on a construction project there, Dad and Grandpa lived in a tent along a river bank in southern Indiana. The food they had to eat was the fish they caught.

---

1   Many of my stories are shared throughout the book within the context of conversations I have with various members of The Columbus Crew.

Every day Dad hitchhiked the twenty miles to and from Columbus looking for work. He finally landed a job. He and Mom were married and moved to my hometown.

From as far back as I can possibly remember, if Dad said this to me once he said it a hundred times, "Son, if I could do any part of my life over, it would be to get an education, and you're going to get yours." From the get-go, I knew Dad and Mom expected I would go to college. Somehow they scrimped and saved to make that happen—perhaps one of the greatest gifts I received from them in my early years. My parents could just as easily have assumed I would graduate from high school—if I even made it through twelfth grade—and go to work in one of those three big manufacturing plants in town. Because they never told me why, I will never understand what allowed them to realize that a college degree was the one way to break our family cycle of little education, hard manual labor, and low paying jobs.

For several reasons, I was fortunate to grow up in Columbus. As I wrote earlier, in the '40s and '50s Columbus already had well-organized parks and recreation programs and many extra-curricular programs for kids. I feel certain the educational programs in my community were above the average of other communities in southern Indiana. I was fortunate to have had wonderful, well-qualified teachers from grades one through twelve. Having been in professional education for forty years, I can make that statement with a high level of certainty.

I remember in first grade I fell in love with Rita Haywood. I knew I loved her the day Mrs. Bottorff made us stand on top of our desks for talking to each other in class. The next love was Sandy Corbin, in sixth grade. I rode home with her on our bicycles most days after school. Sandy moved to Columbus in sixth grade. One day during that sixth grade year I hit the winning home run in the school softball game. I got such a big head after that home run—I just thought I was the "cat's meow." Sandy was so upset with me; she wouldn't let me ride her home after the game. Unfortunately, that one experience wasn't enough to teach me some of the consequences of letting my ego get so big I couldn't find a hat big enough to fit my head.

In the fourth grade, my teacher was Mrs. Fulp, whose son I would get to know in high school. She was great. Being in class with her was always a fun day. For a week during the summer between my third and fourth grades, I attended daily vacation Bible school at my church. One day I was showing off for a girl (of course) and rode my bike through some loose gravel across the street from the church. I was swinging the front tire back and forth and fell off. I hit my head on the ground and was knocked unconscious. Mable Gordon, a next door neighbor, happened to be driving along right after I hit the ground. She scooped me up, put me in the back seat of her car, and drove me home. I don't remember arriving back home.

Mom took me to the hospital. The doctor said I had fractured my skull. Most of the rest of that summer was spent lying on the couch. Our family doctor, Larry Davis' dad, would stop by to see how I was doing—something most doctors do not do today.

You already know that growing up in southern Indiana means I love basketball. I played on teams from grade five through my sophomore year in high school. I got cut from the team at the beginning of my junior year.

While talking to Mom for those two days after Dad died, I better understood why I didn't play beyond my sophomore year. I was a starter every year I played. I got my growth spurt early and was close to six feet tall in eighth grade. I was a starter on our junior varsity team my sophomore year.

Because I came from a working class family, I had my first job as a paperboy when I was ten or eleven years old. I can still remember the day Mom took me to the appropriate office on my fourteenth birthday to get my work permit. I've been working ever since that June day in 1956.

WOW! Look at that handsome Number 10! This is our sixth grade team at State Street Elementary School in 1953-54. Richard and Larry Bray, my next-door neighbors, are Numbers 5 and 4 respectively. The cheerleaders are Anita Walker, Marietsa Theobald, and Phyllis Dobbs.

Our high school varsity basketball coach, Bill Stearman, was the director of the Donner Park recreation programs each summer—a nice way for Coach Stearman to "supervise" the high school varsity players in the evening program held on the two basketball courts at the park.

The summer between my sophomore and junior years I worked at the local A&W root beer stand, and I often worked at night. According to Mom, one night while I was at work, Coach Stearman stopped by my house to talk with Dad. In effect, Stearman said, "Mr. Poole, Eddie really needs to be playing in our summer league program at Donner Park. This is the time he can really improve his skills and make a contribution to our varsity club next year." Again, using my own words, Dad said, "Well, Eddie can't play in your program. He has to work." End of story. After varsity tryouts my junior year, I was the last person cut from the team. I felt <u>re</u>jected and <u>de</u>jected for quite some time—after all, basketball was my passion. After I worked through those feelings, I became an avid supporter of our varsity Bull Dogs, guys with whom I was a teammate for many years.

I loved, loved my high school experience. I was fortunate to have a wide and diverse group of friends, and we shared many fun experiences together.

I grew up in a very strict religious environment. By strict I mean a very literal New Testament interpretation of the Bible. Even though I had those beliefs imposed on me, I often pushed the envelope in high school and made many trips to my "shadow side." In fact, I soon discovered that those trips often were more fun. Since I'm a Gemini, I began to blame those trips on my "evil" twin.

I bought packs of cigarettes and hid them in a small loft in our garage. When Mom and Dad were gone, I'd retrieve my cigarettes and enjoy a few smokes before they returned. Sometimes my steady, Donna, and I would slip out to the parking lot between classes, hop in my '52 Chevy and grab a smoke. As with many high schools, we had a senior research paper requirement in our college preparatory English classes. Bill Spicer, Cal Brand, and I would drive twenty miles to Franklin, Indiana, and use the library at the college. On our trips back to Columbus we slid through the drive-up window of a liquor store, grabbed a six-pack of beer, and enjoyed our libations as we drove home.

Since I got cut from the basketball team, during my junior and senior years I worked part time at the largest department store in town—Major T. Jester's. I worked in the men's department, and Jester's carried a lot of name brand men's clothing. I made a **lot** of bad decisions as a teenager. One of the trips to my shadow side was while working at Jester's.

As I said, I grew up in East Columbus, considered by many as living in the wrong part of town. During my eighth grade year, my parents moved into that home I mentioned, on the north side of town. As a teenager, it was important to me to run with the "in crowd," those who lived on the north side of town. Silly me, I thought one of the ways to be in that group was by wearing brand name clothes. During the winter months at Jester's, I always wore a large, over-sized, long coat. On occasion I would tuck a nice shirt, pair of slacks, or sweater under my arm, button up my over-sized coat, and walk out of the store—such a stupid thing to do. If I could go back and "unring that bell"' would I? You bet I would—in a heartbeat. I didn't feel guilty at the time—although I was raised on guilt—because I felt the end justified the means. One day at school, someone even commented on the nice clothes I wore. Well, that single comment solidified my actions at Jester's. Looking back on those decisions I made to steal clothes, positive lessons were learned and stay with me. For example, today if I accidently receive too much change for an item I purchase, I automatically return the overpayment to the clerk.

I was fortunate to graduate in the top ten academically in our class of 432, and I was also a member of the "Top Ten Seniors." I have absolutely no idea what criteria the school used to select those top ten seniors, but somehow I was in that group, announced at the end of our senior year.

I grew up loving music. Mom and Dad both sang in the church choir. I loved hearing my mom's soprano voice and Dad's low, bass voice—which, fortunately, I inherited. Before we got a TV, every Saturday night was spent sitting on the living room floor. We turned on our huge, floor model radio and listened to the Grand Ol' Opry, having to turn the knob once in awhile to retrieve the fading station.

The Modernaires

When we were in high school, Rob Schafstall and I played in a dance band, the Modernaires. During our conversation, Rob said the following about that experience, "The first time I can ever remember feeling I had really accomplished something that I wanted to do was when I got to play with the Modernaires. I remember just thinking what an honor that was, for me to get to play with that bunch of musicians."

Like Rob, I felt honored to be invited to play with this dance band. I was in the tenth grade when I started playing with them. All the other guys were six or seven years older than me, and were more experienced musicians than I.

The band was formed by Jim (James K.) Dickey and Bob Losure. James K. lived right across the street from me when I was a young lad in East Columbus. Another member of the band was Max Gordon, my next-door neighbor during that same period of time. The band had a huge trailer that carried all the instruments. On each side of the trailer was a very nice logo design, announcing to everyone, "There go The Modernaires." Bob always drove the trailer.

Periodically, if I was going to be home for a weekend from Hanover College and the band had a dance to play, I'd play with them. Just sitting next to James K. and watching him play the Big Band era, especially all the Glenn Miller songs, was very special. I don't know how many times I've seen the movie *The Glenn Miller Story*—more than I can count on both hands. Watching James K., I learned all the trumpet "rides" and improvisations for the Big Band era music. He and I would trade off playing those improvisations.

The band played lots of New Year's dances as well as others that were always attended by adults. It was such fun for me to sit in the back row and watch all the couples on the dance floor. That experience was probably the beginning of my own love of dancing.

Because the guys were older, they would buy me bourbon and cokes wherever we played. I also smoked when I was with them. Because Dad and I were never very close, the guys in the band became my adopted dads. I learned to drive in James K.'s '57 Chevy. A short time after our family moved to that northside home, Bob and James K. bought homes next to each other, and right across the street from mine. That was a wonderful, wonderful period of time with nice guys.

**In this picture of the Modernaires, Rob is second from left, playing the accordion.
Yours truly is second from the right in the back row--the guy with the flattop haircut
and those black, thick, plastic glasses frames--blowing away on my trumpet.**

Steve Everroad
Early Work

Steve: I was a paperboy when I lived in Mead Village. I had the largest route in the whole Columbus area. I had to put papers on the front of my bike, on the back of my bike, and around me.

Ed: What paper was it?

Steve: *The Evening Republican.* When I look back on it, delivering papers was one of the great experiences of my young life, because it taught me some responsibility and a good work ethic. I remember one time I was peddling the bike and all of a sudden I got this pain in my ankle. A dog had attacked me. I remember we had to check out the dog, check me out, see whether I had to get shots, and kill the dog. Another time, I was going along the road and all of a sudden something was hitting me in the leg and my bike—bing, bing. I looked over in the field. Some guy had his BB gun and was taking pot shots at me. I thought, "You idiot. What are you doing?" Another time I was collecting. I went inside this fenced yard and I got up to the door. It was almost dark. I knocked on the door. Here came this vicious dog around the corner after me. I had to jump off the porch. I don't know how I got over that fence, it was pretty high. But I dove over this fence and ended up in the shrubbery. One time, during winter, I saw all this water on the road and I had all these papers. I thought, "Well, this will be fun. I'll just hit that water full speed." It wasn't water. It was ice. I straddled that bike, went down, and papers flew all over the place. I probably laid there for fifteen, twenty minutes. I had to put all the papers back, get the bike up, and keep going.

Ed: I remember when I delivered the *Indianapolis Times*, which was an evening paper. Back in those days they had these little collection books with perforated tabs.

Steve: Oh yeah, that's what I used.

Ed: The tabs had a date on them and whenever you collected the money you pulled off that little tab and gave it to the subscribers. The subscribers had proof they paid you the money.

Steve: And if they weren't there and you didn't get back within a certain time, you were another week late. You didn't get that money until you got that collection.

Ed: Exactly.

Steve: I got to meet a lot of people. I got gifts at Christmas. I remember some older people that couldn't come to the door. I went inside and collected. I saw life a little different than how I had seen it before. I appreciated a lot of customers. Others were a little gruffer. I sort of hated to go up to their doors. But I learned there are some things I had to do.

Ed: Like you, the newspaper route taught me responsibility. I had to be at the manager's garage every afternoon at a certain time to start folding the papers.

Steve: When I was really sick those few times, it was Mom or Dad who had to back me up. Sometimes going way down the road in the dark I thought, "What am I doing out here? It's cold, there are dogs, and I'm pretty far from home, on a bicycle."

Ed: The Sunday paper of course was so big. I do remember Dad drove and helped me deliver those papers. But *The Evening Republican* at that time didn't have a Sunday paper.

Steve: Yeah, I was going to say I didn't have the Sunday paper, but I did for the *Indianapolis Star.* When we moved into town on Newton, I took the morning route. That was a little tougher because sometimes I had to be in the gym to shoot baskets before school started. I had to get up around four o'clock or so, get on my bike and ride it several blocks to the store, where I got my papers. Then I had to fold them and make the deliveries. Being a quarterback, I got pretty good throwing the papers.

Ed: I'll bet you did.

Steve: I could nail it pretty good. But then I got hurt in football. I broke my finger and I had a big cast around it. I was getting paid for workman's comp, but I still had the papers to deliver. Dad had to get up every morning and made me go with him. But we would go in a car—how much easier that was. The *Indianapolis Star* route didn't last quite as long because I was moving on in high school—more clubs, more athletics, and I just couldn't do it all. It was a lot of work but it sure paid off and I liked the money I earned. Even more valuable were some of those characteristics you learn and the people you got to meet, building relationships and being able to deal with different types of people. That's helped me throughout all my life.

Ed: I look back on those experiences and realize the lessons I learned. In fact this conversation right here about our newspaper jobs brought back some of those memories—the importance of being responsible, learning how to deal with so many different personality types, and trying to keep people happy so they wouldn't drop their subscription. This talk is a good example of the importance of storytelling in our lives.

Steve: And I knew people way beyond my neighbors. I knew who they were, I knew where they lived, and I knew so much about their lives. A lot of people were surprised by how much I knew about all these people.

Friends and Fun at the Lagoons[2]

Steve: I lived in town during junior high and high school, and I remember The Lagoons. We ended up over there in our friends' homes and during the summertime we went swimming there. I played a little ice hockey there when I learned to skate. Several of us were always around and The Lagoons were easy to get to. You felt safe there.

I ended up swimming on the summer swim team. I wasn't as good as the Thompsons. One time we went to Broad Ripple and I remember the pool there. The pool got water from a well and it was ice cold. I'll never forget that. We went there for an AAU meet. I was next to the alternate of making the final ten and man was I proud. I wasn't number eleven; I was number twelve. I was next to the alternate. As you can see, I was a good swimmer, not a great swimmer. I learned to swim a lot of different strokes, but the backstroke was my favorite and I got pretty good at it.

Ed: That was cause for celebration.

Steve: For me being next to the alternate was almost like getting a trophy. I just went along because it was something to do. I enjoyed water sports, swimming, just being with the kids, and all the girls in their bathing suits.

Ed: I knew about your playing football, but I didn't know about the other sports.

Steve: Well, basketball, football, track, and swimming—that's about it.

Ed: I can remember when I was a little guy going to Donner Park to take swimming lessons. One day we were supposed to swim under water. When I got close to the side of the pool—with my eyes closed—my hands weren't out in front of me. I had just taken a stroke and so my arms were down at my sides. Smack! Right into the side of the pool. I stood up and blood

---

2   The Lagoons were two lakes in Columbus surrounded by a beautiful subdivision. Lots of fun times were had swimming and ice skating on The Lagoons.

was running down from my forehead. I dropped out of swim lessons for awhile. I finally went back, but that incident scared the heck out of me.

Steve: Practicing at Donner Pool was hard work. That flat wore me out. But it was good. It led me out to Harrison Lakes where Ron Gallaway, Dana Essex, and my cousin Wayne Tanner lived. They all had speed boats and I learned to water ski. I liked to be around water—diving and going in between the seaweed down below, with no fear.

One night a bunch of us were swimming at The Lagoons. I think we were at the Wells' house. It was just past midnight and we were making way too much racket. The neighbors called the police. We were out in the middle of the water on a float, diving in and carrying on, and here came the police with their flashlights. "Boys, get over here; get over here right now." Someone asked, "What should we do?" I said, "We're dead meat. They've got us here."

Ed: Pardon the pun, but you guys were dead in the water.

Steve: Dead in the water. I said, "Let's just swim towards them and take our medicine." The six of us started swimming over. I got about halfway and the policemen's flashlights got off me and went on a couple of the other guys. I dove right down underneath, swam underwater all the way back to the other side of the dock, and hid there. The other guys didn't turn me in; they didn't rat on me. I hid out there and I knew I was going to get it from them. I was laughing. Here I told them, "Well let's give up." Then I thought, "Well wait a second, I might be able to get back to the dock." The darkness helped me out.

Ed: I'll bet the cops gave them a…

Steve: …Oh the cops wore them out, took their names, threatened them, and let them all go. Good friends though. They didn't give my name away. They were just going to kill me.

Working at the Stone Quarry

Steve: I worked at Meshbergers Stone Quarry in the summer between my junior and senior years and then a couple of years during college. The money was really pretty good for back then. I remember one time we were working at Everroad Park. My grandfather built that park. I remember one Saturday I was out there, and we were loading steel forms onto a low boy. We used these real heavy forms to build roads. There were three real muscular men working, who were all a lot shorter than I was. We had put up two levels of forms and we had a few left. They wanted to go for a third level up and I could see they weren't going to be able to reach the top. I said, "We're going to have to pitch the forms there at the end." I was a lot taller and I kept saying, "You know, I'm not sure this is a good idea." You didn't fool around with these guys. They drank beer and they'd level you. Against my advice, they were going to do it. So here I was on the end. They threw the form up there but then it left their fingers and I still had hold of it. My little finger got smashed all to bits. As a matter of fact I'm looking at it today where it got cut, just into my small, little pinky.

Ed: The end of it got ripped off?

Steve: Well, it cut it pretty good. The pain was excruciating, unbelievable, and they said, "We have to take you to the hospital." I've got this hard hat on and no shirt. I went to the emergency room and I didn't get in right away. The pain got a lot worse. An hour later, I was still sitting there. Finally, the doctor looked at my smashed finger and said, "You know it's really a bad cut but I don't think we can stitch it. I think we're just going to put a butterfly on it and tape it up." I was sitting there feeling a little embarrassed because here I got a hurt little pinky and all these other people were sitting there with these bad things happening to them. All of a sudden I said, "Hey, you know, I'm a little light-headed. I think I'm going to faint." And down I went. I remember how embarrassing that was to have so much pain with such a small injury and also how angry I was at those guys because they thought it was a big joke. I ended up in the emergency room wishing I was somewhere else.

Another time at Meshbergers this guy was swinging me around on a crane. The workers had built a little seat that I got to sit in. This guy gave me a paint brush and a bucket of paint and swung me up real high against this wall to paint it. When I finished, he started swinging me back and forth way up in the air. It scared the daylights out of me. I mean it was dangerous as all get out. I was hanging on and I wanted to kill him. He puts me up on the top of a big rock pile. He jumped out of the cab and ran away.

Ed: And left you up there?

Steve: I remember grabbing a shovel and coming down that rock pile after him. I chased him all over the stone quarry.

I remember another time; we were going up the hill to put these big sticks of dynamite, sixteen sticks down into the holes. They started throwing the dynamite sticks to me out of the truck—scared the daylights out of me. But I didn't realize, as long as they weren't wired together with the firing pins, they weren't dangerous. These guys were laughing as they threw pieces of dynamite sticks to me and I was jumping around before they hit the ground. I remember twenty-five, thirty holes, sixteen dynamite sticks in each one of them and then we'd blow off the side of the mountain. That was fun! And we'd have to get far away from it. I learned a lot about that kind of work.

At another job I traveled to Indianapolis at five o'clock in the morning to work in cement. I got cement poisoning sometimes. We spent twelve hour days building roads. It was hard work. The boots I was wearing weren't high enough. They ran out of rubber boots and the cement would get around my ankles. The rocks cut my ankles and I ended up getting cement poisoning. Long days, hard days, throwing that cement around with shovels—oh my goodness gracious. The big trucks kept coming in and going out. There was just a variety of accidents.

One time I was cutting weeds around this big hole at the stone quarry. They were putting water in there. I had this big cutting tool in my hand and all of a sudden I started sliding down this rock, which looked like a snow cone. Just as my feet were hitting the water, I swung that tool over my head and stuck it in the rock. I was holding on and yelling for help, with my feet in the water. I don't know how far down I was—ten, twenty feet—and finally had to work myself up the slope because I was alone out there. I thought, "I'm going to die."

Another time they had me in a big underground gas tank that was on top of the ground. I had to crawl through the hole, ninety degree weather outside, and clean it with some kind of stuff that had fumes. They had a little hose they used to pump in oxygen to me, but it didn't help me breathe better. I was using this chemical to scrape the insides off. It was just too much. It should have killed me. I'm hanging there, trying to get oxygen through this little hose and was almost asphyxiated.

There were really some dangerous jobs around rock quarries. I got to use jack hammers. I found the secret was not to grab it tight, just let it work itself. We had rock spills on these belts. I'd drop a hammer and had to run up straddling the belt with both feet up in the air to grab the hammer before it went into the rock crusher. Those hard hats saved my head two or three times with rocks flying off those belts.

Ed: I'll bet back in those days when you were using the jack hammer they didn't have the ear protectors to muffle the sound. You didn't have those did you?

Steve: No I didn't. And come to think about it, maybe that's some of my hearing problems today. I was really fortunate to have all these work experiences because not only could I make some money, but also I got to interact with people from different socio-economic levels. The crews at those rock quarries and on the road crews were some really tough, tough people that I hadn't interacted with before, interesting people from a variety of jobs and I learned a lot about people.

A Close Call

Steve: I remember during my high school years, I was coming back from a date in Nashville. It was late at night, close to midnight, and I was driving into town too fast. The police came after me. When I saw them I thought, "Oh, I can lose these guys." I can't remember what kind of car I had, but it was pretty fast. I went through some alleys in Columbus to avoid the police. Sure enough the guy caught me. I don't know where he came from. He pulled me over and gave me this big lecture about it being Halloween night and little children out trick-or-treating. I smarted off and said, "Look, if these kids are out at midnight, etc., etc."

Ed: Not a good thing to say, Steve.

Steve: I know but that's the only thought that came to my mind. I thought, "You dummy, they shouldn't be out at midnight."

Ed: What happened to you?

Steve: Surprisingly enough, he just gave me a strong verbal warning and a warning ticket and let me go. I don't know if it was because I had my sports letter jacket on or what. I deserved a ticket.

Ed: One of the nice things about the cars back in those days was you could turn the lights off with the engine running. I can remember a few occasions where I turned off the lights when I was driving here or there. If there weren't street lights, the only problem you had was when you hit the brakes and your brake lights went on.

Steve: Oh, hey, one time I turned the lights off. I was in Dad's Plymouth, and we were out in East Columbus. I ran into this parked car. It jarred all of us. I thought, "Oh no, I'm in for it now." At least I ran into the back of it, the bumpers, but it about killed all of us. Okay, I'm lucky to have survived my teenage years. God was merciful to me.

Jim Battin
Age 10 (1953) My Love of Reading Begins

Jim: I remember it like it was yesterday. It is very clear in my mind. I was in the old Bartholomew County Library at Fifth and Franklin Streets. This trip was my first. I was told by a classmate that with a library card I could check out books free. I couldn't believe it…free?

Ed: You must have thought, "You mean I can get books in here to check out, take home, and read?"

Jim: That's right. It was quiet there and fit me well. I continue to enjoy solitude and draw strength from it. I got my card. I just fell in love with the library because it was quiet. I am an introvert. I love solitude and this environment fit me well. I felt very powerful as I walked through the rows of books. I could hardly go more than a foot or two. I'd pick up a book and think, "I want to learn this. I don't know what it's about but I want to learn it." I started panicking a little bit. I thought, "How can I make sense of all this? How can I decide what to learn?" I immediately became enthralled with the Dewey system of organizing books by topics. That system fit my need for structure. The immenseness of the library just overwhelmed me, as well as the psychological impact it had on me. I thought, "I've got to figure out a way to sort out what I decide to read." It was then that I became very organized in the way I did things. I came to grips with the notion that I could only learn new things one step at a time. It just seemed natural to start with something I was very interested in—sports. I loved basketball, so I went into the sports section and gravitated toward an author named John R. Tunis, who wrote many, many sports books. I ended up reading them all. I remember reading at least one a week. My mother said, "If you could only read your school books that way!" I've continued reading a book a week since that beginning.

Dan FitzGibbon
Life is a Series of Building Blocks

Dan: Our senior year especially was just a wonderful year in so many ways. When I think back on our 1959 undefeated football team, I made very little in the way of a contribution to it. What that team and season contributed to me far, far outweighed whatever little bit I contributed to it. It's funny, going through two-a-day summer practices and getting battered around in practice on the scout team the way I did, prepared me for some of these later challenges I had to deal with in life. If I hadn't had that experience I don't think I could have made it through West Point. I don't think I would have had the mental and physical toughness I needed, that I picked up on that team.

As a boy I was a pretty soft, timid, and undisciplined kid. Football and the discipline we were taught by our coaches made a big difference to me. I believe we have building blocks in life. Something boosts us up a little bit, and I think high school football did for me, to enable me to meet the challenges of West Point. And West Point, in turn, boosted me up a little higher in my mental, emotional, and physical toughness to prepare me for things like Airborne Ranger and Special Forces in the army. Ranger training was clearly the most physically demanding challenge I ever went through. All that training ended up making things like Vietnam seem comparatively easy. And Harvard Law School wasn't difficult at all, having gone through all of those other experiences.

Ed: Well, you know it's interesting you use the word "easy." That would have been one of the last words that came to my mind considering how difficult Harvard Law School must have been.

Dan: Another thing that occurred to me about that football team, Ed, is how successful all these guys later became, or at least virtually all of them. I don't know what happened to everybody, but I would guess in our high school graduating class as a whole, maybe twenty percent of our graduates went on to college.

A lot of people went back to the farm, the factories, or into the military. But I'm guessing that well over eighty percent of our football players went on to college and most of them actually graduated from college, and many earned post-graduate degrees. If you look at these guys, they have really achieved an awful lot of success later on in business, in law, education, the military, and other professions. That's pretty extraordinary for guys on a football team that you don't normally associate with that kind of motivation and intellect.

Ed: Yeah, and especially from a little southern Indiana town like we were from. You look at the swim team our senior year with their second straight state title and undefeated season. A lot of those people, like Charlie Schuette and Claude Thompson held state and national records in their events. They went on to do the same at the University of Oklahoma and Indiana University. If you just look at the group of twenty-four of us that Jack has pulled together, there are some amazing educational experiences among us and interesting kinds of work experiences that everybody has had since high school.

Dan: Yeah. That's really true.

Jay Shumaker
My Studebaker

Jay: When I was sixteen years old, which would have been in May of 1958, my grandparents surprised me by giving me their 1951 gray Studebaker. It was probably one of the ugliest vehicles ever made. It had a bullet nose and the back doors opened forward so they could be ripped off if a car hit them. The car was really a treat for me. My grandparents were very special. My grandfather looked like Gary Cooper. I just idolized him. He was a foreman at Cummins. I loved him a lot. So, I got his Studebaker. He purchased one of those new golden hawks that were coming out. I was excited to have the vehicle and make it mine. I put some things in it to make it work for me. I went over to pick up my girlfriend and took her for the first spin, the two of us alone in the car. It was towards dinnertime and so we drove over to Fritch's Big Boy. We ordered a couple of burgers, a couple of cokes, and fries. We sat outside, with everyone cruising around the parking lot. How interesting it was to finally have our own space and not be in someone else's space.

Ed: That is interesting, Jay. I can remember a 1953 Chevrolet Mom and Dad had, that I drove for a few years. I was going with Donna at the time and we would slide through Fritch's and had many good hamburgers sitting outside by those phones that we used to call in our order. Bill Becker's root beer stand there on Twenty-Fifth Street still has those drive-up spaces where you can order your food from the car and a waitress brings the food out to you. Back to the car. It was nice to have your own special space and not be in somebody else's car.

Jay: For us to be alone and not be bothered with other people was a really beautiful time. My parents had a river cottage. A lot of people in those days had river homes. Of course, we thought we were upper-middle class. We weren't. We were relatively lower-middle class. We didn't have a lot of money, but always did a lot of things. My dad always provided well. He made so much less money that I thought he did.

My girlfriend and I decided that after eating our burgers and fries at Fritch's it might be a good time to be alone together. As I said, my parents had this river cottage and it wasn't open yet. We really didn't move into it until right around Memorial Day, so it was still closed up. We're driving back in there. Around this one bend there had been a lot of erosion during the winter and spring. Part of the road was dug out and wasn't safe to travel on towards the cabin. So we backed up, turned around, and parked the car.

For the first time, we were alone in my car. We decided that maybe we'd just get in the back seat and be a little more comfortable. She hopped over to the back seat. I got out, walked around, and got in. We're in the car for probably ten minutes, fifteen minutes. In our day, petting was a big thing. It wasn't the fact that you were going to have sex; it was the fact that you were experiencing your first intimate times with your girlfriend. We were in the back seat. It was so nice. The back seat was quite large. We were just enjoying ourselves and laughing and just playing with each other and having fun. All of a sudden that car went straight up in the air and then bounced down. It rocked side to side. We were actually almost flying around in the back seat. Whatever it was, it was that strong. It continued and we're looking around and I'm yelling. I jumped out of the car. I'm waiting probably to get the crap beat out of me. There was no one there.

I turned the car and the lights on and I went down towards an area where I thought, "Okay a home would be there." I looked and there was no one there. That was the first day in my Studebaker.

More about Car Problems

Ed: I've got to tell you a funny story about the first time my girlfriend ever drove. I let her drive the '52 Chevy. One Sunday afternoon, she and I were driving around on a country road and it had been raining. My girlfriend wanted to drive. Because the road was wet from the rain, the car started skidding off the road and went through a barbed-wire fence. Of course, part of the fence was still stuck on the hood piece, the mounted emblem on the front of the hood. The front of the car was full of barbed-wire scratches. We ended up in this cornfield, trying to get out, and the car just kept going deeper and deeper in the mud. I had to get a hold of Dad, and I told him I was driving. He had to get a tow-truck to come out and pick up the car. I hadn't had that car very long when she let it slide off the road. I think many of us had some pretty interesting experiences with our first car.

Jay: I remember going to a basketball game. The Bull Dogs were playing in Seymour. Graham Updike had gotten this neat car, a convertible of some sort. He and Jack were in that car and I was in mine with another ball player. We were over at the old Memorial Gym on Pearl Street. I stopped in the middle of the road and no cars were there at all. I was waiting for Graham and Jack to come up to the side. Graham wasn't looking forward and he ran into my car. It was just devastating because it was just me waiting for him to come alongside and he didn't see my car.

Janice took my car after the wreck. Because of the impact, the brakes didn't work properly and she slid right through the intersection. She ran into a curb and stopped the car. The impact with Graham had stripped my brakes and she really could have had a serious accident, but she didn't.

Ed: That car went through some beating after you got it.

Jay: When I turned it in we got a '55 Ford, two-tone. It was nice but nothing fancy. We took the Studebaker over to Central Car, a used car lot on Central Avenue. The shocks were totally gone on one side. The car tilted all the way to the left. It was so ugly.

Ed: Did you get any money out of it?

Jay: Ed, I couldn't believe it. The salesman overcharged us on the car we bought, and he overpaid us for the Studebaker. I think the Ford was five hundred and fifty dollars and he gave me two hundred dollars for the Studebaker. That car wasn't worth fifty dollars. That's pretty good.

Painting the Summer Cottage

Jay: When I was fourteen, my mom and dad bought this river cottage. It had a front porch that was like thirty feet long and eight feet deep, all screened in. It was a nice area. One summer we decided the house needed painting. Mom and Dad asked if any of us would be interested in painting it. They could give us a little money and whatever else we needed. So Jack Hinkle, Brad Ayers, Steve Enochs, and I went out to the cottage. For several days we rode our bicycles out there and spent the day. We had sandwiches and just had a great time—a lot of laughs. We jumped in the river and swam. We painted.

My funniest remembrance was of my mom, who by the way is ninety-five and still alive. We were out there painting and having a great time. You know how kids could be when they're fourteen years old. I'll never forget the day my mom drove back there unexpectedly. Jack was up on a ladder painting. He had a cigarette in his mouth. He saw my mom and he looked at her. I looked at him and he looked at me. We both just threw our cigarettes over to the side. Now Mom, at ninety-five years of age, brings that story up about every other year, how Jack Hinkle looked flipping that cigarette away.

Ed: It's amazing how long people remember what they've seen and heard and continue to tell those stories. For me, remembering is a good thing and reinforces how and why stories can stick in people's minds.

Jack Hinkle
My Second Best Year

Jack: It starts out with the junior prom. Graham and I both had dates and double-dated. We went to the prom and then to the after-prom party. Do you remember the hypnotist guy?

Ed: Yeah, I remember him. Are you going to tell me you got hypnotized?

Jack: I went up on the stage but I don't think I was either dumb enough or smart enough **not** to be hypnotized. I don't think I got hypnotized. Whether anybody else did or not, I couldn't say. I remember one guy in the front row kept jumping up because whenever the hypnotist said a word it was supposed to burn him in the butt. Maybe he was in cahoots with that guy.

It was late in the morning and a few of us were in the Rabbit's Club. It's not like we broke a lot of laws. We were the good-guy group. The gang decided that after the after-prom party, we were going to have an after-after-prom party. Our whole group got together and we drove out to Lake Lemmon for a little beer and refreshment. I understand that I was told I needed somebody to drive me back home. Then we moved into the summer and I was one of the people that got to go to the Fellowship of Christian Athletes conference. Bill Spicer, Skip Lindeman, and Steve Everroad were there too.

Ed: I went between my sophomore and junior years.

Jack: You went to Estes Park, Colorado, right?

Ed: Yep. I went to the beautiful Rocky Mountains.

Jack: The year I went it was in Geneva, Wisconsin. Being there was a real big thrill because of the people I got to meet. We had a get together with Fran Tarkington out on the field. He and others demonstrated some stuff and I actually centered the ball to him once. They did a few plays. Back in those days, Paul Dietzel was the head coach at LSU. He was at the conference, too.

Tom Landry and Otto Graham were also in Geneva that summer. My biggest thrill was Bob Feller. He was there and did some batting practice with us. He was out there on the pitcher's mound lobbing them, and I mean lobbing them, but to a high school kid his lob was faster than anything anybody in high school ever saw. He was just putting them up, and wasn't trying to strike us out.

Ed: Did you hit one off of him?

Jack: I fouled two off.

Ed: At least you made contact with it.

Jack: Yeah. I finally did. I said, "Man that was great." He wasn't intimidating because we knew he wasn't going to try to dust us off or anything. He was just there for a good time. I wasn't scared but I just couldn't catch up with that ball. I also have a side story. I played ping-pong against Fran Tarkington and that son of a gun beat me seven to nothing. He didn't even let me win a point. I didn't think much of that. But I rooted for him later on.

He was one of those guys you might call an over-achiever. He wasn't the kind of physical quarterback you're used to seeing nowadays, but he had that thing about him. You couldn't get a hold of him and he was a good passer. He had good tools but it was just like, "What's that little guy doing running around?" He played for a long time.

On the way back from Geneva, which was an exciting trip for high school kids anyway, we stopped in Chicago to see the college all-star game, which was the super bowl back in those days. The champion of the NFL played the college all-stars. We went to that game at Soldier Field and that was the top off of the trip. When we got home it was time to begin our 1959 undefeated football season. That season I didn't start kicking until the second game. After that, I kicked field goals and points after touchdowns in every game.

I used to joke with Dan FitzGibbon. I called him the finger, because he was the holder. As I remember, I was always first out to practice. I would take the tee and a couple of balls with me and kick them. I'd kick a couple, go get them, and come back until it was time for practice to start. Then after a few games, when we hadn't lost any, we got a little more serious about it and Dan was the natural holder. He was the back-up quarterback. In those days the position you played determined offense and defense. The quarterback was usually a defensive back, the center usually was the linebacker, the guards were guards and tackles on defense, and the ends were ends. But I broke the mold on that one because I was the kicker and I was also the center. Quentin Reynolds was the back-up center to me. Quint was left-handed and he had a problem centering the ball because he was a one-handed center. He threw the ball underneath me instead of having both hands on it. Occasionally he would flip it over my head. About five times during the year I went back and had to pick up the ball about twenty yards back. My negative yardage was probably a school record. Our senior year was quite a season because of our commitment to it. The team was an excellent bunch of guys that just played together. That's really what it amounted to. I thought Bill Spicer was the only really good player we had. We had a whole bunch of good players, but I thought he was by far more of a mature player than the rest of us.

Steve Everroad
Athletics and Having Fun When I Didn't Get to Play

Steve: When I was in high school, I played athletics. My senior year, a couple of us got cut from the basketball team. The year before, I was even starting several games as a guard. My senior year is when they allowed the ninth graders to come up to the high school and play. The coaches had two potentially very good players. In fact one of them became Mr. Basketball in the state of Indiana his senior year.

Ed: That had to be Bill Russell.

Steve: I can remember his shot. He played for Indiana University. Two years later I felt better about the guy making the team and taking my place. I loved basketball so much, I put together an intramural team at the high school and we won the intramural tournament. I also went down to the Boys Club. I'd never been to the Boys Club. They had a league and a travel league. That was a whole different world for me. But it was fun. So I was able to continue playing basketball.

I remember this one time we were playing a team from Indianapolis. When a guy would go for a shot, I had the bad habit of putting out my hand to try and poke him in the stomach, if I couldn't get high enough to block the shot. Next time he might flinch and his shot wouldn't be quite as good. I did that to this inner city kid, which was a mistake. I turned around and all of a sudden he just let me have it, right in the kidneys. After that I thought, "Forget about poking him in the stomach any more. You're going to get hurt."

Ed: If you can remember, how did you feel when you got cut for your senior year?

Steve: Oh man, I was just devastated. These were guys I played basketball with all through the years and some of my closest friends made the team. I was coming out of a pretty good football season. I loved basketball, and I was just overwhelmed for a while, shocked, upset about those ninth graders coming in and taking my place.

Ed: Did you talk to Coach Stearman about it?

Steve: No, not that I can remember. I supported the team. Nobody, nobody was a bigger fan than I was at the basketball games when our team hit the floor. I even went to most of the out of town games. I remember going as far as Evansville one time. I was there right in the middle of those that were rooting for our team. That's the attitude I took. And here's what I did.

We came to tournament time and it was the sectional game. We were playing the Shelbyville Golden Bears on our home court. I got a little teddy bear and a long wooden pole and hung the bear on a rope with a placard on it, "Shelbyville Bears." I was on the first row and when the Bears took the floor I pulled that bear out. I would swing the bear in the air every time they did something bad or we did something good. The Shelbyville fans were just booing me and hissing me. Our fans, even the adults, were just going wild as we got ahead. Charlie Faulkner was standing next to me and asked, "Hey, can I hold that bear and swing it?" I looked at him and said, "Okay Charlie." We were getting excited. I said, "But don't do anything with it. Don't run out there on the floor or anything with it. Don't do that." Sure enough while the game was going on, he threw the bear and the pole out there in the middle of the court, ran out there, and started stomping on it. Holy cow! I had to go out and retrieve it in front of 7,000 fans. The referees had to stop the game. Our fans were just going wild. The Shelbyville fans were ready to come over and punch us in the face. We got back to our seats there on the first row, and I looked way down to the end of the row, way past the scorer's bench, and here comes the principal, Jud Erne. He's stompin' mad! I thought, "Oh no. He's coming right at us." He got down there, grabbed the bear, grabbed us by our collars, yanked us around the corner, and threw us out of the game. Our fans were booing and just going crazy. The Shelbyville fans were jumping up and down. How embarrassing was that?!

We won the sectional and the regional was coming up and guess who we were going to play? The Madison Cubs. I called Erne on the phone and said, "Mr. Erne, I'm really sorry about what happened. I didn't do that. This friend of mine did. You knew that. I'd like to bring that bear back in and change the name from the bears to the cubs. I'll change the color of the pole and I'll get some other guys in the stands to help me, making it less likely anybody's going to grab the bear away from me." Mr. Erne said, "Okay, but you'll be out of school if it happens again."

Ed: You know what though? Jud Erne was a taskmaster and that was good for him to do that.

Steve: Well, it was. I got a big old raincoat, stuck it around the pole and the bear and snuck it in the gym. I got up four or five rows in the middle of the student body. When the Madison Cubs came out I waved that bear and started swinging it and the people went wild. There were pictures in the paper and everything. I just cannot believe I had that kind of guts to bring that bear back in the gym without anyone knowing that I already had permission from Jud Erne.

Ed: Good for you.

Steve: I remember some of the fans coming over, some of the cheerleaders, because I got a real little cheerleader cape. It wasn't theirs, but they thought I'd stolen it. I had a bunch of football players around me protecting the bear that was hanging in effigy by the rope. We won the game, and then we went to Indianapolis to the semi-state. And guess who we played? The Muncie Bearcats.

Ed: You kept the mascot.

Steve: Just changed the colors again and the name. Butler Field House—now we go to TV. On the camera, here I go pulling that thing out. What a wonderful afternoon, although this time we got beat. But swinging that bear and experiencing other things the students were rallying around was one of the big deals during my senior year. I never have forgotten that. Just supporting the team was the deal and feeling good about myself, as well as our team, and trying to encourage them in that unique way.

Jack Hinkle
My First Vacation

Jack: My first vacation was either in '51 or '52. I was nine or ten years old. My grandma and grandpa, my mom and my brothers—the six of us—got in Grandpa's 1951 or '52 Chrysler, four door machine. I always remember that car because it had both a standard and automatic transmission. You could actually drive in high gear with the clutch. We took off headed for Detroit, going up Highway 31.

Ed: So you were on your way to Detroit.

Jack: We're on our way. We went up through Kokomo and South Bend. It was about a five hour trip going that way. Our first stop was Greenfield Village. It's like the Henry Ford Museum because they have all these old cars, the Model-T trucks and all that. They had the building where Thomas Edison started inventing things in New Jersey. The people at Greenfield Village had taken that building and moved it to this place. Also there was the original factory of what ended up being General Electric. The last item I always remembered was they had the chair that Lincoln was in when he got shot.

Ed: Is that right? Seeing that chair must have been very special as you look back on it.

Jack: It was on exhibit there and it made a big impression on me. The next day we went through a tunnel that goes under the Detroit River. We headed across into Canada. Doing that took most of the day. We were headed to Niagara Falls. On the Canadian side you can look right over the top of the falls. Down below there were stairs where people could go in behind the falls. But we didn't do that.

Ed: I didn't do that either, but I do remember the view from the Canada side was better than the one from the American side.

Jack: I remember how noisy it was. In the late afternoon, we made the trip over to the U.S. side. The timing was good. At night they turn lights on the falls and that was pretty impressive. Having been there yourself, you probably noticed the same thing—when you walked along, you'd look over and it looked like you weren't getting anywhere. It was so huge and I remember thinking, "Gee whiz. I've been walking for five minutes here and I'm still in the same place." Our big thrill of the day was after we got through visiting Niagara Falls, we didn't have a place to stay. We proceeded to look for a motel and it turned out we drove about two hours back into Canada, to a place called Wellington. We went into the hotel at two o'clock in the morning. We walked into the lobby with Jerry carrying his suitcase and it plopped open. All his clothes fell out. I started yelling at him and Mom said, "Be quiet. You'll wake people up." Then it got even more interesting. When we got up to the room, it had one great big poster bed that you practically had to climb into. There was this one great big bed in the middle of that room. That was all that was in the room. There were no bathrooms. The bathroom was down the hall.

Ed: Could you all fit in the bed?

Jack: Yeah. I think it was two of us with Mom. Grandma, Grandpa, and Ronnie were in another room. So not all six of us were in that room. Over in the corner was the topper to the story—coiled up rope.

Ed: The fire escape?

Jack: Yeah. I lay awake all night waiting for the fire to start. I remember thinking, "How am I going to climb down that rope?" I could have climbed any tree in town, but I was worried about being able to climb down that rope.

Ed: This sounds like a great trip.

Jack: Oh, it was. Some of Grandpa's family still lived over there. We stopped by and visited my grandfather's first wife. Her sister was my Aunt Edie and they lived in Kenmore, New York.

I always remember that name because we had a Kenmore washing machine from Sears. We spent the afternoon with them. The next day we headed into New York City to drive around. That's the only time I've ever been to New York.

We drove around a little bit and I think we were on the Brooklyn Bridge. We stopped just before we got onto it. We asked a policeman for directions. This policeman asked, "Where are you guys from?" We said, "Columbus, Indiana." He replied, "I'm from Richmond." It was like in the middle of New York City and we saw somebody from Indiana. From that view on the bridge, I'm pretty sure we could see Yankee Stadium and the Polo Grounds. Next we went downtown to Radio City Music Hall and went to a TV show.

Ed: Which one did you go to?

Jack: I don't even know what the name of it was, but Dennis James was the MC. It was a quiz show. I remember sitting in the balcony. I always remember later on when I'd see him on television I would say, "I saw that guy when I was in New York City." He had two first names.

Ed: One of the two vacations I remember taking was to New York City. My cousin's husband was a cameraman with CBS or NBC, whichever one had the Arthur Godfrey show on it. Herman got us tickets to that show and maybe the Perry Como show. That was a big thrill to actually be in the audience, because back in those days the shows were live.

Jack: Yeah, and remember, they had an applause sign.

Ed: Oh, yeah.

Jack: After we got done there, we took the subway out to the Statue of Liberty. That made me nervous too. I was worried about my brother a lot because Jerry was…

Ed: …Claustrophobic?

Jack: He was kind of absent-minded. I thought we'd leave him on the subway and everybody else would get off and he'd still be thinking about getting off. We walked up the Statue. I used to remember how many steps there were, but I'm not sure anymore.

Ed: What a view, isn't it? Kathi and I were there last year. I remember seeing a wonderful view of the city.

Jack: I remember driving by the United Nations building. Then we drove over to Plainfield, New Jersey. I always remember the motel we stayed in because it was a fancy one. It had a living room and a separate bedroom. The bathroom was all glass, a mirror. We also had a walk-in shower. The next day, we went through the Lincoln Tunnel and on to Pennsylvania, which had a tunnel on the interstate. We were on the Pennsylvania Toll Road and stopped in Gettysburg. We checked out the open field where the cannon balls smacked. We drove around the town of Gettysburg for awhile. Then it was back home. That was quite a week for a guy who'd never been out of town.

Skip Lindeman
Junior High, High School, and Sports

Skip: My family moved to Columbus when I was in the sixth grade. We lived down the street from Doug Emig and John Nay. I went to McKinley school and was in class with Jack Hinkle, John Moore, and Jimmy Taylor.

Ed: You started in the sixth grade at McKinley. Then you went to 25th Street School for the seventh and eighth grades and Central Junior High for ninth grade. Right?

Skip: Right.

Ed: Was the ninth grade a good experience for you?

Skip: That was a little hard. It was a bigger school. I tried out for teams and would be the last person cut. I was not very good in either football or basketball, basketball especially. That would always be disappointing. On the baseball team, I played enough to get a letter. I was so proud of that letter. I had a sweater and I had that letter on the sweater. In the closing days of school it's hot, it's spring, but boy I wore that sweater. I was so proud of that.

Actually, while it was scary at first, I was a pretty good student and worked hard. I remember being in Latin class with Graham Updike.

Ed: Wow! You guys took Latin. That was a gutsy move.

Skip: It was. I don't even know why I did, but I'm glad because it's the basis of so many languages. In a way, going to Central was a passage of sorts. I was able to go through that and it wasn't so bad looking back at that time. We lived at 2009 Home Avenue. I could walk to high school all three years. That wasn't so bad.

Ed: How did you improve your football skills to the point that you started as quarterback our senior year?

Skip: Ed, I was very lucky. For one thing David Myers' family moved away. Dave was a terrific athlete in both basketball and football. He was being groomed to be our high school quarterback.

Ed: Dave moved at the end of eighth grade, right?

Skip: I think the end of ninth grade. On the ninth grade football team I was fourth string end. As I look back, Ed, I have no idea why I even went out for football my sophomore year. Again, I like to think that God's hand was in it.

Ed: I was going to say, Skip, you were supposed to because we were supposed to have that season our senior year.

Skip: But the truth is Dan FitzGibbon, my really good friend, was second string to David Myers, But Dan didn't go out sophomore year. They were grooming me for quarterback. Graham Updike and I would split the B team games. Sometimes he would be the starting quarterback, sometimes I would. We'd rotate in and out. When Dan heard I was being groomed for quarterback, he said, "Well I'm as good as you are." And he was. There's no question about that. But, I went out and they needed a quarterback. I was fairly fast and I could pass a little bit.

My dad was always there with some interesting thoughts. He said, "Skip, it's a good thing you can pass, because you're sure not tough." He was just trying to keep me grounded and not think I was better than I was. The fact that I went out and Dan didn't, got the quarterback job in motion for me. In our junior year, I was hoping to beat out Steve Bridges, who was a year ahead of us, but I didn't. I realized I was going to open up at safety and I remember telling my mother, "Mom, I think I'm going to start on defense." She said, "Oh, Skip, you're not as tough as those guys." And she was right. But if you're a safety in high school, and you've got a little speed, you can play pass defense and the only time you really have to tackle somebody is if the guy gets through the line. I could summon up a little courage for when those times happened. I did start at safety and then I realized what Andress was doing. One day I asked him, "You break in your quarterbacks on defense, don't you?" Andress said, "Yes, to give you some game experience." Junior year we didn't have a terrible team. We were six, three, and one. That's when there were ties. We tied Martinsville twenty to twenty. My senior year I was in line for the starting quarterback job. I remember between our junior and senior years Andress saying, "Boy Skip, I hope you have a good year next year. It would really mean a lot for the squad. I hope you come through for us."

Ed: Was that when you all were conditioning in the summertime?

Skip: Yep. All of us were really in good shape by the time practice started.

Ed: That's what everybody has said. As I've talked to other guys who were on the team, a lot of them said, "Gosh, our team was smaller than a lot of other teams we played, but we were in so much better condition."

Skip: We were small, but we were fast and in good condition. As I looked at the stats of the games during our senior year, I realized I remember all of them. However, I didn't realize in some of those games we were tied at halftime, or ahead by only one touchdown. As the third and fourth quarters came around, our good conditioning helped us win those games.

Ed: I'm sure it did. I remember Bill Spicer saying that by the middle of the third quarter you could tell that the opposing team was just starting to wear down.

Skip: Back to when Andress said, "Skip I hope you come through for us," here's how insecure I was. At the end of the undefeated senior season I talked to Andress and asked, "Mr. Andress, do you think I came through for us?" He said, "Oh, sure." We had an undefeated team and I had to ask that question. We weren't a team of stars. We worked together.

Our junior year I told Spicer, as we were both parking cars out at the 4H Fairgounds, "You know, Bill, if we could get up for every game, we could win every game." That's what an idealist I am. He asked, "Are you crazy?" I remember my junior year, we would be up and down, up and down and when we were sky high, boy were we tough. Our junior year we beat North Vernon 41-0. We played Franklin the next week and it was only six to nothing at halftime. We had those let downs. I had this idea if we could get up for every game we could win. Bill Spicer said to me, "You know, Skip, I hope you don't think less of me, but I just don't see how we can get by Bloomington." I said, "Well you may be right." Bloomington had beaten us five years in a row and they were always good. When we played them we were only ahead seven to nothing at the half. We ended up beating them twenty-one to six. Gosh, that was great Ed. I remember at that Bloomington game, we're ahead seven to nothing. At halftime Andress said, "You know boys, this is too soon to talk about an undefeated season, but you know and I know, if we beat these guys, we can go all the way." The locker room just shook, went "**Yeah!**" I still get chills just thinking of it.

Ed: I would too because as I've listened to some of the stories, Max was not all that positive at the beginning of the season.

Skip: That's right. I remember reading something in the various newspapers as we were having this good season: "Columbus, a surprise." A lot of people thought our team was a year away. After the first game, the Franklin game, we won twenty-five to six and Scott Alexander, writing in the Columbus paper said, "Max Andress had a big smile on his face walking off that field."

Anyway, just a terrific bunch of guys that really pulled together. One more thing. Nobody had ever scored on us first. In the Southport game, and they were undefeated too, the score at halftime was nothing to nothing. They scored in the third quarter. We got the ball and we punted to them. They moved down the field and I remember asking John Moore, "Moore, do you think we're beat?" he said, "Hell no!" And I said, "Good, me neither." When we got the ball, Updike made that great, long run and Hinkle's point made it seven to six. Southport didn't make their extra point. Ed, I think back about all the unsung heroes. Southport didn't score their extra point because Gene Critzer got through the line and tackled the ball carrier.

We went back for a twenty-fifth reunion of the team and Paul Pringle had a tape of the Southport game. He's in San Francisco and I'm here in L.A., so we got together and made a tape of the game to watch at the reunion. I did the narration of the Southport game. When I saw Critzer I said, "You know what? We wouldn't have been undefeated without you." I also think of Updike because he was so fast. He could change directions without changing speed. That long run he made that tied the score and then Hinkle's boot that made it seven to six—we couldn't have beaten them without Updike and Hinkle.

Ed: The common thread that runs through everybody's thoughts about that year is about a great group of guys, nobody out for the individual glory. All you guys just created your own team commitment.

Skip: Thank you. I'm glad you said that.

Ed: The team took it a game at a time and didn't project on down the road about much of anything. It turned out real well for you guys, for the school, and for the community.

Skip: I'm glad you said what you did about how we all pulled together. Whenever we'd get close to the goal line, I was bound and determined not to call my number, to be, as Spicer would say, "A white pants quarterback." I never scored a touchdown the whole season, until the Connersville game. I scored the very last touchdown. Andress said, "Lindeman, score one for yourself this time." That was really sweet. We were on the ten yard line, and we had a play that was quick moving. On this play we wouldn't call signals. I just tapped Hinkle on his crotch and he hiked the ball. I had widened out and told both guys to split out and make a big show, and I tapped Hinkle's crotch. He hiked me the ball and zing. I went right through. Andress said later, "Lindeman went untouched into the end zone."

Bill Spicer
The Hero for a Day

Bill: This would have been the spring of 1956. I was on what the kids these days call Spring Break, but we used to call it Easter vacation. I lived in a place called Eagledale which is on the very west and north side of Indianapolis. In fact, this housing development was where my parents bought their first house. You could see the Indianapolis 500 mile track from where we lived. It was only about four hundred yards away.

I was home. My stepfather was working nights, so he slept during the daytime. I was home and I tried to be quiet. I was in the kitchen doing some dishes and putting things away, tidying up. I had lots of chores with the new house. I tried to give my parents as much help as I could. The road that the housing development was on came off 30th Street in Indianapolis and made a huge U to the south—went down and came back up. It was just about symmetrical. We lived right at the bottom of the U and the workers hadn't quite finished that section. There was supposed to be a bridge across the creek. They hadn't put the bridge up yet. So I had neighbors across the creek, on the other side of the road that made the rest of the U.

Ed: How big was the creek?

Bill: It varied in size. It was anywhere from about thirty yards wide down to about ten or fifteen. In the spring of the year, when there was a lot of rain, the creek would get pretty swollen and extremely muddy. There was a smaller creek that ran right behind our house and into the bigger creek a couple hundred yards downstream. In the winter, the little creek would freeze over. We'd go down there and ice skate. The big creek beside the house never froze. It ran all year long. On this particular day, I was standing at the sink doing some dishes and cleaning up. I was looking out the kitchen window at a typical Indiana day—cold, gray, rainy, drizzle. The weather was going to mess up my plans to go out and play basketball. I had a new basketball goal that I put up in the backyard.

It was windy—good old March in Indiana. All of a sudden I hear this banging on the kitchen storm door, which was on the back of the house. There's a little kid out there. He's about eight years old or so. He's screaming, "Sissy's drowning. Sissy's drowning." He was pointing in the direction of the big creek. I reacted without even thinking and went out the storm door. We had a small chain link fence, about four feet high. It suddenly dawned on me that maybe I needed to tell my stepfather what was happening, so I said to this little boy, "You go in and tell my stepdad I'm going down to the creek." I jumped over the fence running toward the creek as fast as I could. It was probably a dash of about fifty yards or so.

Ed: What'd you have on?

Bill: I had on a t-shirt with a sweatshirt over the top of that, blue jeans, and my brand new—that I'd saved up my money for—Converse all-star basketball shoes. You weren't cool unless you had a pair of Converse high-tops. I was running as fast as I could. The construction workers had broken up some large pieces of concrete from somewhere and these were scattered along both sides of the creek.

Before I moved to that part of Indianapolis, I lived right off Memorial Circle in an apartment in downtown Indianapolis and I was a member of the YMCA swimming team. As part of that membership we were given a free life-saving course. You were really cool because you got your trunks and a jacket that said you were on the swim team. By looking at the jacket, people knew I was a life-saver.

As I approached the water I could tell not only was it really muddy, but also the current was moving very fast and the creek was swollen very badly. I knew I didn't want to dive into that. So, I leaped off one of the big pieces of concrete and did the old lifeguard jump, spread your legs forward and back and put your hands out to the side, so you wouldn't sink. In the process I was looking for the little girl.

Ed: How deep was the water where you jumped in?

Bill: Where I jumped in, the water was over my head. Further downstream it would have been about chest high. I didn't see her initially, but then, out of the corner of my eye to the left I saw this little blonde head bob. I made a leap in that direction as far as I could. As soon as I hit the water, it was going to take several strokes as hard as I could go to catch her. She was going downstream.

Ed: Were you going with the current or against it?

Bill: Fortunately I was swimming with the current. The current was ripping her along. I managed to get into the vicinity where I thought she was. I was frantically looking around. Of course the visibility in the water was zero from all the mud. I was grasping around. I felt some hair, or what I thought was hair, run over my left arm. I latched onto it and then immediately a little hand grabbed my wrist. I managed to find her body with my right hand. I pulled her up. I flipped over on my back so I could get her up and out of the water as much as I could. We were rocketing down the creek.

As soon as I got her up, what she started to do was say, "Thank you, thank you, thank you." She was spitting up water and trying to say, "Thank you," and had a death grip on my neck. I managed to get her in a position where I could handle her. I realized as soon as I'd hit the water, that with the swiftness of the current and the temperature of the water, I'd put myself into an extremely dangerous situation. The next thought I had was the need to extricate us from the creek without us getting hurt or drowning. I started looking downstream and could see where the stream itself narrowed to about ten yards, about thirty or forty feet across. Of course the current picked up dramatically as the stream narrowed down. I started trying to put my feet on the bottom and I would touch occasionally, but couldn't get a foothold. One of the big pieces of concrete had hit a small tree, a sapling. The concrete had pushed the sapling out over the edge of the creek. We were moving toward it very rapidly and I knew my best chance for getting out without going downstream any further would be the sapling. I locked on to that. I knew if I didn't get a hold of that limb I was in deep trouble. I let the little girl keep a death grip on my neck. I kept trying to find the bottom of the creek with my feet. As I approached that sapling, I made a lunge for it and got a good grip. It took a minute or so to stabilize. I thought for a second I was going to run out of strength. Eventually adrenaline took over and I managed to pull us both up out of the water and onto this big piece of concrete.

Ed: Bill, at that point, roughly how far were you from where you jumped in the water?

Bill: I was probably a good fifty yards downstream from where I jumped in. And now I'm on the opposite side of the creek. I came out on the opposite side.

Ed: On the opposite side of where your home was.

Bill: Right. It took a couple seconds to gather myself up. I got the little girl turned around. She had her legs wrapped around my waist and her arms around my neck. She kept saying, "Thank you." She was still spitting up water and had water coming out of her nose. All she had on was a little cotton dress. It was cold, so I don't know why that child was outside in that dress. She had on some little tennis shoes. Of course our clothes looked like we'd been straining mud through them from the water. My sweatshirt was down below my knees, all stretched the hell out.

I looked back up toward where the road ended, where the bridge would eventually be, and there was this huge crowd of women and children standing up there. I kept walking alongside the creek, sloshing over the pieces of concrete at the edge. When I got back up to the road all these women were just standing there staring at us. On the opposite side of the creek, I saw my stepdad standing, along with the little boy that was beating on the door. As I approached this crowd of women, like I said, they all stood there with the strangest looks on their faces, and out of the crowd bursts this woman. She came running up. The little girl recognized her immediately and jumped from me to her.

Ed: That was her mom?

Bill: Yes, and this woman says, "Boy, I don't know who you are or where you came from, but I can't thank you enough for saving my daughter." And with that, she turned around and hauled butt up the street. All the other women stood there for a couple more seconds, and they turned and started walking up the street following the lady. Within maybe thirty or forty seconds, I was alone on that side of the creek. I looked across the creek and my stepdad asked, "Are you all right?" I said, "Yes, I think I'm fine."

Ed: What was the distance across the creek there?

Bill: Oh, this was probably thirty yards. My stepdad said, "Well, you got yourself over there; you might as well get yourself back." At the time I didn't even think anything about it. So I worked my way down through a couple pieces of concrete and went upstream because I knew as soon as I jumped in, the water was going to rocket me downstream. I picked a point on the other side that I was hoping I could reach because it would be easier to get out. I jumped back in the damn water and let the current take me and swam a little bit. I came out and got a hold of another piece of concrete over there, the one I'd picked out. I got up out of the water and walked up to the road. My stepdad had an old blanket or something that he threw over my shoulders. He asked, "Are you sure you're all right?" I said, "Yes, I'm sure." He put his arm around me as we walked back to the house. When we got there and walked around the back to where the kitchen door was, he said, "You strip off here and leave those clothes. You're not coming in the house like that." So I stripped off. He hung my muddy clothing up on the line and said, "You go in and take a good hot shower." I did. I put on some other clothes. I came out and he tidied up my mess on the back porch. He came over and patted me on the shoulder and asked, "Well, how's it feel to be a hero for a day?"

Ed: What happened to your new Converse all stars?

Bill: They never were white again. They had turned that good, high quality, Indiana reddish mud color. I never saw that little girl again. I never heard from her family. I don't know her name. I never knew where she lived. It was something we never talked about until one day here not too long ago. I was visiting my stepdad, who is eighty-six years old. He lives about four miles from me, across the lake. He and Mom moved down here about three or four years after I retired. We found them a place across the lake. Mom died a few years ago. This particular day I was over visiting my stepdad. There was a program on about somebody saving somebody's life and he asked, "You remember that little girl you saved in the creek that day?" I said, "Yes. You know I hadn't thought about that for a long time."

Entered from Shortridge High School

Bill: If you look at the senior pictures in the high school *Log* book it says, "Bill Spicer, Football 3 and 4, Basketball, such and such, and then the important phrase is, "Entered from Shortridge High School."

I was born in Columbus in 1942. My parents were both members of the Class of '41 at Columbus High School. My father was Robert Spicer. He was killed in 1944. He was a member of a B-24 crew. As a young man, nobody ever talked much to me about him. I don't know whether they thought that would upset me or whatever. He was a person I never knew. I was two when he was killed.

What little I did know about him was that he was an aviation enthusiast and would do anything to get a ride in an airplane, go out to the local airport, and stuff like that. Before the war broke out, he wanted to go to England and be a member of the Eagle Squadron, you know the Americans that went over there and volunteered.

Ed: Was he still in high school at the time or had he graduated?

Bill: I think he probably had graduated. My grandmother wouldn't hear of dad going to England. He stayed in Columbus and he and Mom were married. He entered the service shortly after Pearl Harbor. My grandmother said, "When the United States gets in the war, you can do whatever you've got to do." He wound up in army aviation and he wanted to be in pilot training. He managed to get part of the way through the school, but when you had bombers with seven or eight gunners on there and only two pilots, and you're losing thirty percent on a ten thousand man raid, you need gunners more than you do pilots. So he fell out one morning and the officers said, "Okay, everybody from here over is now going to gunner school. He was in that group. But my mom said he was still enthusiastic about it. After dad was killed, my mother remarried when I was five. She married another guy that was a graduate of the Class of '41, a fellow named Chet Brown, who'd been an athlete. He knew my father and had played football with him. But he never told me this. Just about the time they were married, I was attending kindergarten at McKinley school.

Within days of their marriage we moved to Phoenix, Arizona. I started the first grade out there and in the twelve years of formal education before I went off to college, I went to nine different schools. The fortunate part of it was I went two years at Shortridge High School and two years at Columbus High. The two years at these two high schools constituted the most time I ever spent at any one school.

In my first grade in Arizona, there were only three Anglo-Saxons in my class. The rest of the class was Japanese, Native American, and Hispanic. The Native American kids were much older, eight to ten, because they started school so late. The rest of us were all six and there was a major size difference. With the exception of the Native Americans, my classmates' families were all vegetable harvesters there in Arizona.

Ed: What took your family out there?

Bill: My mother had some siblings in Arizona and she wanted to get away from Indiana. So we went out there and I attended my first and second grades, one year in one school and the next year in a different school, because we moved. My stepfather really wanted to get back working as a journeyman machinist, which is what he did before he went in the navy in WW II. There were some opportunities back in Indiana. So we came back and didn't have any money and no place to live. We moved in with my maternal grandmother. We briefly stayed in Columbus. I started third grade at McKinley. Chet got a chance to work at Allison's again up in Indianapolis, so we moved there. We stayed there for the next eight years, until I left Shortridge and moved to Columbus High.

In Indianapolis we lived on the south side, the west side, and finally settled out there in Eagledale when I was in the eighth grade, the year I was a hero for a day. I actually lived in the Washington School District. That's where I was supposed to go to school. I didn't like that school. It was a trade school and it had a lot of rough, tough kids, a lot of ducktails and cigarettes rolled up in the sleeves. It didn't have a very good academic reputation. It also didn't have a very good athletic program. I was a pretty good grade school basketball player. I wanted to play for a good team. Cleon Reynolds was the coach at Shortridge. At that time, Shortridge was sixteenth in the nation academically. I told my mom, "I don't want to go to Washington." I lived so far out that no matter where I went it was going to be a trip. We checked into it. The Shortridge school district said the fact that I lived so far away, I would have to petition the school board of Indianapolis for permission to attend Shortridge. I did and they accepted. So I went to Shortridge. It was a marvelous school. However, at that time it was under siege from a demographic shift. I would say it was thirty percent black, thirty percent Jewish, and then the rest of us were just poor white Anglo-Saxons. For me this was not anything new because all the different schools I attended in Indianapolis were very racially mixed.

Ed: Did you play football there as well as basketball?

Bill: I played freshman football and basketball. My sophomore year I started on the varsity football team as a linebacker. I played middle linebacker. On the basketball team, I was on the reserve starting five and was the tenth, eleventh, or twelfth guy on the varsity team. My greatest thrill in basketball there was getting to play most of a game against Crispus Attucks at the Butler Field house.

Ed: What happened that brought you back to Columbus High School your last two years?

Bill: I grew up on the mean streets of Indianapolis. I learned what it was like to be in the minority and be discriminated against. I got exposed to a lot because I had such a long commute. Essentially I had to travel from the Indianapolis Motor Speedway to North Meridian Street and back every day. I didn't have money for the bus so most of the time I hitchhiked. It was a long way. I was a pretty street-wise kid and had to be to survive. I learned to spot perverts, hookers, hustlers, and most of those types of folks you found in a large metropolitan area.

Ed: Those experiences had to be a little scary I would think.

Bill: I got pretty street tough. I also got in a few scrapes. I certainly wasn't a choir boy by any stretch of the imagination. My stepdad had a chance to work at a better job back in Columbus. The company was looking for people and he had a buddy that was down there. The move was a good chance to get me out of Indianapolis before I wound up in some type of real trouble.

So, there I was. I moved into this idyllic little community. You couldn't imagine a more ideal place after you've been dragged around to some of the places I'd been. It was really a life-saver for me. However, after realizing what a great place it was to be a kid, I also realized it was a little bit more hypocritical than I had been exposed to.

Ed: Tell me about how you define that word in terms of what you're talking about.

Bill: There was a very rigid class society. There were those that had, those that worked for those that had, and those that didn't have. It was going to take an act of nature to get you out of your class no matter what you did. If you ever thought you were ready to make that move, you'd better be careful because somebody was going to slap you right back in your place. For me to come to Columbus and not have anybody in the whole school—fifteen hundred kids—who were black, and only one Hispanic was different. I got chided when I played basketball at Columbus because I played like a black guy. And I did, because I grew up playing basketball with blacks.

All that having been said, moving to Columbus was a wonderful thing for me. The school was good. The athletic program was amazing. Compared to what I'd been used to, in Columbus the care they gave you, the trainer and the equipment, were absolutely amazing. But I never thought much about the fact that I had transferred in from Shortridge. After I had been retired from the Marine Corps for several years I went back to visit my aunt who lives in Linton, Indiana.

We were getting ready to leave and she came out and said, "I think I should give you this information about your dad." It was a big manila envelope full of newspaper clippings about my father and his death, along with his senior high school *Log.* I said, "Nobody ever talked about him." My aunt said, "I know." Hell, here I am in my fifties and now someone wants to give me this information. I decided that the good news was at least someone finally did give me some information. However, this certainly wasn't the time to open it up and go through it. I went back to Florida. After a few days, I sat down with the damn envelope. It was full of newspaper articles and all sorts of other documents. I learned more about what happened to him than I ever knew. The last thing I opened was his Columbus High School senior *Log.* I looked up my mom's picture and then his. Right there under his senior picture it reads, "Robert Brooks Spicer, football 3 and 4, HiY, and then 'Entered from Shortridge High School'."

Ed: Oh my gosh.

Bill: My blood ran cold. I can't really explain it but I actually felt a chill run through my body. The fact that somehow we both attended those two schools for the same amount of time, that

I had subsequently felt a desire to enter the military, became a pilot—all the things he wanted to do—was too much for coincidence. This whole array of thoughts and feelings is something I've never gotten over.

Boiled Shrimp

Bill: After the '59 undefeated season, there were a few of us that had some scholarship offers. I got notified that Hink and I, and I believe John Moore and Graham Updike were invited up to DePauw University in Greencastle, Indiana. I borrowed my mother's old station wagon to drive up there. I was a kid that had lived in Phoenix and many other places, but I didn't have a wide dietary intake. I was pretty much your basic meat and taters Indiana guy. Shrimp, I don't think I'd ever seen a shrimp.

Ed: I didn't see a shrimp until I was at Hanover College.

Bill: I remember people talking about somebody building a place in Indianapolis called The Key West Shrimp House, but who had the money to eat there? I wouldn't have known what to order. My only idea of seafood at that point in time was a Carmichael's fish sandwich, which was probably the greatest fish sandwich ever made in the world.

Ed: It sure was.

Bill: Often imitated, never duplicated. We got invited to go up to DePauw and were to get there on a Friday night, go to some team meeting and then watch a football game the next day. Our hosts were to take us to dinner and a dance on Saturday night. We were going to come home Sunday morning. Hink rode up with me. Of course we didn't get away from Columbus on time. It was raining. We got there late. I think one fraternity house was going to host John and Graham and the other one was going to host Hink and me. These guys are wearing coats and ties and they took us into the fraternity house. We went down to the bottom end of their dining hall. One fraternity member gave us this big welcoming speech and said, "I'm sorry you guys missed dinner, but we saved you some food. We had a special treat tonight. We had Caesar salad and boiled shrimp."

I looked over at Hinkle and of course he's giving me his best poker face because he didn't have a clue either. I said, "Well that sounds good." They took us over to our seats and sat us down. There was as much silverware as I'd ever seen at a place setting. Out came one of the fraternity members with this big bowl of shrimp. He said, "Here's a bowl of cocktail sauce if you want that to dunk your shrimp in." I took some cocktail sauce and put it on my plate. They passed this big bowl of shrimp to me and I put some of it on my plate. The shrimp was boiled, not peeled.

Ed: Did you eat your first shrimp with the peel on it?

Bill: I ate all of them with the peel on. I started dunking them in the sauce and eating them.

Ed: Did Hink do the same thing?

Bill: Oh, no. He hung back to see what was going on. I'd eaten three or four shrimp and these guys were watching me. Then they started peeling their shrimp. This one fellow said, "Do you always eat your shrimp with the shells on?" Of course at this point I'd gone too far to back off so I said, "Oh yes, this is the way I like them." The guy said, "Really? I've never tried them like that." I said, "Oh you ought to try them some time, they're pretty good." I ate the whole meal of boiled shrimp, shells on. Hinkle was trying to keep a damn straight face.

Ed: You made a good comeback, I'll tell you that.

Bill: The rest of the weekend, I'd be standing around and there'd be some guys looking at me and pointing. I finally asked Hinkle, "What the hell do you think they're saying about me?" He said, "They're talking about some dumbass from Columbus that ate a couple dozen boiled shrimp with the shells on. That's what the hell they're talking about."

Charlie Schuette
A Life-Long Gift from my Asthma, and the Early Years

Charlie: I had asthma from birth. That's why I started swimming. I would be really bad, almost hospitalized, until the day I started swimming. About two days after workouts started, everything was fine.

I remember the first year that my doctor told me to try out for the swim team, I tried out with Duane Barrows and the Columbus High School team. We were All-American that year. I was All-American in four months. That was mainly because I was on a relay team with Claude Thompson, John Roethke, and a couple other guys. A special event was the annual trip in a van with Duane Barrows to a place call Cuyahoga Falls, Ohio. It was the preparatory swimming event for the big nationals. We'd go to Cuyahoga Falls and sleep in tents, because we had no money. We couldn't afford to get a hotel room. We'd just come out and kick everybody's ass and they were asking, "Who are these kids?" I remember one relay race with Claude, John Anderson, Wayne Thompson, and me. It was a big race with New Trier High School. They held the American record and we were right beside them, because we qualified second. One of the guys on our team was standing there and he takes off his shirt and his sweatpants. He takes off his bathing suit, hangs it on a hook, and is standing there buck naked. I said, "Put your suit on man. It's time to swim." And we beat them and broke the American record. We were state champions twice. We went a couple of years undefeated.

Ed: Weren't you state champions both our junior and senior years?

Charlie: We were. I was the first guy to break two minutes in the two hundred yard freestyle and set that record. We rode on the fire trucks and had all this recognition, just like the football team.

Ed: I remember that. Talk a little bit more about the kinds of things you remember from high school. Didn't you have a '55 or '56 Ford?

Charlie: Yeah, sure.

Ed: I remember riding around town with you. Was it a convertible or hard-top?

Charlie: Hard-top.

Ed: What are some other memories you have from high school?

Charlie: Well, I do remember the car, but I really dedicated my life to swimming. I didn't get to know that many people in school. I knew you and Jay Shumaker pretty well. I knew Cal Brand pretty well. Swimmers pretty much stuck together and did their own thing, like the basketball and football teams. I tell you one guy I really remember was the doctor. He died recently, and I forget his name, Ed. He just died a year ago in a plane crash.

Ed: Larry Davis?

Charlie: Larry Davis. He and I ran around a bit. He was very smart but kind of a goofy one. And then I saw him at our first high school reunion.

Ed: Did you enjoy Columbus while you were there?

Charlie: Well, that's all I knew. Of course I did. I had fun. I had a horse and I'd ride the horse. I used to jump trains.

Ed: I didn't know you owned a horse. Were you a little guy?

Charlie: Oh, little guy probably through about eleven to fourteen. I used to ride in the horse shows at the 25th Street Fairgrounds. We did what's called the Rescue Race. I was a little guy, so I stood at the end of a run and this guy would take off on a horse coming at me, and round the corner. I grabbed the saddle horn and centrifugal force would throw me up on the back of the horse. Then I had my own horse. When the fair came to Columbus, those that had horses stabled at the fairgrounds had to move them out. We rode them to Brown County State Park and stabled them there until the fair was over. My horse, a palomino—I mean Trigger looking—broke his leg on one of our trips and we had to put him down. Then I started swimming and I got rid of the horses, because swimming took up a lot of time.

Dave Steenbarger
My Mother's Influence

Dave: I remember what a great person my mother was to me and what a special influence she had on my life. I was an only child. My mother was a surgery nurse at the Bartholomew County Hospital. She was a real mom; you know the mom that you knew loved you but also was a disciplinarian. Her mother was the wife of a Methodist minister who I didn't know. My grandfather passed away early in my life. My grandmother was a very godly woman, as was my mother. They kept me on the straight and narrow. They taught me things of God and made sure I went to church. My father also attended church with us. He was a good father, a good provider, but he was not the spiritual leader. My mother was the spiritual leader. She and I were real close and I think if we are honest about it, we usually choose one parent that we're closer to than the other. In my case it was Mom.

I literally looked up to her for guidance and leadership in everything. That's how my story started. While I was in high school I thought, "Well what am I going to do?" For my first job, Jim Battin and I worked as caddies at Harrison Lake Country Club. That was such a great time, just carefree. What a great start that was. We were juniors. We just thought we were living on top of the world. We hardly got paid anything, but we both enjoyed golf. The pro out there, Mal McMullen opened a driving range and a miniature golf course. Do you remember that?

Ed: I remember Mal McMullen, as well as the driving range and miniature golf.

Dave: That was my next job. I worked for him at night selling golf balls and during the day we picked them up. We could play free miniature golf. It was a great summer. But I realized I couldn't work at a driving range and miniature golf course for a living. I wasn't that good at golf. As I said, my mother was a nurse and she wanted me to be a doctor. I knew I just didn't feel good about that. Blood made me squeamish. I remember one time I went to the hospital when she had an operation. The nurse came in to give my mother a shot. I fainted.

Ed: So there was a message in there.

Dave: Yeah. Right then and there I knew that being a doctor was not for me. My mother got a book somewhere about pharmacy. She said, "You know, I think you would make a good pharmacist, David." She knew Wade Shanower, the owner of Carpenter's Drug. She was in there a lot because he gave discounts to nurses. She asked if there was a job opening for a high school boy. Wade said, "Yes, there is, coming in as a stock boy to clean up."

At that time, if you were going to pharmacy school, you had to have so many hours of apprenticeship time. You filed, had to write a formal letter to the state board of pharmacy, and you kept track of your hours. You needed four hundred hours before graduation. I worked at Carpenter's Rexall Drug Store and just loved it. Instead of playing baseball, I was at the drug store my senior year—each day after school and on Saturdays. I decided I'd go to Purdue, because Purdue and Butler had the only two schools of pharmacy in the state. Purdue was a lot less expensive. I went up there and the dorm I chose, Ed, was closest to the co-recreational gymnasium. I went over there every night and played basketball and my grades reflected it at the end of first semester. I was in serious trouble. After your first year, you're accepted into or rejected from the school of pharmacy, based on your pre-pharmacy year—your first year. I was failing four of the six classes. They didn't count how many free throws I could make. I didn't understand it. I was desperate and I knew what to do. I called mother and sure enough she had some wise advice for me, encouraged me, and sent me some scripture verses from the Bible. She said she'd been praying for me, which I know she did.

Tom Taylor
Memories of Dad

Tom: I really don't much want to talk about memories of Columbus. My wife, originally Linda Kay Followell, and I were born in Columbus, graduated from CHS in '60 and '61 and went to I.U. where we both graduated in '65. Then we moved to Boston for our grad schools and never looked back at Columbus. I didn't enjoy Columbus schools much. Except for Linda, I didn't make a circle of life-long friends. I didn't pick up whatever it is that makes people love to look back at their home town.

Instead of talking about Columbus, I want to talk about my dad. The most important memory out of Columbus in my life is my father. My earliest memory back when I was still one year old, just before my second birthday, is of crawling over the Bombay in my father's B25. I remember waking up in a tent on a sandbar along White River and smelling the wood fire, coffee, and bacon. I was on a canoe camping trip with my father. I asked him about that a few years ago and he said the trip was in 1947. It was canoe camping with him and the Methodist church Boy Scout troop where he was a volunteer. I didn't realize how much affect and influence he had on my life until fairly late in his. But I did realize it while he was still alive and we were still seeing each other frequently. Fortunately, I was able to tell him about the influence he had.

Ed: You know Tom, I never had that opportunity with my dad because he and I just didn't talk much at all. I grew up in a real non-communicative household, period.

Tom: Well, you know so did I. We didn't talk. I remember when my dad told me the facts of life. We were driving home from Indianapolis. My mother must have been saying, "Tommy's underwear is kind of messy sometimes. It's time you talked to him." He must have taken a minute and a half to explain.

Ed: That sounds like my own sex education experience. I played in a dance band. I remember Dad took me to a Sunday afternoon practice. My entire sex education occurred while we were sitting in the front seat of the car. It consisted of fourteen words. Dad looked at me and said, "Son, if you ever get a girl in trouble, just don't bother coming home."

Tom: In my case we were driving along and all of a sudden he said, "You know what your sister looks like?" I've got a sister who's seven years younger than I. I said, "Well, yeah." He said, "I mean what she looks like when she's taking a bath." I said, "Yeah." He said, "Well, you know, sometimes in the morning you,"—I called it my "go-go" then—"your go-go's kind of hard and stiff?" I said, "Yeah, until I go to the bathroom." Dad said, "When you get older sometimes your go-go will get like that at other times too. It goes inside the place where your sister's different and kind of sticky, milky stuff comes out. That's how babies are made." That was it.

Ed: Well, you did a hell of a lot better than I did.

Tom: We didn't talk much, but otherwise Dad did it all with me. He and I played trumpets, sitting next to each other in the city band. We played sitting next to each other in our church orchestra. The church orchestra rehearsed on Wednesday nights. We attended the First Methodist Church. Dad went for ten years without missing a Sunday concert or a Wednesday rehearsal. We didn't play for the three summer months, so we could take vacations without missing. I remember when I was in the seventh grade. I was back in the rehearsal room one night, the instrument room, getting my horn out of the case. I looked around and Dad had already gone out, so I went out too. When I got out, Dad's sitting in the second seat. He left the first seat for me.

Ed: What an amazingly thoughtful thing for your dad to do. He sure had confidence in your ability to play.

Tom: Those kinds of things were what we did. He and I camped together when I was four and every year of my life thereafter until I was married. We still got a camping trip in once in a while. I think the last time I camped with him was in 2004—Dad, me, and one of my granddaughters. Nothing was ever said about the importance of the outdoors or the need to be in tune with nature, the health of it. No lectures about Teddy Roosevelt and being a rugged he-man and learning how to make your way. He just **did**, not talk about, and he taught me by his example. He taught me how to build a fire because it was necessary to build a fire to fix breakfast. We never talked philosophy. It was just by example. He loved the outdoors and the woods. By taking me out there, he passed that love on.

Dad was helping the Boy Scouts. A fellow named Forrest Woods was the scoutmaster at the First Methodist Church. He asked Dad if he could use Taylor Brother Construction Company's trucks to take their canoes down to the river. He also asked Dad if he would help get them out. Dad said, "Well, you can use them if you let me go along on the trip." Dad got very involved with the Boy Scouts. When I was in Boy Scouts, he was always my scoutmaster. I realized well into my adult years his example was why I started being a Cub Scout assistant master when my son was a Cub Scout. I was a cross-country ski coach for a children's cross-country ski team in my suburb outside Boston. My son and daughter were both on that team at different times. I realized Dad was my scoutmaster, but he walked a perfect line between doing me no favors and making it harder for me. He didn't go either way. He was just absolutely neutral. The only difference between me and the other boys was that I'd be riding home in his car.

I went to two national jamborees, one in '57 at Valley Forge and one in 1960 at Colorado Springs. Dad was the scoutmaster of the Council Troop for both of those. He was given a

Silver Beaver Award for volunteer service on the council level. My sister came along. Mom was Scoutmaster of her Girl Scout troop. Dad did so much to help them that he was made a Girl Scout. He actually has a fancy, official certificate that reads, "This is to certify that Virgil Taylor, in honor of the work he has done at the local, regional, and state level, is declared a Girl Scout, member of the Hoosier Hills Girl Scout Council."

Ed: I'm sure there are not too many males in the country who have that certificate.

Tom: That's right. That kind of service, the fact that he was involved in scouting when I was four years old—he didn't do that for me. That was for the scout troop.

As I said earlier, Dad and I played in the church orchestra and the city band, but I was always given the understanding that playing in the orchestra and the band wasn't playing for ourselves. We were playing for the people that were listening to us. At church we were playing to assist the service and to improve people's enjoyment and understanding of their church service. Never really said too much, but the feeling was there. He didn't stand up and take bows.

My trumpet hobby has made enough money to be self-supporting. I always have done it humbly with the sense that it's for the audience, not for me. I got to thinking about the time when Dad was sixty years old and playing a solo at the Baptist Church, after he moved over there when my sister got married. He's not standing up there playing that trumpet because he's sixty years old proving he can still do it. He is actually doing it because the people in the church love to hear it.

Ed: It sounds like your dad, and now you, realize some of your dreams by helping other people realize theirs.

Tom: That's true. I'm an amateur astronomer. My father and I built a telescope from scratch for a science fair project when I was in the eighth grade. He showed me how to find Saturn and look at the rings, and the moon. We didn't do a lot of astronomy together, but I now volunteer as an astronomer at Chaco National Historical Park giving night-sky programs for the campers. That's a pretty major observatory. I haven't discovered anything, but I have done confirmatory observations of planets around other stars. I did a confirmatory observation of a super nova in the galaxy we call M51. Two days after it was discovered I made photographic images of it. I don't think I'd be out there doing that except for the campers who get to see a really dark sky and get to look through a 25" telescope for the first time.

Ed: Where is that observatory, Tom?

Tom: It's near Farmington, New Mexico. Four or five times my wife and I have spent up to six months there as volunteers doing programs for people who camp in the park. In New England, I loved to hike in the mountains. I adopted a trail. I maintained a trail up on the top of Mount Washington in New Hampshire in the National Forest. I went up a minimum of four times a year to check the trail markings and clear any blockages and maintain the trail. Like Dad took his love of the outdoors into scouting, I took my love of the outdoors into trail maintenance for the National Forest.

Ed: Do you remember what kinds of things you said to your dad when you realized the influence he had in your life? You said you had a chance to talk with him about it.

Tom: There are phases. In my formative school year days—pre-school, elementary school, high school, and my year at music school that wasn't successful—I looked to him as the support I needed. His support continued as I made the transition and decided what I was going to do after music didn't work out. A couple years later I got married, on New Year's Day 1964, in the Methodist Church in Columbus. That time, up to when I got married, was the period where he affected me. Then there's a hiatus. Linda and I went off to Boston. She would bring the kids back to Indiana to visit the grandparents and I wouldn't even go. That was a period that lasted for maybe twenty years. My dad and I contacted each other and we saw each other once a year. When Dad was seventy-two, he had a heart attack. He was still a pilot then. He lost his pilot's license because of the heart attack. He recovered from the heart attack just fine. He died at the age of eighty-nine, in 2006.

After dad had his heart attack, I realized he was not going to be here forever. I started making more contact with him, started inviting him over to help us when we were remodeling our house. He had retired from the construction company, but the idea that he could come over and help us build shelves was something he enjoyed. So I reached out a little bit and started making occasions for us to get together, doing things he enjoyed. After I retired in '98, we bought a place on a lake down in Texas as our legal residence. He and my mother came down there and visited.

I don't actually identify my mother as a very big force in my life. I know she was there. She loved me. She cooked my meals and did my clothes. She was very traditional, very conservative, and very in the background all the time. She wasn't the one that was taking the scouts to Colorado Springs and she wasn't the one driving trucks down to the river to get the canoes out. She wasn't the one that was out with me with the telescope. I felt supported by her, but I don't identify her support as an active part of my life. I taught myself to read before first grade, and I think I accomplished that mainly sitting on my mother's lap as she read me books. So she was there, but she somehow wasn't my influence.

My parents would come down to our place in Texas. Mom and I still didn't connect. Dad showed me the way into what was important to him and I started inviting him into my life. Sometimes we invited them to come out to where we were skiing. We'd go for a week to Steamboat and say, "Hey, why don't you come out for a couple of days? It's beautiful. Come out and join us." So I made that kind of outreach.

Meeting Louis Armstrong

Tom: In '59 or '60, Louis Armstrong came to Columbus and played in the high school gym. Our band director, Elwin Brown, arranged for Jimmy Butler and me to meet Louis in his dressing room.

We were the first and second trumpet players in the high school band. Jimmy had already made his decision to dedicate his career to jazz and I was very interested in it. We went down after the show to see Louis. Jim knew more names than I did and did most of the talking. Jim said to him, "You know, they said there are three trumpet players. There was you and Bix (Bix Beiderbecke) and Red Nichols. After the New Orleans era, you three were the three that did it." Louis smiled from ear to ear and said, "Oh yeah, I used to jam around with those boys. Ah yeah, I remember Red Nichols coming in." Then Louis said, "Some people think that I'm tommin'[3] a little bit. I want you boys to understand this. There is one thing human beings do that the apes don't do. The apes use tools. They live in families. They have wars. But there's one thing that humans do that the apes don't do. They make the decision to entertain people. People say I'm tommin' out there. I made the decision to entertain people. I'm a trumpet player. I may be the best there's ever been." Louis gives a great big smile and he said, "But what I'm proud of is that I entertain people." That comment never left me. Ever. Sometimes at night I still dream about meeting Louis Armstrong. I made contact with Jimmy Butler a few years ago and his version is a little bit different but he remembers the night with Louis.

Ed: Sometimes when I've heard stories about people like you and me having a chance to meet and talk with someone of the stature of a Louis Armstrong, folks come away from those conversations real disappointed that the person they talked to is a different person than the

---

3   The word "tommin' denotes the black man's extreme submissiveness towards a white person or white people.

one they saw in the movie, saw on the stage, or whatever. It sounds like maybe he was just who he was.

Tom: He was who he was—nothing phony or fake. At that point he had nothing to prove. The amazing thing was he was there alone in his dressing room with us two high school students; we were the only ones that came.

Louis was one of three black men my father just really, really admired. Dad couldn't believe I had met Louis Armstrong. It made me start looking at entertaining very broadly, so that it'll fit a church service too. Music doesn't have to mean playing "When the Saints Go Marching In." It could mean playing "The Holy City" on Easter.

Speaking of Music…

©Time/Life, Inc. The Jive "Kennel" in downtown Columbus.
It was a gathering place for CHS students in the '50s and '60s

Ed: Our high school mascot is the Bull Dog, hence the name "Kennel." Students met there. They could dance and eat. There was a TV room and an area to shoot pool. I'm not certain how many communities of 20,000 were far-reaching enough in their thinking to provide such a social place for high schoolers to meet. The Jive Kennel was a wonderful place that no longer exists. Although I have no data to support my next statement, I feel the Jive Kennel probably not only provided a safe, fun place to hang out, but it also kept many CHS students from driving around the streets of Columbus—perhaps getting into trouble.

...Savoring *Your* Memories...

1. Who was your favorite elementary school teacher? Why?

2. What part-time jobs did you have growing up?

3. How did you feel when you went to junior high?

4. What **two songs** from the '50s and '60s hold the most memories for you? Why these two particular songs?

5. What memories come to mind about your experiences in high school?

6. Who was your first girlfriend/boyfriend?

7. Who was your high school sweetheart? Whatever happened to her/him?

8. What was your relationship like with your parents while you were growing up?

9. What was the first car you drove? What "adventures" did you have with that car?

10. What was the **worst** trouble you got into? How did it turn out?

11. Who were some of your friends? What did you do for fun?

Chapter 6   The Divergent Paths We Followed Beginning May 26, 1960

I t's Thursday, May 26, 1960. It's 5:30 in the morning and the alarm clock just rang, waking me up to spend my first day at my summer job, working on the assembly line at Hamilton Cosco, Inc. I leave in August for Hanover College. Our 432 senior class members graduated last night from Columbus High School. I was honored to have been asked to give one of the commencement speeches. The title of my thoughts was "*Today—The World*." Some others from The Columbus Crew participated in last night's commencement as well. Dan FitzGibbon gave the Invocation. Tom Taylor played his trumpet in the Concert Band for the Processional and Recessional. Class President, Skip Lindeman presented our class gift to the school. Principal Judson Erne read each of our names as we walked across the stage at Memorial Gym and received our diploma from Superintendent Dr. Clarence Robbins. Last night I remember sitting with my classmates and thinking, "This group will never be together again, **ever**, just as we are right now, tonight." I was overtaken by that thought. I have known some of my friends who graduated with me last night for eighteen years. Others I've known for much less time, but the friendships are no less strong.

To be honest, I'm not really ready to be finished with high school. I have had such fun these past three years at CHS—I just didn't want it to end so soon. My girlfriend is going to be a senior this coming year. I'm a bit envious she will still be here. I do know, however, that it's time to move on to the next phase of my life, the one Dad told me about many, many years ago—"you will get your education." I'm sure someday I will be very grateful my parents didn't leave me a choice about going to college. It's just that I'm gonna miss ol' CHS.

Today my classmates have taken off for the four winds. Some have decided to stay in town and work at Arvin's, Cummins, or Cosco. Many of my friends, like me, will head off to college this fall. Most of us won't see each other ever again. Some will be fortunate enough to run into each other at the various class reunions over the years—at least I hope so. I know we're following 432 different paths. I just hope those chosen paths will allow some of us to come full circle and reconnect again. I'm counting on it. Let me share with you sixteen of those divergent paths.

George Abel
An Unexpected Athletic Career

George: I went to Purdue University in the fall of 1960. While there, I went out for football. I just walked on. I had to go up there a month early, in August. Jack Mollenkopf was the head coach.

After about a month, the coach called me into his office. I knew I was getting cut. The coach could have had an assistant tell me I was being cut, but he personally called me into his office. Mollenkopf said, "I can tell you love sports. You just love to be an athlete and you love to run. I'll tell you what's going on. We're starting a soccer program here at Purdue. They need players." I said, "I've never played soccer."

Ed: I was just thinking that was a pretty long time ago for colleges to have soccer programs.

George: Purdue was one of the early schools to initiate soccer. The only two I remember in Indiana at that time were Purdue and Ball State.

Ed: You tried out for the soccer team, and I'll bet you made it.

George: Yep. I did it because of Mollenkopf's advice. He told me, "You can stay with this football team if you want to. You'd be third, fourth string. The only time you'd probably get to play much would be at the end of a game, or blow outs." But I knew I was in trouble when I went to Purdue. I was a dash man for Columbus High School. I was pretty fast. I thought I was pretty good. I got up there and I was running forty yard wind sprints against a two-hundred-sixty pound fullback from Chicago. I'll never forget it. He could outrun me.

Ed: Well you were pretty thin and scrawny at the time.

George: A hundred and sixty-five pounds. Yeah, I wish I was that size now.

Ed: I know what you mean.

George: Playing soccer was a good experience for me. I got to travel. We went to St. Louis. We played the University of St. Louis and Washington of St. Louis in the same weekend. I went to several places I wouldn't have otherwise gone. And I actually got a letter as a soccer player.

Ed: Wow. That's great, George.

George: Yeah. And I never played the game before. I actually started out as a halfback. I didn't do much except try to tackle the ball in the midfield. I finally got moved to outside corner which is in the line position. I got to score a goal and it was quite an experience. I was glad I played soccer. That was the only big attraction I had to returning to Purdue. I really screwed up my first year. I didn't make good grades. I would have gone back on probation.

Going Down Some Wrong Paths and Finding my Way Back

Ed: Did you return to Purdue after your freshman year?

George: No. And that's when my life really took a big downturn. I pretty much knew I wasn't going back for the second year at Purdue because the next year for me was the year my brother was supposed to graduate. My dad was just up against it financially at the end of the year with both of us being there. Dave was going to finish and I could go back the next year. You know how that goes sometimes. Before the year was up, I was in debt for a car, my girlfriend was pregnant, and my life had taken quite a downturn.

Ed: It sounds like a very tough year for you.

George: Yeah. And it was all my own doing. I tried to keep my nose to the grindstone.

Ed: Where did you work?

George: I worked for Arvin Industries. I went to work for them in 1961 right after I left Purdue. It was actually just a summer job. The people at Arvin thought I was headed back to Purdue because I was a college kid. When it came time to go back to school, I wasn't going. I talked to the human resource people and they said, "Sure, you can stay on." I stayed with them until I just decided to quit one day. I suppose from the time I quit that job, until I went in the air force in 1963, I must have had ten or twelve jobs. I couldn't tell you all the different places I worked.

Ed: Why did you decide to join the air force, George?

George: I was dealing with some issues. I had gotten in trouble and was arrested for public intoxication and illegal possession. I was under twenty-one. I had to go to court for that. Another incident came up. I wasn't charged with anything, but the police knew I was involved with the crowd that was in some real trouble.

Ed: Some heavy stuff?

George: Right. The prosecutor said, "Before you get in any more trouble, before anything happens , if I were you I'd very seriously consider joining the service." A lot of times back then, if somebody joined the military, they would suspend the sentence. I said, "Okay that sounds like a good idea." I went to join and did the paperwork. Information came back that I had two misdemeanors within six months. That's because both misdemeanors were on the same day and I was charged with both. I had to go before Judge Lienberger and get a waiver to join the air force. I want to San Antonio for my basic training. It was the best thing that ever happened to me.

Ed: Why's that?

George: I got my head on straight as far as schooling and studying. I was an honor graduate in my class. I got some really good assignments. I came back to March Air Force Base and was the only one in my area of inventory management control that had been through the new computer concept and the process the air force was going to use to track and inventory things. I was put into a position about four levels above me just because I could answer the questions and help them set things up. For me it was a really good situation. I started going to a couple of college classes off base.

Ed: George, where is March Air Force Base?

George: It's in California. It's probably sixty miles due east of L.A. San Bernardino is near the base. There was a situation that came up because I was married at the time and we had a baby.

In addition to having to get the waiver to go in the service, I lied to them because you weren't allowed to enlist if you had more than one dependent. I had a wife and a child. I had to keep it secret about our child. Therefore I didn't get an allotment for my daughter and that really made it tight financially, especially when she came out there in January of '64. We were getting ready to have a second daughter. The air force knew I had one daughter, but my records didn't show it. The whole story came out. I had to go before the commander and tell my story.

The military had two choices. They could either discharge me as undesirable or they could retain me and basically say, "Wipe it out." They chose to exercise their second choice. What I didn't realize was they would give me back pay for all the time my daughter was not on the records—for about a year I guess—and it amounted to probably thirty, thirty-five dollars a month. That was big bucks back in 1965. When I got discharged from the service I had a new perspective. It got me out of the crowd I had been running around with. It gave me an opportunity to think, start seeing my life in different lights.

Ed: Especially with the family now.

George: My wife and I had two kids by the time I got out of the service. Within less than a year after I got out of the service, we had a third. I worked with Dad. Dad had the greenhouse and I started a landscaping business and did that for a couple of years. I would work other places in the wintertime. I worked one year for Coca-Cola doing relief route deliveries. I did whatever I had to do to get by. In '68 I went back to Arvin. I was planning on just being there for the winter. I was going to do the landscaping business again the next year. I got into what I was doing at Arvin and saw an opportunity for a career there.

My Career

George: I was at Arvin for thirty-eight years. I started out as an operator, hired in off the street. At that time they had different levels of jobs they moved people into. I was a fixture loader and a welder. Then I got a set-up job. After four or five years, I took some tests and got into a toolmakers apprenticeship program. I was a toolmaker for four years and worked first shift. Arvin was getting ready to move me back to second shift. I didn't want to go back to the second shift because of the three children. It was just pretty hectic not being at home.

I went to real estate school with the intention of quitting my job at Arvin and selling real estate. But about the time I was getting ready to quit, the plant engineer had a position open for a tool designer. I had never done any design work, but I figured I could handle it. I went in and talked to him about the job. Also, it was a first shift job. He said, "Yeah, I'd be glad to consider you, but you're going to take quite a pay cut. You're not going to get the overtime that you get." I said, "Well it's either that or I'm going to be leaving." He said, "Okay."

I took that job thinking I could also sell real estate. I hooked up with a broker that would let me work the hours I wanted. I got involved in that and from there I was just very fortunate. My career just took off. I started going to Indiana University/Purdue University at Columbus, taking courses in engineering. In the middle of this, I got promoted to a project engineer's job. So, like an idiot, I quit going to school. I thought, "Okay, I've got a good job now." I was able to advance. Throughout my career, it seemed like every time I was a little frustrated, another opportunity would come along. I was very fortunate. I ended up being a facilities manager for two different plants in Columbus. That was as high as I could go, because I didn't have my college degree. I had twenty years of a career left and had I gone back to school I could have done more. Back in the days I was working, if you showed an aptitude, a desire, and could handle it, a lot of times they'd give you a chance. They don't do that much anymore.

Ed: Were you guys unionized at the time?

George: Yes. I wasn't affected by that because from 1980 on I was in management and was non-exempt salaried for awhile.

Ed: The same thing happened to my dad. Having dropped out of school at sixth grade, he finally reached a point at Cummins where he went as far as he could without a high school diploma.

George: I think that wasn't uncommon in our parents' era. I have no doubt my dad could have been a manager with a company and done most anything, but he would have never been given an opportunity beyond being a machinist and being out there in the shop. Those were the kinds of jobs that were available for someone with no more education that he had.

Cal Brand
Hanover College

Ed: I know you thought about a career in law. When we were at Hanover did you major in political science?

Cal: I started out at Hanover as a business major. As you probably remember, I hated accounting so much that first semester. It was awful, boring, just totally uninteresting. I switched to a major in English. I ended up with a double major in English and Theology. Later I decided to go to seminary. I felt like I had a really good high school education. I also felt like the first semester at Hanover I pretty well coasted. I discovered I didn't want to practice enough to make the golf team at Hanover. I only played third in high school. To get on the Hanover team, I'd have to play a lot better. The idea of being out there every afternoon practicing my chip shots until I was blue in the face just…

Ed: …didn't appeal to you.

Cal: That first year I was at Hanover, I had to hitch-hike to Indianapolis to see Betsy. I hitch-hiked right through Columbus and never said anything to anybody. I spent the time with Betsy and hitch-hiked back to campus.

Ed: I don't know if you remember, but that first semester at Hanover was really difficult for me. In fact, I packed up all my stuff and took it back home at the end of that semester with the idea I wasn't going back second semester. I don't know if you remember a red-headed guy in our fraternity, Larry Thomas, who lived in Columbus. I talked to him over the break. He knew I had brought my stuff home. I was fortunate to have a Cummins Foundation scholarship while I was at Hanover. Fortunately, I talked to Randy Tucker at Cummins during that semester break and got the same message from both of them—it's too early to make that decision. So I packed everything up, and you and I were back together for the second semester.

Cal: You remember that little brown jug lamp we had on the desk that I kept full of vodka?

Ed: I most certainly remember that brown jug. You know at that point in time, it was so easy to get a fake ID. I remember spending a lot of time at the Oasis Bar in Madison.

Cal: Amen. We stuck all those beer bottle labels up on the ceiling—peeled them off, laid them on our wallets, and pitched them up there. Quite a few stuck! I don't know if you were there that particular night…

Ed: …I think I know what you're going to talk about.

Cal: A bunch of us Phi Delts were sitting in the back room and Charlie, the bartender, came back and said…

Ed: …"The feds are up front. If you have a fake ID, get out the back door right now." You and I were there together and ran for the back door.

Cal: Standing out there in the cold. He finally came out about fifteen minutes later and said he was just kidding.

Ed: It was April 1st and he came outside and yelled, "April Fool." He had a big smile on his face.

Cal: I also remember during that year making a few trips down to the University of Louisville to see Spicer.

Ed: Bill and I have talked about the one time the three of us went to a bar in Louisville. We were there a long time, drinking a lot of beers. We were getting ready to leave and I stood up and proceeded to throw up all over the table. The three of us made a quick exit. I don't even know if we paid our bill. When I recently reminded Spice of that bar story, he said, "Oh yeah, they put a memorial 'Ed Poole' plaque on the wall in that booth in your honor."

Cal: Do you remember going to the burlesque show one time in Louisville?

Ed: How could I forget that?

Cal: I remember one girl in that show. I still thought about her for years after that visit. Speaking of getting drunk, I remember going to a debate in Terre Haute with Corky Atkinson. He was my debate team partner. That rascal brought a fifth of Old Forester. When we got done with whatever we had to do the first day, we stopped in the restaurant in the hotel and got two giant cokes. We took them up to the room and poured out about half the coke and filled the cups up with Old Forester. I got so drunk.

I had heard if you put your foot on the floor the room stopped spinning, but it didn't work. So I decided I'd go take a bath. I got in the tub and spent about ten minutes trying to catch the soap. It kept running away from me. I never puked and I finally got back in the bed and went to sleep. When I got up the next morning, I had the worst hangover I'd ever had in my life. We had to walk from the hotel across campus to where the debate took place. It felt like my head was going to explode with every step I took.

My first event was extemporaneous speaking. I went into a room and they give me a topic and five minutes to prepare. Then I gave an eight minute talk on that subject. I mean it was a joke. I was trying to keep my wits about me under those circumstances. I just loved that.

Ed: I have an extemporaneous speech story for you. When I was principal at Columbus High School, the speech coach invited me to go to Indianapolis with the team one Saturday morning and be a judge. I didn't know much about judging a speech contest but I said, "Sure, I'll be happy to go." My assignment was to be one of the judges in the extemporaneous speaking category. I will remember this story until the day I die. This was back when the country was becoming aware of mercy killings. The word for that day was "euthanasia." In this instance, the kids stood outside the door and when they came into the room they were given the card with the word on it. The student turned his or her back to the group and had three minutes to prepare. This one poor kid came in, saw the word, turned around, got his thoughts collected, turned back around, and here's how he started. "Youth in Asia, compared to the youth in the United States…" In those days, after you gave your extemporaneous speech you got to sit down in the room and listen to the rest of the presentations. The next kid came in, went through the same routine, and gave a very good extemporaneous presentation on euthanasia. As soon as he started, I looked over at the kid who had just finished. He had this really unhappy look on his face. I just shrugged my shoulders like, "What can you do?"

Cal: That's funny. I remember in the first year at Hanover we had fraternity rush. When we were pledges, we weren't supposed to drink in Jefferson County. So that was part of the reason for going to Louisville. Do you remember any of the drinking parties at Clifty Falls State Park?

Ed: Of course. I remember them very well.

Cal: I had that old Ford. I remember one time I was so drunk and it was snowing when we headed back to campus. I had to open the car door and lean out to watch the road go by the side of the car. I couldn't see to get down out of the park.

Ed: Do you remember during Hell Week when Wes Keller sent the pledges out to Clifty Falls to get, I don't remember how many, buckets of horse shit from the stables where they kept the horses?

Cal: I remember going to get the Beta Shield. I don't remember which of our actives did it, but he chained that damn thing up on top of Parker Auditorium. That created quite a stir.

Ed: I remember stripping our clothes off and the actives put this little piece of carrot on a block of ice. We had to bend down over the ice and pick up the carrot between our cheeks.

Cal: It was crazy, wasn't it?

Ed: At the time it didn't seem like much fun, but looking back on it all, it was hilarious. Also, we had to wear a burlap bag underneath our clothes one day during Hell Week and go to classes that way. We had to wear an onion on a string around our necks one day, but not to classes. Anytime an active wanted us to take a big bite out of it, that's what we did. I remember the pledges had to throw the actives in the shower when they didn't get up after third call. Those were some fun times that second semester.

Cal: Do you remember the Hanover College choir singing at the Presbyterian Church two out of every three Sunday mornings?

Ed: It was during the four years in that choir loft at the Hanover Presbyterian Church that I first discovered a loving God. At the East Columbus Church of Christ it was all about hell, fire, and damnation. I learned about an "I'm gonna get you" God. If I hadn't spent those Sundays in the choir loft at Hanover, I wouldn't have come to that understanding about a loving, forgiving God.

Cal: I also remember a few of those Sunday mornings when we'd been out partying on Saturday night and the people in the front rows of the church could smell it.

Ed: Yep. I remember that. And I don't think our college choir director, Don Morrison, appreciated it very much either. Do you remember our choir trip to Carnegie Hall in New York City?

Cal: Oh boy, yes.

Ed: That's an experience I shall never forget.

Cal: We all went to Mama Leone's after the concert.

Ed: And stayed up all night to see what the critic review was in the *New York Times*. It was a good review. We got a standing ovation at the end of the concert. I remember the college reprinted the critic's review in our senior yearbook.

Cal: Quite a thrill wasn't it.

Ed: Absolutely.

Cal: That whole tour was a thrill. When I think about that choir, I always think of Henry Bishop, and the time he showed up with his mustache shaved on one side and his beard shaved on the other. Funniest guy.

I remember Steve Krohl teaching me how to play the guitar. One day I had a faith experience in the study room Steve used. I was on the couch. It was dark and nobody else was in there. All of a sudden, something drew my eyes up toward the corner of the ceiling in front of me. I saw blue illumination. Now my mind is telling me it was about the size of a basketball, although it wasn't spherical. I had this feeling that somebody had actually been there speaking to me and saying, "I love you." I knew it was God. All of a sudden, all that stress just went away. I closed my books and went to bed.

I got up the next morning and called Jack Matthews in the theology department. I asked to have a delay in taking the test. I told him I wasn't ready. He gave me a week. I felt a lot of grace at that moment. I went and sat for my test. Knowing I was headed home for semester break, I told Donna, my new Hanover friend, I was going to see Betsy. She seemed very understanding and didn't try to control me. When I got home with Betsy and told her I'd had several dates with Donna, she hit the ceiling. She felt there was a big difference between her going out at Butler and my having regular dates. I wasn't too surprised, but her reaction drove me closer to Donna. When I got back to Hanover, Donna and I became pretty serious, in a fun way. Then after Donna and I were settled early in my junior year, I was taking more theology courses. I remember a conversation with her. I was making this shift from law school to theology and asked her what she was hearing from me. She said, "Well you really have more interest and excitement when you're talking about theology than anything else." That was a pretty strong signal for me. So Bill McGoughy and I jumped in his car and drove out to Princeton for their junior convocation. I really liked what I saw out there. Matthews and his theology colleague, Ed Huenemann, were both pushing Princeton. When I switched out of the pre-law track into the theology track, my grades got a lot better.

I don't know if you remember this, but when we were sophomores I got hooked up with some of the other Phi Delts to try and get the national organization to get rid of the "socially acceptable" clause. I don't know if I was hanging out too much with Bill Laws at the Columbus Presbyterian Church or what. I didn't like being in a segregated organization. We got turned down that year. Our junior year we tried again, and again it was voted down. The head council decided they wanted to keep that clause in the constitution, which meant no blacks. So I moved out of the house.

Ed: Cal, I do not remember that.

Cal: I lived in the new men's dorm my last year there.

Ed: Did you come to chapter meetings?

Cal: No. I just left the fraternity. I don't remember signing anything, but I was gone because I didn't feel like I could stay in it.

Ed: Good for you for living out your beliefs about that. I admire you.

Cal: If I had been a lost, single person I might not have been so eager to leave. As it was, I just didn't feel like I could stay. That turned out to be a good thing in a way because I got to meet some people that I wouldn't have met otherwise and formed a good friendship with a guy from Kenya, Arthur Nduro.

Ed: I remember Arthur.

Cal: I brought him to Columbus a few times to visit with my folks. In later years, his daughters were in the United States studying. One of them got into some kind of difficulty. The next thing I knew, I was on the phone with Arthur and his wife, trying to help figure out what to do. Now there's a good opportunity that in January I'm going to Kenya to do some teaching.

Ed: Wow, that's great. Through the Presbyterian Church?

Cal: Actually through the ACPE. It will also be with the Presbyterian Church. I'm just hoping Arthur's still alive and I can find him over there.

Ed: Wouldn't that be a great reunion?

Cal: It sure would be wonderful if I could see him again.

By the time I was out of the sophomore year, and dating Donna, I had cut way back on how much I was drinking and partying. I got so interested in the course "Man's Dilemma and Biblical Understanding" and some of the other coursework I was doing. The last four semesters there I made the Dean's list. By the end of the first semester our freshman year, I was half a grade point from probation.

Ed: You did quite a turn around. How did that happen?

Cal: One of the experiences that came out of Campus Fellowship was deputation teams. I went out a couple of times and preached at little country churches in the area. That was such a disaster. I was out there with my head full of all this academic theology.

Ed: The "disaster pastor."

Cal: Exactly. Bless their hearts, the people were pretty patient. I'm sure they were glad when the sermons were over.

Ed: Probably not. But at least that time gave you the opportunity for a clinical experience.

Cal: It did. It did indeed.

Ed: I'm sure those experiences allowed you to have a continued interest in going to Princeton, which is good.

Cal: Yes; however it also confused things because I began thinking I did not want to be a parish pastor. I thought I wanted to be a missionary, if anything. Mostly I just wanted to learn about this God who loves me. Donna and I got married. The summer between Hanover and Princeton I had a job with the Indiana State Republican Central Committee. I organized the precinct education and training program for the whole state which meant going to all the courthouses in all of the counties, getting all the election records for the three previous elections, and entering the data. We had training events and the candidates would speak. I would pass out these books and tell them how many votes they had to get from their respective precincts if they were going to win. That was the year Barry Goldwater was running.

Ed: I sure do remember that. The fall election that year was my first year teaching. I remember taking my social studies class to Louisville to see Goldwater speak.

Cal: We had a pretty decent state ticket. But they got washed out with Goldwater. In that regard, the summer was a disaster but it was also a nice summer for Donna and me. I had a good income and we were living in Columbus. I was commuting to Indianapolis. Whenever I went out for meetings and trainings, she could go with me. We just toured the state and had time together.

Princeton

Cal: I got to Princeton and that was a really big change. One of the first things I ran into at seminary was a course that was basically a repeat of "Man's Dilemma and Biblical Understanding," the course I took at Hanover. I got excused from that course. Instead, I took a course called "Christian Mission and the Problem of Humanization." It was taught by a professor named Richard Shawl, who was six months at Princeton and the other six months he was in Brazil working in base communities. There was some suspicion back then that these gatherings were Communist, but they were socially, active-based community churches. He really turned me onto the church. I had decided I was not interested in the parish. But during that year I realized the whole deal was, what does it mean to be human? What's Christian mission about if it's not helping people to become more human? So much of the history of the church has been dehumanizing. I spent some time at the Southern Baptist Seminary in Louisville because they have a good missiology section in their library.

Ed: Is Princeton non-denominational?

Cal: It's Presbyterian, with a significant enrollment of folks who were not Presbyterian—kind of like Hanover.

I also had an identity crisis. I got into my second year at Princeton and I got so discouraged. It didn't come out with my counseling with Dr. Loder, and that was how I ended up calling it an identity crisis. My crisis focused in some way on the sense that I didn't want to be like my dad and I didn't know it was possible for me, as a young man, to be like my mom. I had one moment in the therapy experience when Dr. Loder asked me something about the interests I shared with Mother. Just before he asked that question, I was sitting with my arms and legs crossed—a more feminine seating posture—and guarded as well. After I finished responding to him he said, "Well it sounds like you want to be more like your mother." Unconsciously I uncrossed my legs, put my arms on the armrests of the chair, and assumed a very male posture. He asked, "Why did you do that?" I asked, "What?" He said, "You changed the way you're sitting." That statement began a period of time where I actually tried to explore and practice some of the things I enjoyed that were similar to the things Mom liked. I took up painting a little bit. I mixed some recreational reading in with my academic reading. I listened to music and did activities I knew were important to her. In the long run, I realized I didn't want to be like Mom **or** Dad. I wanted to be my own person. I needed to work through a process so I wasn't being reactive. I think that's why Dr Loder eventually recommended I go into the CPE program and begin practicing being the different person I thought I wanted to be.

Ed: Did you go into the CPE program right out of Princeton?

Cal: Actually, I finished two years at Princeton and then took a year out to gain some clinical experience. The hospital where I had my experience was on the west side of Philadelphia. You remember 1966, '67? It was like a war zone. We were in the middle of Black Power and urban renewal, or urban removal. I rode the train downtown into Philadelphia, caught a subway up to the stop where I got off, and walked three blocks to the hospital.

Ed: That had to be a little scary.

Cal: I didn't worry about it a lot, but I knew that it could be scary. The staff at the hospital told us early on to stay out of the alleys, the dark places, and we would be fine. Of course I saw stuff in the emergency room that you wouldn't believe, from the gang fights and domestic violence.

But I loved the ministry in the emergency department, working with the staff there and helping them manage when patients were having problems. I remember a guy who was brought in dead from a heart attack. He was sixty-five and had just retired. His wife was in hysterics. She kept talking about how hard her husband had worked. They waited all these years for retirement and then he died. The first reaction on the medical team was to give her a shot of Librium, a sedative. I said, "Let me take her down the hall to a quiet place and just spend some time with her first and see what happens. Maybe she won't need to be drugged." She and I sat and talked for about half an hour. She finally got enough of it out that she was able to calm down some. I took her back and she signed the papers she needed to sign. I felt like it was a good thing I was there.

One night when I was on call, a guy came to the door after visiting hours were over. He was in New York for business. He learned his mother was hospitalized, and the staff was not going to let him in. I happened to catch what was going on. I called the security officer and we got him inside. He told us who he was and who he'd come to see. I called the head nurse on the unit where his mother was located and she said, "Well, I suppose, even if it's after visiting hours. If you bring him up and stay with him, it's all right." I took him up to his mother's room. That visit was important for both of them. I walked him back down and saw him out of the hospital.

These were signs to me of this motif about humanization that the real ministry is about—making a place in the world for people to be human, instead of being dehumanized. I had just a world of good learning experiences during that year with my peer groups, my supervisor, and my patients.

When I went back to seminary I had this challenge to try and understand intellectually what I'd been learning emotionally, so I might be able to talk about it in an articulate way. We had this wonderful New Testament professor, Chris Becker. He was a Dane, kind of a wild and wooly guy and a lot of fun. He agreed to work with me on formulating a biblical anthropology and Jim Loder was willing to work with me on formulating a personality theory that included systems thinking, which in 1968 was still pretty new. I had to scrounge to find textbooks in the field. I found enough books, got my paper together, and felt satisfied with it. I graduated and it was a good year. I mean a good three, four years actually.

The first call I had was as an assistant pastor at the Presbyterian Church in Newtown, Pennsylvania, which was Quaker area. We had a historic colonial church, the original Presbyterian Church had been maintained, although we didn't worship there except in the summer. The basement had been used as a prison for Hessian troops and the sanctuary floor was the infirmary for wounded revolutionaries. It was pretty neat. I learned a lot there and thought I might be interested in a master's degree in organization development. It seemed to be where this systems theory idea was going.

Ed: At the very same time you were writing your paper at Princeton, I was writing my dissertation at Indiana University. The dissertation was based on organization development as a way to bring about lasting change in an organization. Like you, I had to do a lot of looking for books on the subject.

Cal: One of the avenues I could follow was systems theory. I interviewed at Drexell in Philadelphia. They said, "We think you need to stay in the church." They felt I was too committed to involving everybody in making decisions, and their program was not interested so much in conversation and dialogue as theory and practice. Then my senior pastor up and decided to leave, and I had to go on. I got admitted to the CPE training program in Chicago, to do supervisory training.

Jack Hinkle
All This to Play Football

After a fabulous senior year in high school, I was honored to be offered a full scholarship to play football at Indiana University. My high school coach, Max Andress, helped me. He sent information to such schools as Dartmouth, Syracuse, and the University of Pennsylvania. Thus began my year of higher education.

I got to campus in Bloomington, went to the athletic department, and talked with Mr. Dalsasso, one of the assistant coaches. As a reminder, in 1960, IU was under a four-year probation for recruiting violations.

After I signed the required papers, I was directed to the towers dormitory, which was a fairly new complex on campus. Towers had five buildings, one that was nine stories high and four smaller three-story buildings on each corner. The athletes were put in Building "D". I got a room on the second floor with Dick Klepper, who was from Tinley Park, Illinois. I always remember Tinley Park because that's where the Bettenhausen Indy race car drivers lived.

Being a scholarship guy on the football team was a great situation. When it came time to sign up for classes, I had a priority note to get my classes early in the day, because practice was in the afternoon. My scholarship included room and board, books, tuition, thirty dollars a month for laundry, and a Sunday evening meal. The cafeteria wasn't open to other students on Sunday evenings.

In 1960 there was no freshman eligibility. When you were a freshman all you did was learn the system and be the opposing team against the varsity. My year was strange, because Indiana University was running the "Wing T" offense, but the freshmen were running the single wing. For those who might not know the "Wing T", the center hands the ball to the quarterback, while with the single wing, the center hikes the ball three yards back to either the tailback or the fullback. Since I had played both offenses before, I didn't have a problem with either. It just didn't make sense to run a freshman offense that was different than the varsity's.

Three things of note happened to me during my stay at Indiana University. One, I played with Doug Lackey, Steve Obremsky, Gary Ryser, and Bob Boroff who were opponents during my senior year at Columbus. Another was I played against Earl Fasion, a senior, who would later be a very successful pro with the San Diego Chargers. Finally, I was there the year IU dedicated the new Memorial Stadium. We got to go out onto the field and practice. We also got our pictures taken individually and as a team out on the new field.

For the most part, September, October, and November were class, football, and rest. We celebrated with an intersquad game at the end of the football season. All of this sounds exciting, and it was. But when football season was over, I proceeded to take myself on a journey that would eventually lead me to finding my carccr path.

Here is the reality. After football season ended, I pretty much screwed around for the rest of the school year. During the week I played bridge. On weekends, I hitch-hiked to Ball State University and played pinochle at my brother's fraternity house. I went to class some, but didn't apply myself at all. I almost didn't graduate from high school because of a term paper, and then I wrote a term paper at IU that probably deserved a failing grade, but I got a B-. The catalyst to my demise was a letter from the coach saying I was to weigh 210 pounds when I reported to spring practice. I weighed 235 at the time. I worked at it by playing handball and other activities. When spring practice rolled around I weighed 218, so I didn't report. For the rest of the school year I didn't do much of anything. But I was also never questioned about not being at spring practice.

I remember the holiday break during my only ycar at IU. Graham Updike and Bill Spicer picked me up in Bloomington. We stopped by a refreshment stand for supplies ('nuf said) and headed for Nashville, Indiana. There is a road that goes by The Little Grand Ol' Opry close to Nashville, Green Valley Road. We turned left and drove about a block. We found the driveway up a hill to a log cabin. The cabin belonged to an aunt of either Bill Ryan or Larry Davis— high school classmates. Did I mention the snow was about a foot deep and the temperature was around zero? We turned on the oven and burners. There was an Arvin's heater, made in Columbus, and we built a fire in the fireplace. Dan Mobley made it to the party, along with some others. We partied all night and we were loud.

My future wife lived a little farther down that road. Years later I told her about our party. She had heard about it. She told me her brother said the sheriff received calls about our party but it was too cold to follow up on. I'm pretty sure we had a good time!

A few years after I left Indiana University I was talking to Coach Marston, one of my coaches at Columbus. He said the university had called when I didn't show up for the next year. I don't know much about eligibility, but my grade point average may have been a negative.

In reflecting back, I have some personal thoughts about my higher education. One is, I went to IU with no preparation or direction. My major was Health, Physical Education, and Recreation because that was my brother's major. The football season wasn't what I expected. As I look back, I think the head coach Phil Dickens put in a system that was not appropriate for his players. I also received an injury that the coaching staff didn't seem to be interested enough in to take care of.

As a final thought, you have to take the good with the bad. Even though I didn't do well, I'm glad I had the experience, and I wouldn't be where I am today if I didn't have that one year at Indiana University.

Data Processing Evolution

As I just shared, I didn't apply myself very well during my one year at Indiana University. I tried to blame it on IU football, but I really wasn't meant to get a college education. I got a job working on Interstate 65 which, at the time, was being built close to Columbus. When cold weather came, that job became nonexistent, so I applied for a job at Irwin Union Bank in Columbus. It took about eighteen months for a job to materialize, but my career path finally opened up before my eyes.

Sometime in late 1962, the people of power at the bank decided to keep up with the big banks and proceeded with a plan to install a computer. In searching for people to work on the computer project, the bank offered an opportunity to take a programmer's aptitude test. I took the test and came in third. First was my boss to be and second was Leslie Bluhm, who was ranked either first or second in the 1959 class at Columbus High School. As it turns out, Leslie didn't want to work on the project, so that's how I got my start. During the next year, we proceeded to prepare for the conversion from manual work to the computer. For the next thirty-five years I was involved in system design, installation, and training.

That introduction leads me to the purpose of this story—to comment on the progress of computer technology over the last fifty years, according to Jack. First, the generic terminology has evolved over time. No more IBM 80-column cards. No more wired board calculators and interpreters. No more key punch machines. No more card sorters.

Our first computer was an IBM 1240 system, which consisted of a processor with 8,000 characters of memory, two disk drives with disk packs that initially held 2,000,000 characters of data, a card reader, a printer that would print out about two hundred lines per minute, and a MICR Reading 7 Pocket Check sorting unit. The computer took up about sixteen square feet of area. The processor was about five feet by five feet by three feet, like two double-wide refrigerators side-by-side.

Because of the memory size, the jobs had to be strung together a little at a time. The programming was what impressed me the most. I started with auto-coder, which was an assembler language. The syntax was simple and pretty easy to learn. I had to set up an area for working data and then integrate the data, make the changes, and store the information.

The first step in using an IBM card was to punch holes in it. The interpreter would figure out the holes and print the letter or number at a particular place on the card. The government refund checks were done the same way back in those days. The program would read those same cards, capture the characters, print the data on the printer, and store the detail in various ways on the disk packs. I might also note that with the first computer, I could only do one process at a time. For example, step one was to set up an account. Step two was to capture the checks and deposits for the accounts. Next, I read the check data and updated the account. The last step was to print paper reports, one at a time. With the conversion to the second computer in 1969, some of these functions could be done at the same time, by a multiprocessing capability that was created.

That first computer disk I described held two million characters. It took ten of those disks just to hold the Irwin Union checking accounts in 1970. Now you can store that same information on a flash drive the size of a pack of cigarettes.

When I started at the bank in 1961, everything was done by a bookkeeping machine. In 1964, the bank converted to a computer that would capture information and update accounts, supplying paper reports daily. In 1972, the bank moved to the phase which allowed the tellers to access checking and savings account information in real time at their stations. Through the 1970s, the banking and credit union industry moved into the ATM machine technology. In the late '70s-early '80s, banks started with automatic money transfers known as

EFT (electronic funds transfers). During the eighties, the banking industry moved forward in the area of consolidating all accounts together to give the customer a statement which showed all account information. We now can operate our accounts completely from our homes, thus almost eliminating paper.

One final thought. Think about how many social security checks are deposited every day into many, many checking and savings accounts. Most companies automatically put your paychecks into your account. How do they do that?

Jim Battin
A Surge of Personal Growth (1966-1979)

Jim: I realized after four years, life as a golf pro was not the environment to someday raise a family. Although I had not dated much at all, it just seemed instinctual that family was important to me. I met Charlotte and we've been married forty-three years. We dated for ten weeks before I proposed. We got married eight months later by Reverend Laws at the Presbyterian Church in Columbus. Charlotte graduated from Columbus High School in 1964. I had never met her until I went to apply for a job. She thought I was a salesman. I joked with her later and said, "When I heard you say, 'I thought you're a salesman here to see me.' I said, 'I got you fooled'." To the day we joke about her desk being closest to mine, as a reminder of our chance meeting. This period is a tremendously powerful time. Charlotte encouraged me to go back to college at the same time we were expecting our first daughter, Samantha. I went back to school. It took thirteen years at night to get my degree. I took two or three classes a semester at night, worked full time, and Charlotte and I raised our two daughters. Stephanie, our second daughter, was born in 1971. I felt a strong sense of responsibility to do everything I could for our family.

For the first time, I saw the connection between education and what it could bring to all of us. I became immersed in learning all I could. I read constantly beyond the textbooks. Personal growth and development became a very strong part of my educational process. That growth and development also carried over to how I wanted to model my behavior for our children's sake. In looking back, it's amazing to remember the good feeling of this period of time. Of course life was physically demanding with tight schedules, but at the same time, it seemed like we made time for family—recitals, picnics, vacations, and in general just a lot of time together. Charlotte and I agreed we would never leave the kids alone. She stayed home while I got my degree. When I finished, I stayed home and she got her degree, in three years. Our beliefs about family are what brought us together. To this day we have such good memories of that period of time. There are times when I have dreams. I wake up and I can't tell exactly where I am. Am I back there? Or am I here now? You know what I mean when I say that?

Ed: A little bit, Jim. Waking up with those kinds of questions may have happened to me a few times. I never did learn, or I never took the time to learn, what everybody says should be done—which is to have a journal by your bed. As soon as you wake up, write down the dream. For me the dream always floats away very quickly. I wish I had kept a journal because I know I've had some dreams that have had that kind of impact on me, and probably through my subconscious had some messages in them that I just let go and forgot about.

Jim: The dream was so authentic. Charlotte and I didn't have a lot of money, but we had all we needed. We taught and instilled those values in our kids. And they know that, and talk about it. It is a great source of pleasure to hear our kids talk that way.

Ed: I can imagine. How old are your girls?

Jim: My girls are forty-two and thirty-eight, and they each have two children. So we have four grandkids. They live close by. We go on hikes together.

Ed Poole
Hanover College, Beginning Forty Years in Education, and an Unanticipated Gift that Saved My Life

After I graduated on May 25, 1960, I went to work for the summer at Hamilton Cosco Company—one of those three manufacturing firms in Columbus. I worked on the assembly line, boxing products right before they were stamped and shipped off to their final destination.

In the fall of 1960 I enrolled at Hanover College, a small one thousand student college in southern Indiana. I knew myself well enough to realize I would not have survived at a large university. Fortunately, I was accepted at Hanover, which had a demanding academic program.

When it was time to student teach the second semester of my senior year, I was fortunate to be able to return home and have that experience at Columbus High School, a place I had just left four years earlier. Further, I was able to have as my supervising teacher Jack Nussbaum, who was **my** United States History teacher my junior year. What a great semester we had together, and a very positive learning experience for me. When my family moved to our home on the north side of Columbus, Jack and his family lived three doors from us.

I'm going to jump ahead a bit in my story. As you'll soon read, I began teaching in 1964 in a small town on the Ohio River, just across from Louisville, Kentucky. One evening in 1966, Jack called to tell me there was an opening in their social studies department for the upcoming 1966-67 school year. Because of the opportunity to once again return home, I interviewed for the job and subsequently was appointed to fill that position.

The next part of my story is a "pay forward in kindness" story. Jack Nussbaum and his five sons all graduated from Wheaton College in Wheaton, Illinois—a west Chicago suburb. In 1980 I went to a western suburb very close to Wheaton, as principal at Naperville Central High School. In 1982, a young man walked into the school and introduced himself to me. "I'm Andy Nussbaum." I quickly realized Jack's son, Andy, was very well qualified to teach mathematics at Central High, a decision I've never regretted.

After graduating in 1964, I began my wonderful forty year career in education. During those forty years I was a high school social studies teacher, middle school principal, high school assistant principal and principal, associate superintendent for instruction, and superintendent of schools in five communities in Indiana and Illinois. After finishing my doctorate at Indiana University, I was a college professor at The University of Georgia, Indiana University, Northern Illinois University, and Aurora University—gifts that came full cycle back to that one, sage, oft-repeated, single sentence from Dad. "Son, if I could do any part of my life over, it would be to get an education, and you're going to get yours." I'm glad my parents were so insistent and that I listened to their persistency.

When I was fifty-four years old, I had an experience that changed my life forever. Because I wore many masks during my adult years—as a husband, father, son, educator, neighbor, member of several civic organizations—outwardly it appeared to others my life was on cruise control. I had always obtained the jobs I wanted when I thought I wanted and needed them. I was making my climb up that ladder of success in education. Because of those masks I wore, I've imagined some of my friends and others saying something like, "WOW! Look at Ed. He's had such success during his career and affected so many lives. I only hope my career comes close to matching his." What none of those people could have known was that, on the inside, my life was falling apart around me and I didn't even know it.

During the late summer, early fall of 1996, many issues were impacting me, both personally and professionally—issues I had conveniently ignored for several years. At that time my job was an hour drive from where I lived, some of that drive being on a two-lane highway. As I drove back and forth to work, I began noticing cement trucks and eighteen-wheelers coming at me on that two-lane highway. I noticed those vehicles more and more until one day I thought, "Ed, if you just unbuckle your seat belt, turn the steering wheel a little to the left, floor the accelerator, and plow head-on into one of those huge machines, there is no way you'll survive that crash, and most likely the other driver wouldn't even be hurt." The day I took off my seat belt, I got scared.

I didn't show up for work the next morning. I was afraid to get out of bed. Finally, I got up the courage to call my doctor's office and make an appointment for late morning. After a brief conversation with Jim, he put me in touch with a psychiatrist friend of his, with whom I met in the early afternoon. By four o'clock I was admitted for four months in a psychiatric care unit, diagnosed with clinical depression—an experience I **never** thought would happen to me. Why didn't I see that coming? After a long period of reflection I knew the answer. There were two results from wearing my masks for much of my adult life. Wearing those masks kept others from knowing Ed Poole. More importantly, wearing those masks also kept **me** from knowing Ed Poole.

One day while in the hospital, I recalled all those cowboy movies I watched growing up in Columbus. You may remember at one point in every one of those movies, the good guy would come slowing riding into town on his beautiful horse, passing all the storefronts—the hardware store, the saloon, the bank, the dry goods store, the church, etc. I thought if I would ever go onto one of those Hollywood sets back in those days and look behind all those storefronts, I would find nothing but big pieces of lumber bracing up those "buildings." The storefronts were facades, just like the masks I wore.

When I was released from the hospital, I realized several gifts resulted from my stay. For the first time, I discovered I had no idea who Ed Poole was stripped of all those fancy job titles I had during my professional career. I had conveniently avoided getting to know myself, because I thought I knew who I was behind all those masks. One gift of that hospitalization was coming to the realization it was way past time to get to know myself.

I took a two year hiatus from **everything**. I read a lot; I reflected a lot; and I wrote down those reflections. Out of that time came my second gift, my first book, *Lessons from the Porch: A Gathering Place for Telling Our Stories*. I never, ever thought of myself as one who could write a book. If I hadn't spent that time in the hospital, I'm quite certain that first book would never have been written.

As I began destroying my masks I realized that as I climbed that ladder of success as an educator and got to the top rung—superintendent of schools—the bricks to build that wall were mostly put there by people who had **their** expectations for my life and none were placed there by me. I realized this because, during my two-year timeout, I understood that for most of my adult life I had "wandered" before I "wondered."

You may be thinking, "Okay, Ed, what do you mean by this little play on words?" It's not a little play on words. For me, I've learned there is a huge distinction between wandering and wondering, and the difference goes back to that ladder I climbed in my profession. For most of my educational career I wandered willy-nilly from this job, to that job, to another job, without wondering why I was making all those moves. At that time in my life, there was no wondering to be done, because I didn't know myself. Therefore, I could not sit in the silence with myself and wonder if this or that move was one that met my **own** expectations for what I should be doing with my life, rather than how others thought I should be living my life.

The Big Dog manufacturing company has been a friend of mine for the past few years. You may have heard of them. Initially Big Dog only manufactured t-shirts and has since expanded to all sorts of software products. I own two of their shirts, each of which found me at just the right time. Right after I finished writing *Lessons from the Porch*, I bought the shirt that reads: "If ya can't run with the big dogs, ya better stay on the porch."

In 1997, my life slowly came back together. I went back to work teaching at a local university. In July, 2004, my life again fell apart around me and once again I was hospitalized. Although my stay wasn't as long, one of the results was a new diagnosis, BiPolar2. I was put on a completely different regimen of medications that began to work. Once again two gifts came from that second hospitalization. First, I realized I hadn't learned all the twenty-two lessons I discovered while writing my first book. I also knew I had more lessons to learn. My second gift was again calling a timeout in my life—not as long—but just as important. After I once again spent time with myself, I wrote my second book, *Lessons from the Crossroads: Finding My Authentic Path*. While writing this book, I came to an even better understanding of Ed Poole and my own expectations for myself and my life. You have to realize this inward journey process is ongoing. It is a process which for me I hope will never end. As I was finishing my second book, my second Big Dog shirt found me. On the back it reads, "I'd like to care, but my 'give a damn's' busted." Now, don't jump to the wrong conclusion. I care very much about many aspects of my life and the people in it. But I do know myself well enough now to distinguish among those happenings in my life I do care about and those about which I really don't give a damn.

Recently, I published my third book, *Lessons from Empowering Leaders: Real Life Stories to Inspire Your Organization Toward Greater Success*. Although I've loved writing each of those three books, and learned much from the process of putting my thoughts onto paper, this fourth book, *60 Going on 50,* is my favorite. I loved having the opportunity to touch base with twenty of my friends and classmates from our 1960 graduating class—some of whom I had not communicated with for forty-nine years.

Jeff Crump
Virginia Military Institute, Law School, and the Army

Ed: What was your experience like at VMI? Was it a hard school?

Jeff: I had to be a masochist to stay there!

Ed: What was your freshman year like?

Jeff: It was very physically rigorous, as well as mentally challenging, because I still had to do the college curriculum (in four years) plus the military training. I was a math major and I guess I was smart enough to pass and still do the military stuff. This was in the '60s when everyone else was loosening up our moral fiber. If you passed the military training and graduated, you earned a commission in the Armed Forces, assuming you otherwise qualified.

Ed: Did you get harassed a lot?

Jeff: Push-ups, harassment, shine shoes. Plus learn all the military stuff.

Ed: And then on top of all of that, you were playing basketball.

Jeff: Yeah, actually my "Rat" (freshman) year, I played both basketball and baseball. At VMI, first year students are called Rats. Actually, in some respects playing sports was better because I got out of doing some of the normal military training things Rats had to do.

Ed: I wondered if you were given any kind of break because you were in athletics.

Jeff: I got to travel a little bit so I got away from some of the military harassment. Then they had what was called the training table. I could eat there regularly and not have to "square" my meals. I got to know the upperclassmen that played ball and they were friends with me. They helped me and took care of me. So in that respect, it was positive.

Ed: What made you choose VMI?

Jeff: My dad went there.

Ed: Did you play basketball all four years?

Jeff: I was good enough to make the team, but I didn't play much.

Ed: Was there a military obligation after you graduated?

Jeff: As long as I completed all the requirements and otherwise qualified, I graduated with a commission. My commission was in the Army Air Defense Artillery.

Ed: How long were you in the military?

Jeff: I had a two-year commitment. I actually got a deferment to go to law school and then I went on active duty. I was promoted to First Lieutenant while I was in law school without a day of active duty.

Ed: Did you stay in the United States or did you go abroad?

Jeff: I was in Korea for a year, which was a lot better than Nam.

Ed: I just finished reading Dan FitzGibbon's book. The Vietnam experience was a horrendous time for our country. He does a nice job of balancing his sense of pride and honor and duty to serve the country, while at the same time identifying some pretty stupid decisions the leadership in this country made when they were fighting that war.

Jeff: Yeah, well it was micro-management. If you're going to fight a war get out there, win it, and then go home. I was in Air Defense Artillery; specifically my MOS (Military Operations Specialty) was Nike Hercules missiles. Right after I graduated from law school, President Nixon signed Salt II and we couldn't have Nike Hercs anymore, except in the United States and maybe one or two other places in the world.

I went to Korea. Korea was a really great tour. I was in what's called the Korean Military Advisory Group. I worked for the U.S. Advisor to the Deputy Chief of Staff for Personnel of the Republic of Korea Army, which is like their pentagon. We actually were there on a Department of State passport, as opposed to a military passport.

Ed: Where were you stationed?

Jeff: Seoul.

Ed: You had the amenities of a pretty good sized city.

Jeff: There was a base there and we had most of the amenities of home.

Ed: You never were faced with battle of any kind?

Jeff: No. I was nervous while I was there and had my bag packed ready to head towards Pusan.

Jim Battin
The Flight from Nashville to Raleigh

Jim: In 1992, when I was fifty years old, I was on a flight from Nashville to Raleigh. The flight was about an hour long, and I took that time to lay out the rest of my life. I had been reading a book that I still have, called *Living on Purpose*. On that flight, I took out a piece of paper and laid out the next fifteen to twenty years of my life. I described what success would look and feel like. I decided the day I would retire in 1998. I wanted to have a six-figure income. I wanted to have a work setting that allowed me to stand up at any time, go to Brown County State Park, and take a hike. I wanted to work when **I** wanted to work. I often wake up at 1:00 o'clock in the morning. I work until four or five. I take naps during the day. I read. I write. I've achieved almost to the letter all I wrote on that piece of paper that day on the flight from Nashville to Raleigh, except for the health goals. I'm struck by that. While I've always espoused wanting to be healthy, I've gained about thirty pounds in the last five years. I'm beginning to lose it now, but doing so has been a challenge.

In 2006, I reread the list and was stunned by it. In fact, it took me several days to find the letter. I knew I had stored it someplace safe; I just couldn't remember where that safe place was. I defined success fourteen years ago and I think I've got it and don't know it. I wrote this letter in the present tense, and it was eerie how accurate it was and made me realize we really do become what we think about. Ed, do you know the book *The Secret*? I believe there is something to the Law of Attraction. Whatever you think about—whether it be positive or negative—that is what you'll attract. How often does that happen? Reading that letter raised a lot of questions for me. Do most of us really know when we've arrived at where we want to be?

Ed: Your questions are interesting. I believe a lot of people don't realize that the journey itself is the destination. We get to a point and ask ourselves, "Well, is this what it's all about?" We don't stop to realize, "Yeah, this may be what it's all about for right now." My own belief system says I was placed on my own unique authentic path before I was born. At several times in my life, especially before I began my inward journey toward understanding Ed Poole, I would stray off my authentic path. That path doesn't change. In my case, I have wandered away from it on many occasions. At those times I have to stop, stand in that stillness, and realize that somewhere I took a detour that I probably should not have taken. Yet even when those occasions continue to occur, there are lessons I take away from those experiences.

Jim: I know exactly what you're talking about. When I drifted away from what I would call the authentic self, I was living in a world where I was paying too much attention to what I **should** be doing versus what I **wanted** to do.

Ed: I was listening to you talk about the flexibility in your schedule. You know from your own life's work, and I know from mine as a school administrator and college professor, I had a lot of structure in my days. That structure, however, was usually **somebody else's** structure for my time that was imposed on me. When I left that last university position over three years ago, I find I still have structure in my days, but what I love now is the structure is my own, not somebody else's. Like you said if I wear down a bit and want to take a nap at one in the afternoon, I can crawl into bed, set the alarm clock, take that snooze, and then get back to my work. You and I just never had that opportunity before. I have to say I'm still trying to turn that corner from being a "recovering university professor" to becoming an entrepreneur. When I began turning that corner I experienced a very difficult time. I wouldn't go back and change any part of my journey because every stop along the way has been full of learning experiences. I think God puts me in one spot until He thinks I'm ready for the next one and then somehow He gets my attention to let me know. By "spot" I don't necessarily mean geographically.

Jim: He creates new situations. I keep looking for the next situation. If I'm doing it right now I say to myself, "Okay, I think I know what it is. It's research. It's writing." It's happening, because I'm researching and writing right now.

Dan FitzGibbon
West Point, Vietnam, and Letters from a Green Beret

Ed: I would love for you to talk some about your experiences at West Point and in Vietnam. I've always been fascinated and admiring of you for making that commitment to both your education and to serving your country. You talked about this a little bit when you described the senior year football team being a building block for West Point. What was that experience like for you, Dan?

Dan: Wow! It was by far the most difficult overall challenge in my life. The academics, the discipline, the physical and psychological demands, the requirements to do so many different things at once and do them all correctly just created a lot of pressure and emotional strain that was almost overwhelming at times. The first year, Plebe year, was certainly the worst. All the way through that year, the pressure never let up entirely. There was always something going on. Some cadets just got overwhelmed by everything they had to do and dropped out or flunked out.

Ed: Did you ever think of quitting?

Dan: No. You know I really didn't. I was scared I might do badly and not make it, but the idea of voluntarily quitting never did enter my mind. Ed, I think the reason was that going to West Point was my idea. It wasn't something my parents encouraged me to do. It was a decision they ended up supporting, but it was not their idea. As a result, having been the one who put myself in that position, I couldn't allow myself the luxury of failure.

Ed: How did you decide West Point was the place for you?

Dan: That's interesting. As a child, I loved to read and spent hours and days at the good old Bartholomew County Library. I read a lot of boys' books, novels, and when I was about fourteen or fifteen I got into military history, reading a lot about World War II. That reading got me interested in military service and that got me interested in service academies. I looked at West Point as a prestigious place to attend, get a good education and good training for later life. In those days we had the draft in effect. You could just about count on spending two to four years in the military anyway, so going to West Point and having a four-year military commitment afterwards was not a big deal. I felt patriotic and wanted to find a way to serve our country. I thought that was a neat thing to try and decided that was what I wanted to do.

Ed: Can you recall the most memorable experience you had there?

Dan: I had some successes, but I think what probably is most memorable was the near failure I had my first year as a Plebe. I felt that Columbus High School prepared me well in English and history. I did well in those subjects at West Point, as well as foreign language. But I didn't do well in mathematics. Math is an important area at West Pont. In those days, during Plebe year one was required to take math six days a week for one and a half hours each. Our work was graded every day. I almost flunked out in math the first year. Differential and integral calculus almost did me in. I did do much better after my Plebe year and ended up graduating around the top twenty percent of my class, but it was still a long way to work my way up after my first year, especially my first semester.

Ed: Did you get some help with math during your Plebe year?

Dan: I did. West Point had a program where professors regularly met with students for extra instruction at five o'clock in the afternoon. The program was for those who were struggling with a particular subject. For several weeks I took advantage of the program in mathematics. I went to one particular professor who was a major in the army. Most of our professors were active duty officers. He got me through it. Ironically, about four years later, I was a lieutenant or captain in West Germany. This professor was in charge of some kind of operation for U.S. Army Headquarters in Heidelberg and I ran into him. It was really neat. I certainly thanked him profusely for all he did for me. I would never have made it without his help.

Ed: I can imagine that had to be a wonderful reunion.

Dan: It was. Since I wasn't in the army all that long after West Point, I didn't get a chance to link up with a lot of people that I went to West Point with, or professors that I learned from while I was there. Speaking of the guys I attended West Point with, as you can probably expect with people who go through a process like that, we feel a real bond with each other. I've developed some wonderful lasting friendships among my classmates. There are probably a dozen or so guys that I'm especially close to and then virtually everyone else in my class I feel that bond with. It's almost like having five hundred brothers out there.

Ed: Do you still stay in touch with some of them?

Dan: I do. A dozen or so and I stayed together. We link up periodically, physically. We stay together through email, letters, and postcards. We have reunions at West Point, the whole class, every five years. My forty-fifth year reunion is coming up later this year.

To Bear Any Burden

Ed: Tell us a little bit about the book *To Bear Any Burden: A Hoosier Green Beret's Letters from Vietnam*. I'm assuming by talking about the book you'll be talking about your experiences in Vietnam. Do you tell it like you felt it was over there and maybe not always so positive about Vietnam?

Dan: Absolutely right. The book is a compilation of letters about my experiences while there. The letters were sent to my parents while I was stationed in Vietnam from the first of February, 1968 to the end of August, 1969. I was an Army Special Forces captain over there. After graduating from West Point, I went through Airborne, Ranger, and Special Forces Training and spent three years as an infantry officer in West Berlin—a neat thing to do and a great place to be stationed in those days. Then I volunteered for Vietnam and spent my first ten months as an A (alpha) team leader in two different Special Forces camps. In those two camps, we had six hundred local villagers we had recruited into an armed force that we used to conduct military operations in the area. Then I was at group headquarters, the Fifth Special Forces group headquarters, working as a staff officer in the operations and training section for the last nine months there. I returned to the U.S., resigned from the army, and entered law school. I had decided to get out of the army while I was in Berlin. I'd gotten a little bit jaded with all the self-generated and often meaningless activity I found myself doing and observing while I was in the army. It just seemed too often the enemy was higher headquarters and not the Soviets on the other side of the wall.

Ed: As the old Pogo saying goes, "We have met the enemy and he is us."

Dan: Yeah. I decided that I could probably do something more meaningful for society as a lawyer. I had also thought about being a lawyer as I was growing up. So that seemed to me to be a logical thing to do. At one point, I thought it might even be possible for me to get involved in politics. By the way, I quickly ended that idea once I got out of law school and took a hard look at political life and my personality and concluded they would be a bad fit. After Berlin I went to Vietnam and there were a lot of mundane, a lot of scary, and a lot of funny things that happened to me over there. I tried to recount them all in my book. It's a pretty complete record of everything I did, everything I felt, everything I saw and experienced, everyone I met and interacted with to any significant extent while I was stationed over there. Incidentally, my book cover has a picture of me as a twenty-six year old army captain. I've had the pleasure of giving a lot of book presentations around the state to school groups, public libraries, and others since the book came out in 2005. It's been fun but has had its humbling aspects. You'd be surprised how many young people ask me whose picture that is on the cover of the book! The last forty years have been good to me in so many respects but one of them obviously is not my appearance.

Ed: Join the crowd, Dan. How many letters are in the book?

Dan: Really not that many. I'd say eight or ten. The letters were written in stages. Every night, whenever I was back in my bunker in my Special Forces camp and not out in the field on an operation, I would write a few pages. After I had a few weeks worth accumulated, I shipped the letter back as one letter to my parents. They were pretty long and somewhat disjointed because of that writing style. I'd go from one subject one night to another subject the next night, and I might be in a completely different mood. So the letters have some rough transitions in places, but it really is a pretty complete summary of everything from the mechanical aspects of constructing a camp and building perimeter defenses, to some of the civic action programs I was involved in and especially the military or combat operations I was tied up in.

Ed: If you had to think about some lessons you've taken away from your experience there, what comes to mind?

Dan: I can think of a bunch, but certainly one of them is the importance of teamwork. I led a team that consisted of myself, two other officers, and ten very experienced and highly professional, highly trained sergeants. We functioned well and achieved a lot as a team. You can't get that done sitting back giving orders to people. I think that affected a lot of my subsequent management style as a partner of my law firm and my training style working with young lawyers and law students. I think that lesson has been very beneficial to me.

I certainly learned a lot about myself in terms of what I was capable of and what I was not capable of. I felt, as I said earlier somewhat facetiously, Vietnam was easy. It wasn't really easy, but it was more manageable as a result of all the training I had and the fact that I was twenty-five when I went over there, instead of eighteen or nineteen. I learned I could handle combat situations not because I was brave, but because I had so much to do, so many things on my mind, so many responsibilities and people to watch out for, that I couldn't think about my own safety until after the fact. I also learned that I could screw things up occasionally.

Ed: It's nice to know we're human, isn't it?

Dan: Yeah. In my book, I recount a case where I put four entire companies of soldiers down on a landing zone that was three or four miles farther out from where I thought it was, and I was in there with the group. I was the first one to land. I realized my mistake as soon as I got down there. We ended up running across a North Vietnamese unit we would never have seen had we not landed in the wrong place. As a result, we had a big military success. It was all due to my map reading blunder. I talk about that in my book. I talk about the amusement of my team members when they found out the circumstances. There were some other things I did that weren't too bright, that I learned from. It's wonderful to have the resource of experienced and competent people around to help bail you out of these situations, as was the case with me.

Ed: I remember hearing a high ranking army officer talk about how the army has taken a whole new look at leadership—not so much top-down, but more about cooperation, collaboration, shared leadership, and giving people responsibilities and assuming they are capable of doing them. Did that happen while you were still there?

Dan: I don't think so far as the army as a whole was concerned. I think in large part though, that different style was very true of the Army Special Forces experience. There we had a team concept. It's not a typical military unit where you have a commander who gives orders to people. We did function as a team and in fact, they're still doing the same thing in Iraq and Afghanistan these days, the same kind of thing that I was doing when I was in Vietnam. I really learned an awful lot about how to motivate people, how to get people to do the most they're capable of doing and still enjoy the process while they're at it. It's funny and I do want to make this point, because this may be surprising. As I look back on my time in Vietnam, I consider it to be an enriching experience for me.

Ed: It's really good to hear you say that, Dan, because as a country we did hardly anything to recognize you and the others who were in harm's way for a good deal of time. It's both interesting and good to hear you say that.

Dan: Thank you, Ed. I really feel honored and privileged to have served in Vietnam. I actually look back on that time period in my life with a great deal of pride and even some fondness. I discussed this not too long ago with some guys who served with me and they have the same feelings. You would think people would look back on that as the most horrible part of their lives. It was a very intense period in our lives but we were young, we were motivated, we were working as a team with people we respected and trusted, and we were doing something that was bigger than all of us, that we thought was important and worthwhile. We were achieving some real tangible successes through our efforts. It's kind of funny, but what I just said sounds like a description of our 1959 football team.

Ed: Dan, as you went through each subsequent experience and each of those building blocks you mentioned, it seems your self-confidence and self-image grew, which always allowed you to say, "Hey, I can do this."

Dan: That's absolutely right. I never considered myself a tough guy by nature, and still don't. I think I forced myself to become one, or at least act like one, by enduring and meeting all the challenges I put myself through or found myself in a position of having to do. I think that's exactly the way it worked out.

Ed: Let's talk about your attending Harvard Law School and how all your previous experiences helped you there. Why did you choose Harvard?

Dan: As I mentioned earlier, I had decided before going to Vietnam that I wanted to get out of the army and go to law school. While I was in Vietnam, I had a law school admissions test preparation book that my sister sent over to me, which I was able to look at from time to time. I actually took the LSAT, the law school admissions test, while I was in Vietnam. Not ideal circumstances, so I had come up with a great sob story. I was going to tell all the admissions people at these law schools about why I had such a poor score on my LSAT.

Ed: But you didn't get a poor score.

Dan: Much to my shock and surprise, I got a really good score and was able to get into every school I applied to. Based on conversations with some people I knew, I decided Harvard was the best place to go. I just thought it was too good to turn down despite the cost. Incidentally, Tom Taylor in our class went to Harvard Law School ahead of me, though we didn't overlap. He thought it was wonderful and was really impressed by the professors. I really didn't share Tommy's fondness for the experience. I felt a little more isolated from the professors and from my classmates, partly because I was five years older than my typical classmates and partly because my experiences during those previous five years were so radically different from those of my classmates. In the fall of '69 there was a lot of anti-war hostility going on at many campuses. Harvard was certainly no exception to that. I never had any of that personally directed at me, but I certainly felt it—anti-military, anti-war, and just an unpleasant environment. Those attitudes didn't help. Also, Harvard is such a large school that my classes were typically a hundred and fifty students each. It was not a great opportunity to get to know professors individually and consult with them about questions and issues. So I didn't feel that fond of Harvard while I was there and was glad to get out when I finally graduated.

Jim Battin
Living My Dreams

Jim: After high school, I went to Franklin College for a year or so. It was clear to me early on that I did not know what I wanted to study or be. I played golf competitively in high school and enjoyed that a lot, so I continued playing at Franklin, actually more than going to classes. I didn't like college at all. I was miserable. At the end of the first year, I was on academic probation. During the summer I struggled with even going back. It was a very difficult period of time, not knowing my direction. Finally, I decided to return and after two weeks I just quit. I went home. I felt badly because my parents had worked very hard to support me financially. They never once said they were disappointed. They were very supportive. It was years later that I truly realized how hard that must have been, as a parent myself looking at our kids. In looking back, I think I lived in a world of "should" and relied heavily on what others said I should be or do versus looking within myself and determining my own interests.

Steve Bush and I tried to join the army. We both flunked the physical and we left saying, "Now what?" We were good friends. What were we going to do? We both played golf, and decided to go to Florida. I followed my dream, turned pro, and went to the PGA Business School. I became a golf pro and I did that for four years. I kept hearing older adults saying, "You're only young once. You should not grow older and wish you had done something." I took that to heart and I've done that ever since. I've always trusted my intuition and my gut on what I needed to do, and that's what I did. No regrets whatsoever.

Ed: Isn't it good to be able to say that? Did you manage a golf course for awhile?

Jim: Yeah, I was assistant pro for two years. Then I became head pro at a course west of Indianapolis. The key lesson was following my dreams. Only I know what they are. They will lead me in the direction I need to go.

Ed: That last statement you made is important. "They will lead you in the direction you need to go." Sometimes people are afraid to just stand still in the silence. For some people, silence can be deafening at times, but we need to stand still in the silence. Years ago a friend told me, "Ed, you can't be any place other than where you are right now. Sometimes you have to stand still and let it hurt. Sometimes you have to stand still and let it feel good. And sometimes you just have to stand still."

I'm continuing to learn how to just be still and figure out what it is I'm supposed to be doing next. In this fast-paced world we live in, where people go at break-neck speeds, we don't take time to dream. When you talked about your gut and your intuition, personally I think one of the strongest characteristics of an effective leader is relying on that intuition. You and I have both known really good leaders who can gather together around them every single piece of information that they could possibly find about a particular issue or problem, but they're still frozen in time. They don't know what to do. They don't realize one of the greatest parts of themselves they have to work with is their insight. Yet, some people just don't trust it.

Jim: I often tell groups that I think are in a frenzy, "Don't just do something. Stand there." That statement throws them for a loop for a moment but it serves its purpose, because it's simply, "Just slow down." I want to emphasize a couple of important points. It's easy for us to be influenced by what others want us to do or be. But at the end of the day we must listen to ourselves, because only we know what direction we need to take at that moment in time. Secondly, the other key lesson is to follow your dreams. Only you know what they are. They will lead you in the direction you need to go.

Larry Long
Cummins Engine Company, Harvard, and a Cummins' Lesson I Learned While Working With Other Countries.

Larry: I was trying to think of some things that characterize what I learned and talked about earlier. One of them was the time I was in Nebraska where we had our own small company. This was after I'd been at Cummins Engine for fifteen years. The company was called Nebraska Engineering. We sold irrigation systems and pivot irrigations to Saudi Arabia. This was during the time the Saudi's were subsidizing food because they'd just had the oil embargo in the early seventies and they were afraid we were going to embargo food from them. We were a little fifteen million dollar company trying to compete with the giants. I studied all about Saudi Arabia. I read part of the Koran so I could understand their religion, and I read this book about the history of King Ibn Sud. When we were trying to figure out how to get into the market, we realized everything's controlled by the royal family. We couldn't compete on a corrupt practices act—how people donated money to them—we just didn't have the ability to do that. I had to find one of the leaders of the Shammar group in the north and play on the fact that they wouldn't have to deal with the royal family if they dealt with us. They'd have to pay more for their pivots to buy them from us, but they would be working directly with a U.S. company and not have to pay homage or commissions to the royal family. It worked and we ended up getting the contract. The giants couldn't figure out why we were getting our little eight percent of the market. It was because I took the extra time to study. That's just the kind of lessons we learned growing up, whether on the playing fields or at school. I learned from those experiences.

Ed: Larry, how long were you with Cummins?

Larry: Fifteen years.

Ed: And within those fifteen years you went to a lot of places. You must have been on the fast track at Cummins.

Larry: Yes I was. Because Cummins sent me to Harvard, one of the things I didn't like was every year, year and a half, I would get promoted and get a new job. Usually the first year you're learning a job and then the second year you're really good at it. I would usually be moving on by then. I was responsible for North American sales, and then got Europe and Africa. I had the construction and every other market except trucks, which was what I had overseas. I did some really good jobs and liked Cummins. I finally figured out that I probably wasn't going to be president. I called Ted Marston after three years in Europe and asked, "Ted, what do you guys have planned for me? I'm over here in Europe, which I think has done really well. What am I coming back to?" They never really came up with a plan and I was fairly disgruntled. Plus that was the period of time when the United States was in a recession.

Ed: What year was that?

Larry: That would have been 1980 and '81. We were doing well in Europe. Europe was having a little bit of a recession, but we were taking market share from Mercedes and Deutz and all the other companies. We were doing well. Cummins had a companywide bonus, but none of us got any bonuses. We had really kicked butt over there. I said, "Guys, you have to change this. You've got to have European bonuses and you've got to have U.S. bonuses. You have to have two levels of bonuses. We're dying in Europe."

Ed: You didn't get a bonus because you were in Europe?

Larry: That's right. Carter was President and we were paid in dollars. When I went to England, the conversion was two dollars and forty cents to a pound. They were worth a lot. After Carter had been in office eighteen months, the dollar was worth less. I had a forty percent pay cut in pounds, which is what we lived on. I was not a happy camper. Cummins sent an "American invasion" to Europe. We were the Americans to go to Europe and get things going again. As I've thought back about things, when I got out of grad school and the company asked, "What do you want to do?" I said, "If I'm going to be head of marketing at Cummins, I need to sell at the very bottom level." I got the New England territory. The leaders at Cummins said, "Your other option is to be an assistant to Henry for a year." I said, "I've been an assistant to a vice president before and I don't think I'll learn much." In hindsight, I probably should have worked as Hank's assistant for a year, because I probably would have gotten a distributorship.

Ed: Was Hank Schacht president at the time?

Larry: Yeah, Hank was president. I don't know if it really made any difference, but I probably should have thought about working as his assistant. I finally realized there was no presidency for me in the long-range plans. Cummins was very highly valued in the '60s and its market cap on Wall Street never went up over a twenty-year period. We never made any money off our options. In fact, all of mine were under water the whole time. I realized I wasn't going to get rich. For those three reasons, I entertained other offers. Before I talk about my jobs after leaving Cummins, there are two stories I have to tell you about our benefactor in Columbus, Mr. Miller. I don't know if you ever got to meet him. I did a couple times.

Ed: I met Mr. Miller one time.

Larry: When I first went to Cummins in 1966, the company was experiencing a tremendous attrition. Cummins had never lost people before, but there was an economic downturn. I think eight percent of the executives left in one year. Mr. Miller set up a committee of senior and mid-level folks. I was on the mid-level committee and actually got to be the chair of the committee. In our second meeting we were sitting there with Mr. Miller. He asked, "And Larry, why were you chosen to be chairman?" I asked, "Do you want the real answer or the politically correct answer?" He said, "No, the real answer." I said, "The group decided I was the only unmarried guy and if I or the group did something wrong, I could get fired and it was a lot easier for me to move on. I was the only one that doesn't have a family." He said, "So, it wasn't because you were the best." I said, "No."

Later, we were in England. I was running the operations there and Mr. Miller came over. I thought he was coming to see us. He sat in on one of our quarterly reviews. At dinner he said, "I'd like to sit with Mary Ann and Larry, because Mary Ann's from Nashville and I'm from Columbus. Everybody else is from somewhere else." So we sat with him, having a nice conversation. During dinner it slips out. He said, "And Phillip said…." I asked, "Mr. Miller, you didn't come to see us did you?" He asked, "What do you mean?" I asked, "You came to see Prince Phillip, didn't you?" Mr. Miller said, "Yeah, but we came to see you, too." "Yeah, I'm sure you did."

The last story is about Mr. Miller when he was eighty-nine or ninety, maybe five years ago. He finally retired as chairman emeritus and was fairly crippled by then. I sent him a hand written note and wrote, "Mr. Miller, congratulations. I never officially thanked you for sending me to grad school." Three days later, I got a letter back from him thanking me and the people in Columbus for the way we did things. I thought, "Here's a guy who has done everything; it doesn't make a difference, but he cares. And he's ninety years old." I think he was the epitome of the humility of the people of Columbus and we all grew up with that. It didn't matter if you were the richest or the poorest.

Ed: As much as he had materially as a multi-millionaire, he modeled that humility. When I think about people he knew from all over the world, he himself was a humble guy.

Larry: You're exactly right. To me he's the epitome of Columbus and the uniqueness we had there. Because of people like Mr. Miller and Bill Laws, the minister of the First Presbyterian Church, we were very racially tolerant even though—as you'll remember—there were few blacks in high school. I'm thinking, "This is strange." I worked at the Golden Foundry for two summers, the worst job in the world I ever had. The workers were all black, with my brother and me integrated in. We asked, "Where do all you guys live?" They all lived in North Vernon and commuted to Columbus to work. I now realize there was a silent agreement about keeping blacks out of Columbus in spite of everything Bill Laws and Mr. Miller did.

Ed: You went to Cummins in 1966, right?

Larry: Yep, 1966. I graduated from Purdue in 1964, which was the height of Vietnam. I wanted to be a pilot and I didn't quite pass the eye exam. My peripheral vision in my left eye would slide on me. I had ten-twenty vision and so I dropped out. In 1965 the government started the draft lottery. I took a year of law school, of all things, to avoid an assignment in Vietnam. I needed to get into grad school. I went for a year and didn't enjoy it at all because the program was not very creative. You just memorized. Then I ended up breaking my leg really bad in an industrial accident. A bulldozer hit some pipe we were laying and broke my femur. I was automatically classified 4F.

I was trying to figure out where to go and get a job. The only four companies I interviewed with were ones where they'd pay for your graduate school. I interviewed at U.S. Steel, Armco in Ohio, Cummins, and Owens Corning. Because Dad died when I was a junior at Purdue, Mom was struggling a little. Dad had started a company so I stayed home, paid the mortgage for her, and lived at Harrison Lake, which wasn't a bad deal either. Cummins had a scholarship program. Once I got admitted into grad school there was a committee that evaluated all the people who qualified and then picked the top three. The three winners got free rides.

Ed: That's amazing—a full ride. I had a Cummins Foundation scholarship for the four years I was at Hanover. It wasn't anything like yours, but my folks struggled financially so every little bit helped. In your case, having Cummins pay for everything was great.

Larry: Yeah, it really was nice and I was lucky enough to win. I was getting ready to go to the Bahamas for a week on my honeymoon. I was the assistant to Chuck Grace, the VP of sales. He called and said, "Larry, got some bad news for you. It's a recession year and we're not going to have the scholarship program for grad school this year." I said, "Chuck, give me a break. Three scholarships are going to break the company? That's bullshit. Tell the committee for me that I wish I hadn't come to work here. That's the reason I picked Cummins." When I got back, Vaughn Bolls, Executive Vice-President and General Manager called me up to his office. He said, "Larry, we reviewed things and we decided to reinstate the program. You're one of the winners." I asked Vaughn, "Was it the memo I wrote?" He said, "No, I threw that away. If I had given that to the committee, you wouldn't even have a job."

I went to Harvard. That's another interesting story. The people at Harvard were interviewing me after I was accepted, and the guy asked, "How many schools did you apply to besides Harvard?" I said, "None." He responded, "That's not very good decision making." I said, "At Cummins, if you don't go to Harvard, you might as well not get an MBA. So I was coming to Harvard or not get an MBA." My first year one of my professors was a guy named Ted Levitt, who was the marketing wizard of the world at that point. That was my baptism into school.

Ed: Were you there full time, or did you work and go to school?

Larry: I couldn't go at night. I either put all my passion into work or into school. I figured I had to take time off. I had just gotten married, so I knew I wouldn't do well on a weekend program. Plus Harvard didn't offer that program. I'll tell you the third lesson I learned growing up in Columbus, that helped me. I learned in Columbus, I was a grinder. The work was hard. It's not particularly about being smart. That's nice, it's helpful, and it's the tie breaker, but it's grinding every day. When I hear Tiger Woods say he's grinding and he's the best in the world at what he does, that's what makes the difference.

Ed: It sure does.

Larry: You just keep doing it and a lot of it isn't fun. Growing up in Columbus we were all pretty humble and most of us came from pretty middle class or lower-middle class backgrounds. Our parents didn't have a lot of money. Even though Dad was a director at Cummins, he didn't make that much money. He'd started a business when I was going to school, so he didn't pay for Purdue. He said, "I'll give you the money after you graduate."

Ed: So you paid for your undergraduate program?

Larry: Yep. Of course it was easier to do back then. But I have to tell you about my first day at Harvard. My third class was managerial accounting. The professor was a guy named Bob Anthony. He's written lots of accounting books. The guy is a genius. When he went to Harvard his roommate was a guy named Bob McNamara.

Ed: That Bob McNamara?

Larry: Yeah, **that** Bob. And that Bob McNamara said, "I wasn't very smart compared to Bob Anthony. Bob Anthony was like a wizard." The first day after class Anthony called four people down front—a student from the University of Massachusetts whose name I don't remember, Hank Paulson who was just recently Secretary of Treasury, Goldman Sachs, and me. I'm thinking, "Shit, I said something brilliant already." Anthony said, "The four of you are the only people in this class that never took accounting in your undergraduate degree." I'm thinking, "Uh, oh, this is not good." He said, "In early June, each one of you was sent a thirty-eight chapter self-taught accounting book. I sent you the one I've written. I know you went through it this summer and in two weeks I'm going to give you a two-hour oral exam to see if you can stay in the program."

Ed: Ouch!

Larry: Yeah.

Ed: And of course you probably had read the book cover to cover, right?

Larry: Worse than that. I got it the week before our wedding and honeymoon. I got this package from Harvard and asked myself, "What the shit is this, an accounting book with answers on the side?" I threw it away.

Ed: Oh, no!

Larry: Yep. I didn't even look at it. I got home from school the first day. My wife Mary Ann's five years younger than I am and just a neat, feisty young lady. The first day we were there, she went job hunting. By noon she was hired at the Harvard Faculty Club. The first day she met Henry Kissinger, Ted Kennedy, and John Kenneth Galbraith. She'd had a good day. Mary Ann asked, "How was your day?" I said, "Not too good. I have to do three chapters a night of accounting to stay in this program, and I'm not going to do anything else. I'm not going to work on my other classes." She asked, "Why didn't you read the book?" I said, "Because no one told me it was important. I wasn't exactly thinking about studying at that time in my life." That was my first day at Harvard and I learned how to study. I didn't study at Purdue. I was lucky and I pretty much coasted through the four years there.

Ed: Was your undergraduate degree in engineering?

Larry: After my sophomore year I did not want to be an engineer. I switched over to International Relations.

Ed: What was your focus at Harvard?

Larry: The focus at Harvard was finance. I wanted to be in marketing and run companies. I had seen the finance guys at Cummins just crush the marketing guys because many of those in marketing didn't know their numbers well enough. I wanted to learn it as a defense against the finance wizards. So the three lessons I really learned beginning in Columbus were: no limitations, get a fantastic education so you can compete with anybody in the world, and it was hard work that really made the difference.

Ed: That's what you guys did on the football team our senior year. There was a lot of humility and nobody was out to be a star. Every member on the team was a grinder. You all felt there were no limitations on what you could achieve, and you learned a lot about life that year.

Larry: I have another story from Harvard. When I tell you this next story you're probably going to want to brain me. You really worked hard and probably wrote a really good dissertation for your doctoral degree. Mine wasn't like a doctoral dissertation but I still had to write a major paper, a thesis. I wrote mine in my second year at Harvard. Mary Ann and I couldn't go on spring break that second year because I had not done anything on my thesis.

I knew I had to write it. I checked around and found out seventy pages was fairly appropriate. Mary Ann asked, "Are we going to take a break and drive to Florida for at least a week like we did last year?" At that time, I was the undergraduate director of the placement office at Harvard so we actually had a little money. I said, "No I have to write this thesis." She asked, "Haven't you done that?" I said, "No, but I know what I'm going to do." Mary Ann facetiously said, "Well that's really good, Larry." I was writing about Cummins, the acquisition program, how they'd failed at all those efforts, and how they needed to refocus the company. I had a lot of material and a lot more material was in my head. The week before spring break I had to go over to my undergraduate office. I worked during the day and went to class. I didn't get much done. Then we came to spring break. All I was doing was working at the undergraduate office. I figured I had to write ten pages a day to get it done. I did four all nighters that week, actually got it done, and got a high pass, which was a B. I did not deserve it. If they had ever found out I wrote it in one week, I'm sure they would have thrown me out of school or at least yelled at me. But it was this belief I learned growing up and playing on our undefeated team and I could do anything. You'd just figure out a solution when you had to.

Ed: Our conversation is taking me all the way full circle back to some of those lessons that came out of Columbus.

Larry: I've got to tell you another one. During my second year, Harvard had a course called "The Executive and his Wife." Our professor was a guy named Barry Greif who ran the psychological program at Harvard. The school worried that the divorce rates were staggering the first five years after school. So Mary Ann and I took this course together. It was held at night. I got the grade, but Mary Ann and I were both supposed to do all the work. And remember, I'm interviewing for jobs even though I knew I was going back to Cummins. I was also working across the river at the placement office, so I wasn't reading the casework for class.

I'd pick up Mary Ann and as we drove to class, which was about a twenty minute ride, I'd ask her about the cases for that night. She of course, had read them all, taken notes, and done a good job. I found out what the cases were about. In class, I'd talk a couple of times in the first five or ten minutes. Then, because I knew very little, I wouldn't say anything the rest of the time. Mary Ann knew I hadn't done anything. She was almost at the point of telling the professor I wasn't doing any of the work. I said, "Mary Ann, this is what is called good business practice. I'm delegating to you." And she asked, "Why doesn't the professor call on you later in the class?" I said, "Because I talked already. In the second half, it's only the people that haven't talked that he'll lean on to see if they've done their work." It was a classic case again of figuring out the best way to get through something. I did have to learn a certain amount of gamesmanship.

Leaving Cummins

Larry: As I said earlier, Cummins didn't really have a long-term plan for me, so I left.

Ed: What kinds of career opportunities have you had since Cummins that led you to what you're doing right now?

Larry: There were two opportunities I had after that long time at Cummins. A gentleman who recruited me had a small irrigation and agricultural products company in Omaha, Nebraska. We'd never been in Omaha. I got ownership in the company and we moved to Omaha and stayed there seventeen years. With Cummins, we moved ten times in fifteen years. I didn't realize what it would be like for the family, until I changed companies. We had a whole new grounding. It was much harder than I thought. During the seventeen years in Omaha, I had three five-year stints. One was at Nebraska Engineering, where I became president. I was thirty-nine and I was able to be a young president for a decade, which helped me meet a lot of people. I met a guy name Bill Esping who founded FDR, which American Express bought. Bill hired me after a couple years of courting. I went to work for him and managed some pretty big divisions of American Express in Omaha. They were the largest processor of Visa and MasterCard in the mid-to late '80s.

Ed: What did you do for them?

Larry: I was president of four divisions. The cable group was where we processed cable bills for about twenty million users. We had all the telemarketing. We did all the operator calls for MCI. The third division was a Dunn & Bradstreet database Skip Tracing that we managed for the federal government. We found people who hadn't paid their bills. The fourth was the processing of MasterCard and Visa. After about four years, American Express was going through some tough times and I was very fortunate to join MFS—Metropolitan Fiber Systems—which is a division of Peter Kiewit. Kiewit Company was in Omaha. The only person that rented an office from us was a guy named Warren Buffett. His best buddy was Walter Scott, who was the chairman of Peter Kiewit, an employee-owned construction company. They put over four hundred and fifty million dollars into MFS to form the first fiber-optic telephone company in the early '90s. I worked there for five years. Those were exciting times because Telecom took off in the '90s and we had this terrific company. I focused on acquisitions.

In fact, this is a good story about persevering. I'd been there about a year and a half when the chairman said, "Larry, you need to go to New York. We have to do this. We're not going to get the acquisition in San Francisco you want to work on." I said, "Jim, I know you're the chairman. I'm sure I'm right on this acquisition in San Francisco. I lived in New York once and it's not worth any person ever having to live through it again. So I'm not going to do that."

There was one other issue we disagreed on, so he fired me. Although six months later, he called me and asked, "Larry, how would you like to come back as COO of the company instead of CEO and do that acquisition in San Francisco we talked about before?" I went back there and did extremely well. This is when you talk about timing and thinking you're invincible. I had eighty thousand shares of stock. I got offered a presidency at a really neat company and thought it was worth ten million dollars. In the best case scenario, my stock was worth five million dollars in three or four years. That was right before a guy named Bernie Ebbers, who ran MCI, went to jail. He bought MFS. He paid twenty-one times revenue for the company. He paid fourteen million dollars for this six hundred million dollar company. Unfortunately, I left three months before, leaving lots of valuable stock. In hindsight that wasn't a good decision.

Ed: Why not?

Larry: He was crazy. We had an east and a west coast Internet location where all the Internet traffic went through. We had the fiber to both of those places. He thought Internet was the future, which it was. That's why he paid so much for MFS. But I left in February and the stock was trading at thirty dollars a share. Jim had already said he'd sell for a hundred and ten. In July, Bernie offered a hundred and ten dollars a share, four times what it was trading at. He bought MFS and that was my first lesson in learning to look at balance sheets and not just go for opportunities. I left to go to this other company that was in trouble financially, but I got ten percent of the company. About eight million dollars later, I learned a little lesson on that one. I had to give up the stock when I left. As Jim asked, "How would you know we were going to sell it in four or five months?" I said, "Well, I don't know, but my wife thinks I should have known."

Jay Shumaker
My Early Professional Career

Jay: My professional career resulted from having great mentors, recognizing opportunities, and having lots of **luck!**

Ed: What do you mean "luck"?

Jay: My first job out of college was as a sales trainee with a corrugated box company headquartered in Columbus, Ohio. I remember how surprised I was when I learned that ninety-five percent of all manufactured items were placed in a corrugated box somewhere in its supply chain. I trained in a testing lab in Muncie, Indiana, where my teaching professionals were truly top industrial designers using corrugated as a packing material. John Green and Robert Hoyt were my first contact with the industry. They showed me how enjoyable it would be to work with engineers, purchasing, and management teams.

Ed: Jay, it sounds like you had some great training. What happened after that?

Jay: After three months of training, I was moved to a small town in north central Indiana. Frankfort became my first home away from college. It also was where I first experienced rejection from companies who already had a packaging supplier. They did not want to consider that this young pup would be of benefit to their organizations. I became a fast study on what the purchasing departments expected from the suppliers. It's the money, stupid! Save them money with better ideas on how to package their products and you will be successful. I started bringing in project after project, over and over, and I found success coming faster and faster. I landed two huge accounts in Anderson and Muncie, Indiana. The first was Guide Lamp who made headlights for GM and the second was with Delco Battery, who made all the batteries for GM.

Ed: You surely were a quick study and began helping the company. You got it!

Jay: A new niche was formed as I realized these people wanted me to be like their own son. So I became what they wanted. I became a son who worked smarter for them by finding better ways to set up their packaging lines and better equipment for their production lines. Soon, I felt lucky more often than I could believe. After three and a half years in Anderson, I moved to Ft. Wayne, Indiana, to join a different corrugated company. Ft. Wayne has been my home for the past forty years. My new company was St. Joe Paper Co. It was a manufacturing company started in the 1930's by Alfred I duPont. Mr. duPont left the family business in Delaware, taking all of his money with him and moved all his business to Florida. Mr. duPont purchased several banks, later to be called the Florida National Banks. He purchased a small paper mill in the Florida panhandle in a city called St. Joe. During the next ten years he purchased over 1,300,000 acres of land, making him the largest property holder in Florida. The wonderful thing about this company was that the final destination for the profits was the trust, Alfred I duPont Foundation. The foundation earned money by owning forty-five percent of the stock in St. Joe Paper and Florida East Coast Railroad. This money went to help children, by establishing hospitals in Florida and Delaware. The effects of polio on children created a great need for special hospitals. Can you imagine working and selling for a company that gave funds to help children?

Ed: Having spent my career in education, I can appreciate any company that wants to help children as an integral part of its mission and goals.

Jay: This was a powerful philanthropy and I know this information influenced many aspects of my thinking and selling. I became the number one sales representative in the country for St. Joe Paper Co. which included eighteen plants in sixteen states. Can you see the luck in having a company that you represented being what we wish all companies could be?

Rob Schafstall
Franklin College and Still Living in Franklin, Indiana

Ed: Have you been in Franklin since leaving Columbus?

Rob: Yes. Came to college here and never went back to Columbus. My mother died when I was in grade school and my dad died when I was a sophomore at Franklin College. I really had no reason to go back. Coincidentally, the lady I married was a Franklin College graduate and grew up in Franklin. Her family was all here. So we just stayed. I wasn't a stellar student in high school. You wouldn't have any reason to remember this, but my class standing was two above half.

Ed: Well, you were in the top half of the class.

Rob: I was really proud to be in the top half. It was good enough. I only applied to Franklin. I was ass over elbows in love with a Columbus High School girl. She was still in high school and had two more years at CHS. I couldn't stand to get more than twenty miles away from her. Of course that lasted about six weeks. That's how I got to Franklin, plus one of the admissions directors had been a bartender at my dad's restaurant.

Ed: You have got to love that.

Rob: Yeah. Later on he wound up being mayor of the city and I was city judge. My dad would have had a heart attack if he knew the bartender was the mayor and I was the city judge. Probably the most important thing that happened to me in that era in my life was becoming a member of a fraternity. Didn't you go to Hanover?

Ed: Yeah. What fraternity were you in?

Rob: Phi Delta Theta.

Ed: Me too.

Rob: I thought that was the case. The fraternity really became important. Because Dad died when I was a sophomore, my fraternity brothers became my family. A lot of guys are still really, really close after all this time. I laughed one day when I was at a board meeting at the college. A student spoke and the board announced she had a 3.85 grade point average. My response was I had a 3.85 grade point, but hers was an average and mine was an aggregate.

Franklin, and maybe Hanover as well at the time, had a requirement of twelve hours of a foreign language. The languages offered were German, French, Spanish, and Latin. There were six or seven fraternity brothers in second year German my sophomore year and we couldn't even say "hello." We didn't know anything and weren't interested in learning it either.

I was not a perpetrator, but I was one of the six who drew lots to see who would scale the downspout outside our professor's office to get an exam ahead of time. Personally I didn't win. I didn't have to do that. But the exam wound up in the fraternity, and all six of us took advantage of it. The school decided two of us had exams pretty much alike so we must have copied off each other. It was absurd because we weren't even sitting near each other. But to save everybody else's skin and not make it any worse, we admitted to having had the benefit of the exam. For that we both got a semester suspension.

That was awful. It's awful now thinking about it. I graduated in eight semesters, but they weren't eight consecutive semesters because of that suspension. What was particularly bad about that was I went back to Columbus for that period of time, had a good job at Arvin making more money than I ever thought I'd make, but then my dad died in August.

Ed: While you were home?

Rob: While I was home. He never knew I went back to school. I always felt sorry about that. I was, as many of us were, the first kid in the family that ever went to college.

Ed: I know what you mean. I have a sister and thirteen cousins, although I couldn't tell you where a single one of my cousins is today. My one cousin from North Vernon and I are the only two, out of the thirteen, that went to college and graduated.

Rob: After serving my purgatory at Arvin for that semester, I went back to Franklin. The principal reason I went back to school was because of the fraternity. I didn't care a lot about the school. The fraternity was my family. I got back and in spite of my personal stigma, got elected president of the fraternity, which was a really huge honor to me. It meant a lot, especially with what had happened. My academic career at college was about the same level of achievement as it was in high school. In fact, I was having lunch with the president of the college the other day and I said, "You know, I never did articulate this when I was in college, but I can look back on it now and it is clear to me that my goal as an undergraduate was to graduate in eight semesters with the absolute least amount of effort possible." I succeeded.

Ed: Let me tell you a Phi Delt story from Hanover. Steve Caldwell was two years ahead of me in the fraternity. Since the college was down on the Ohio River with all the caves and caverns, geology was a great science to take.

I was in my first geology class with old Professor Wickwire. We took an all-day trip down amongst the caves and caverns along the Ohio River. Then we had to write a paper about a particular part of the trip. I started talking to Steve, who had taken the same class. They went to the same places and so I just used Steve's paper to write mine.

The thing I didn't know was old Professor Wickwire kept all those papers. He read mine and I guess he thought, "Oh that sounds kind of familiar." He found Steve's paper and I ended up getting an F on the paper. I passed the course with a C. Looking back on that experience, do I wish I hadn't copied Steve's paper? Hell yes, but in those days I was known for wanting to take the easiest way out I could. So I learned a lesson there. I didn't do that anymore, but who would have thought that two years after Steve took that course, Wickwire would still have those papers collecting dust somewhere in the corner of his office. I'm not proud of myself.

The second geology course I took was second semester my sophomore year and was taught by a gentleman who was blind. The campus was small, like Franklin's, so he memorized the route from his on-campus home to the classroom. He had his cane and walked to and from class by himself. Three of my fraternity brothers and I sat in the last row of the classroom. The window, about a foot and a half behind us, was always open. After class got started, it was not uncommon for us to very quietly climb out of that window. Did he know? As sensitive as his hearing must have been I'm sure he knew something was going on. He may even have called our names and we didn't answer, but he never said anything to us about it. Those are two things that I look back on and think, "Those weren't the smartest things I've done."

Rob: What my experience has taught me is the little things that I've either accomplished or good things that have happened to me, they mean a lot more because I didn't just give up ship when that happened. After I graduated, I went to work for a couple of years at Cosco there in Columbus. I remember one day my boss called me in the office and said, "We're going to give you a raise. We're going to raise you from sixty-six hundred dollars a year to seventy-two hundred dollars a year." He thought I'd be thrilled. I said, "I don't want to be rude or ungrateful, but I just got admitted to law school and I don't want your raise. I don't want your job." I left. I asked my wife, "Do you think it's possible that someday I might make that much money practicing law?" I was dead serious.

Jim Battin
1993-1998: Developing a World View

Jim: During the last five years of my corporate life at Cummins, my work provided me the opportunity to travel extensively throughout the world. I was fortunate to be able to visit many places—the United Kingdom, France, Germany, Switzerland, Austria, India, China, Japan, Brazil, Mexico, and Canada. Travel had a profound effect on me in many ways. On one level, I learned that all people are really the same. They have similar hopes, fears, faith in a higher being or purpose, etc. On another level, there are significant differences—what we accept as evidence, value systems, issues of equality/inequality, language, religion, demographics, history, business practices, how we view time, protocol for greeting each other, gestures, dress, and how we address each other. I found that putting similarities and differences together is what life is all about. On the one hand we have a natural propensity to want to bond, share, and in many respects see the world the same. On the other hand, we have a rich diversity through the world that offers both opportunities to learn and tensions to bear. I have fond memories of those days:

- Watching families in Mexico take their children to a central plaza/park in the evening. Watching parents display gentleness and patience toward their children, traits we in the United States could learn from.
- Talking with hikers in the Scottish Highlands who just took a week off work to walk and enjoy their land.
- Watching the French enjoy a meal and a glass of wine on a sidewalk café in Paris. Of course, there were fresh flowers on the table and soft music abounding.
- Seeing the windmills of Germany that are creating natural power. Why can't we do that?
- Seeing scenery in the Swiss countries that had to be from *The Sound of Music*.
- Walking the Great Wall of China and envisioning the bundles of wood being lit to spread the word of impending intrusion of outsiders. Knowing that the Great Wall of China is the only man-made structure on earth seen from the moon.
- Visiting the Taj Mahal in India. Taking our shoes off so we could "feel the Taj" as our guide said.
- Seeing the diversity of Brazil. They live the way we are still talking about .
- The museums and historical places in Paris.
- The wine country of France and Germany.
- The reverence of the White Cliffs of Dover on the English Channel.

Despite all these memories, there was nothing like coming home and appreciating all we have and take for granted. The world is a great place. We take so many things for granted in the U.S. as being the only way to do something and the correctness of that belief. Only after visiting other countries did I see there are many views and while they are different, they are as powerful to others as we hold them for ourselves. It was a humbling experience. Underneath it all is a general desire for peace, to live a good life, to get along, to respect each other, to enjoy family, to be an individual, to be a member of something larger, and to see the human condition. I found a powerful sense of observation and a desire to listen and experience it all. Doing so forced me to continue to learn and appreciate cultural differences. I changed my view of the world and my place in it.

Dave Steenbarger
After High School

Dave: As I said earlier, after graduating from CHS, I went to pharmacy school at Purdue. During my freshman year I met my wife. We went together all through our time at Purdue. After Purdue, we got married and moved to Muncie, Indiana. Donna got her master's degree at Ball State. I worked in Muncie. Then we moved back to Indianapolis. I still worked in a pharmacy. I worked for L.S. Ayers. In fact, I managed their pharmacy. In '87 they were bought out and I got another job with a long-term care pharmacy which services nursing homes. I actually go to the nursing homes now. I get the flexibility of working when I want to and not working when I don't want. It's like being retired, except I get paid for the days I don't work. There's a real shortage of pharmacists. They're very generous and I feel very blessed to be in the position. I'm very content and happy.

A Wonderful, Life-Changing Decision I made in 1961

Dave: On February 26, 1961, at approximately two-thirty that Sunday afternoon, I met a young lady by the name of Donna Daubenspeck, who later became my wife.

Ed: You have got that down to the minute.

Dave: I remember because my fraternity was having a trade party with her sorority and that was our Founder's Day. I met her and there was an answer to my prayers because she said, "I go to the library and study at night." I questioned, "Library?" I had a choice to make, Ed. Do I play basketball with the guys? Or do I go with her? Well, my desire to be with her was greater than basketball. I wanted to be with her and lo and behold, I studied nights. We'd go to church on Sunday mornings and study Sunday afternoons. My grades came up that second semester and I got accepted in the pharmacy school. What would have happened had I not met her? I would have kept going down that same path and who knows where I'd have ended up. I'd probably end up picking up golf balls. What a milestone that was.

Tom Taylor
More Memories of Dad

Tom: Dad's role in the community as a caretaker was important to him. Dad made the decision to die at home. While he was still alive, the Mayor of Columbus declared Virgil Taylor Day, an honor Dad was able to appreciate and value before his death.

Back in the '50s when the new high school was being built, the Jaycees gave Dad the Key Man Award, because Taylor Brothers donated the heavy labor and a lot of the materials for the track behind the high school. That was done with Taylor earthmovers and dump trucks to bring in the gravel, all of which was donated. When Dad was eighty-nine, Virgil Taylor Day was declared. Man, you think about that and try to put it in context.

When I was in school, especially elementary school, I felt like my parents didn't support me at all. They didn't understand the problems I was having. I felt like they weren't there for me. A teacher in sixth grade said, "Well you know, Tommy's just basically not a part of the class. He just sits there. He doesn't participate. He's immature. He needs to catch up." And my folks said, "Oh, oh," and shook their heads "yes," not challenging authority. That affected me too. When my son was in the fifth grade his school called us in and said, "We think your son's very immature for his age. We're going to repeat him." I said, "Not in this same public school that is failing him." We took him out and put him in a school for children with learning disabilities. He ended up with a PhD from Stanford. For awhile I was down on my parents. I wondered, "Why didn't my parents do that, fight for me like I fought for my son?" Now I understand better. My generation stood up to authority and my parents' generation didn't. They were WWII and we were post-Kent State. Their president was Ike who led us to victory over evil. Ours was Nixon who lied to us about evil. I think my parents supported me in their fashion and in a way that helped me. I was never in fear of being unable to go home. After Dad's heart attack, I went home and experienced the realization of how much his life had meant to mine.

In 2006, my dad died at home. My mother had died a few years earlier, and my father remarried. At their wedding, my son and I played jazz ballads from the '40s, the period of Dad and my step-mother. We played "As Time Goes By," "Time After Time," and others. We played those for the prelude music. Dad got married, went on his honeymoon, got sick on his honeymoon, came home, and died. They knew he had cancer but they didn't know how bad it was. He came home and the doctors said, "Well, your choices are a really invasive operation, maybe never get out of the hospital, can't promise you'll live more than six months, tube fed and excrement collected in a bag." He asked, "What happens if I don't do this?" The doctors said, "You can't eat because your bowels are blocked by the expansion of your kidney cancer and you'll die in three weeks." He asked, "Can I do it at home?" They said, "Yes." Dad said, "Well, I'm going to leave the hospital now and I'll come back and tell you my decision."

Dad went to his high school reunion that afternoon, sat down with the eight people from his class that were still alive and attended reunions. He discussed his situation with them and said, "I'm going home." We were called. We came back from the west and went to Columbus. For two weeks I was there in his house with my step-mother and him. My sister, Linda, lives in Columbus and came over every day. We talked with him. We sat with him. At the end, we changed his diaper. A hundred and fifty people came through the house to pay respects. The city declared Virgil Taylor Day because he built Mill Race Park down where the old cannery used to be. Ed, just absorbing by example I got public service, music, and I succeeded in scouting. Everything I learned in scouting I learned because he was in scouting with me. And I learned a work ethic. I don't ever remember his saying, "If you're going to do it, do it right." But it was clear. Mom would ask Dad, "It's three o-clock in the morning. Why are you going out?" And the answer was, "Well, because I have to check on that concrete floor. The temperature's dropping." I saw it. I didn't even think about it at the time. My own work ethic is there because of Dad. You do it, you do it right. You take responsibility for it.

And I saw him die. He died with me there, with my wife there, by his own decision. An orderly, peaceful death at home with his loved ones around him. How much more could you wish for? One day, Dad was crying a little bit. Linda asked him, "Are you afraid to die?" Dad said, "No, I'm not afraid to die. I'm crying because of what I'm going to miss. I was just thinking about the great-great grandkids and when they were going to be graduating." Not afraid of death? I mean, geez. I'm not a Christian, but if anybody was ever going to heaven, Dad's there, and I don't have to worry about that. I may not make it to see him, but he's there.

Jack Hinkle
One of My Favorite Years

Jack: In 1967, I went to the Rose Bowl with a friend of mine, who worked at the bank with me. That was the year Indiana University played USC. He got tickets for the ball game and asked if I wanted to go. I said, "Sure." We made some quick arrangements to get a flight out there. The night before we left, I went to a dance—a New Year's dance at the Ramada Inn in Columbus. The next morning, Curt and I hopped on a plane and flew to Pasadena. We talked on the way out about what we were going to do when we got there, because all we had were tickets to the game. We didn't have a place to stay or anything. We landed at the airport, got our bags, put them in a locker, and headed for the Biltmore Hotel, which was where all the Hoosier fans were congregating to have a little hoot and toot. We walked in, checked our coats, and were walking down the hall. Curt looked to the left and there was a guy in the room that we recognized was his roommate at IU. He lived about two blocks from the parade route. So we stayed at his place. We watched the parade with the Hells Angels. We didn't have seats. We walked along, got to this one place, and there must have been a hundred motorcycles parked in there. It was the Hells Angels.

Ed: At that time the Hells Angels were not a real friendly group, were they?

Jack: No. They weren't. That's why we were concerned. After the parade we went to the Rose Bowl and found our seats. We were about two rows down from the top in the end zone, away from the cameras. The scoreboard was at the other end and we had a good view of the field. It turned out that my grandpa and my brother Jerry were at the game too. They were sitting about thirty seats away. We ran into them, and they had a car. The strange thing was that Jerry's wife and my grandmother sat in the car during the game.

Ed: Oh my gosh, because they only had two tickets?

Jack: Yeah, so they sat out there and Grandpa and Jerry watched the game.

Ed: Did you know they were going to be at the game?

Jack: Yeah I knew, but I didn't know if we were ever going to see them. We didn't make any plans to meet. But it ended up that we piled in the car, Grandpa took us out to eat, and they took us back to where we were staying.

The guy we stayed with had tickets to the game but he went separately because his tickets were in a different area, and he had some other people to go with. Curt's friend showed us around town for a couple more days. Back in those days most bars were topless, which was a big deal in California. We joked that we went to about ten different places and they were all topless. We verified that. We went to one place called The Body Shop. They had a girl there called the Fan Dancer. She danced with the fans in front and back of her. I think she was probably sixty. We were right up at the front of the stage. It was one of those walk-out stages and I could have reached out and grabbed the fan out of her hand. While we were in there, we turned around and saw Rex Harrison sitting there at a table by himself. We went to Santa Anita to the horse races. The whole trip was really a neat, neat thing. We came back, returned to work, and shortly after that I proposed and became a married guy. That was the end of my first wonderful year.

Charlie Schuette
The University of Oklahoma and Law School

Charlie: I got a full scholarship to Oklahoma, Ohio State, Indiana, and Rutgers. Everything. I mean room, board, books, food, everything. Mom and Dad were butchers, so I wasn't going to college without that scholarship. I went to Oklahoma and was All American, NCAA All American twice, and broke a couple of American records.

Ed: What made you choose Oklahoma?

Charlie: When we graduated from high school, the Indiana coach was Doc Councilman. I talked to Doc because he was very close to Duane Barrows. Doc's the one who coached Barrows on how to coach us. Doc said to me, "You ought to get out of here." Indiana just dominated swimming at that time.

You go to a swim meet with Indiana, and you could be one of the top in the country but finish fifth. So I got out of there. The Oklahoma coach was the 1952 Helsinki Olympic coach. Oklahoma had a couple of national champions and a couple of Olympic champions from Australia. I went there and it just relaxed my mind on the whole Indiana competition. When I went back to a meet at IU, I was actually able to compete well and beat a couple of guys. Because of that experience, Ker McGee Oil Company hired me as the coach of their team. They had been fourth in the state and I moved them to number one. We put several swimmers in the nationals. That's how I paid my way through law school, coaching the Ker McGee swim team. I went to school all day and then drove to Oklahoma City, coached until seven thirty, came back, studied, and went back to class the next day. I did this for three years.

Ed: What kind of team did Ker McGee have?

Charlie: The age group was from six years old to eighteen. It was like the Donner Park swim team in Columbus. It was a helluva lot of fun. When I first got there, the parents were at the bench yelling at the kids to do this, do that. I went to them and said, "Look, I'm coaching this team," and I kicked them all out. I told them, "You can come back when you can sit down and shut up and let me coach this team," which they did. And of course, the kids loved it. They did quite well.

Ed: Going back a bit, our high school years were a special time. I would not want to be a teenager in today's environment. Just no way.

Charlie: But, Ed, we knew no different. We didn't know anything else. You went to Chicago and everything opened up. I went to Oklahoma and then worked in the Bahamas for several years and then here to Miami. All of a sudden you see things that are so much different. What we were exposed to was the way it was, the way we thought it was everywhere.

Ed: Exactly. I've always felt we're limited by the experiences we have. And like you said, when all of us get out and have different experiences, we learn to reconsider where we came from and be grateful for that.

Charlie: I've retired three times and then got back into different things—law firms, chairman of a bank, and interim stuff—so I went back and forth.

Ed: Was your first wife from the University of Oklahoma?

Charlie: My first wife and I got married when she was eighteen. I was in law school and was twenty-three. I don't think she ever went to college. We were divorced in three years. We had a child who died at eleven months. Our little girl had a degenerative disease called nuclear dystrophy. The NFL quarterback Jim Kelly's son had this same disease.

Ed: I remember that particular story about Jim Kelly and his family.

Charlie: When they diagnosed our daughter in 1969, they said there were only two thousand cases ever reported in the world. They requested our approval to study her. She was going to die in one month. The doctors requested to study her and test everything. My wife and I felt, "If we can do that we may help other kids." We told the doctors they could. We seemed to think the fact that Jim Kelly's son did live until he was twelve or thirteen was because we and others made some kind of contribution to his living that long.

...Savoring Your Memories...

1. What did you do after graduating from high school? What were the circumstances that helped you make this choice?

2. What was your initial career path and why?

3. Have you stayed in that kind of career? If you have, what was it about your work you liked? If you went down a different work path, why?

4. Who are some of your dearest colleagues?

5. Who have you stayed in touch with after high school? Why these folks and not others?

6. Do you remember making some wrong decisions at this time in your life? What would you change if you could?

7. If you have a family, what do you admire most about them?

8. What kind of parent have you been? If you could change some of your parenting, what would it be?

Chapter 7   What We're Doing Now

George Abel
My Retirement and New Life

George: I probably would not have retired had I not gotten married. I married Debby five years ago last month. I lost a knee joint six years ago, right before Debby and I met, but I continued working. I struggled the last few years, working on a stiff leg. I was always having back trouble. The cost of insurance with my health history was high, but I couldn't afford not to have the insurance. I looked into what I could do if I quit, what I would have to retire on, and it just didn't make any sense. So, I kept hanging in there. Then Debby and I met, got married, and I was able to revisit everything. She's fourteen years younger than me and had planned on working four or five more years anyway. She had government health insurance, which was pretty good. Her good insurance program gave me the opportunity to go ahead and retire. Because of our new financial situation, we've really been able to fix our place up.

Ed: Did your wife grow up in Columbus?

George: Yes. As a matter of fact her first husband, who's decreased, used to play little league baseball for me. Her brother rented a house from me. Actually, they bought it on contract from me.

Ed: It sounds like the two of you were supposed to get together at some point in time.

George: That's what Debby always said. She once told me, "All my life I heard George Abel, George Abel. Somebody was always mentioning you to me and I had never met you." She and I got to talking one day and she asked my name. She was like, "I can't believe this."

Ed: Where'd you two meet?

George: Debby works in the post office in Jonesville. They have one little post office, a one person operation. At the time we met, being single and trying to buy a new home, she worked several evenings at The Brick, a little tavern in Jonesville.

Ed: I've heard of The Brick.

George: The Brick is pretty well known. Matter of fact, the governor of Indiana stopped in the other day for a burger. It's kind of unique. I stopped there one evening on my way home from work. Debby was working and we struck up a conversation. I was going through a divorce and she was breaking up with a boyfriend. We cried on each other's shoulder. I never really gave us any thought because of the age difference, other than being good friends. It just developed into...

Ed: ...into a marriage.

George: Yeah. We both love the blues. One day I said to her, "I'm going to Memphis this weekend. You want to go?" "Oh," she said, "I'd love to but..." Anyway, she asked the owner of The Brick what kind of person he thought I was and what he thought about her going with me. He said, "The way you love the blues and the way you two get along, if I was you I'd go." She did and we've been together ever since.

Ed: There you go. We have that in common. I absolutely love the blues, especially "Nawlins" and Memphis style. I was in Memphis a few years ago and remember going to B.B. King's and a few other places. I could sit and listen to the blues for most of the day. So, a trip to Memphis and then you got married. Did Debby retire from the post office?

George: No. She has three and a half years left. But it will be an early retirement and that dilutes the retirement. She's not nearly old enough to draw social security. We'll just have to look at the situation – whether it makes sense to retire, to hang on, to do something part-time, or whether we can get by on the income we'll have at that point in time.

Ed: Then she's probably got about twelve years or so before social security?

George: Yeah. I would think by the time she gets the chance to at least get seventy-five, eighty percent of social security and with her retirement from the postal system and my retirement income, and hopefully our savings, we can get by and get her out of there.

I'll tell you what, and I know you've seen it too. We lost sixty thousand dollars in our 401K this past year. On the one hand, it's killing me. All along, we were using some of my money to remodel. We added on a beautiful family room, put in a hot tub, and built a pole barn and put lots of tools and things in it to work with. We've been to Cancun and Florida. Now we have to take a look at everything because the smaller your base is, even when it improves, the less you are going to be able to make.

Ed: I can identify with that. When I started my own company three years ago, I pulled the seed money out of some of the investments I had. The money's still flying out the window faster than it's coming in. Everyone has told me, "Ed, it takes five to seven years for an entrepreneur like you to even get to the break-even point." I had a pretty fair investment portfolio, but it's almost depleted now. As they say, "You have to spend money to make money." It's just that I've been doing more spending than making up to this point.

George: Debby and I were in a situation where we knew she was going to be working and having that income for a few more years. We decided we were going to do everything that we wanted to get done to the home and have it ready and paid for by the time she retires. Now we have to look back and say, "Well, we'd better hang on." We have maxed out her savings now so she's buying, and she's buying at a time when the market's low. So, from that point, it's good.

Jim Battin
Making Sense Out of Complex Topics

Jim: I mentioned earlier about my love of reading. So far, I've read close to three thousand books. I can't go very long without reading. I read in a Zen-like manner. By that I mean I'll go into a bookstore with no notion of what I'm looking for. I wander through and make my little notes. After my wandering I say, "Well, I've got to make some tough decisions," and off I go.

Years ago I took an elective course at Indiana University/Purdue University at Indianapolis – speed reading. I was so motivated because I thought, "Oh, boy! Now, depending on the material, I can read as fast as I want." I got up to eight, nine hundred words per minute. I realized you don't want to read that way all the time, but it felt very powerful to me. I kept reading. I started setting up files, writing journals, and it didn't take long until I began integrating thoughts and concepts. I realized that's what I was supposed to be doing.

I learned to make tough choices about what I read. I also found out that the more I read, the less new information I got from each book. It got to the point that I realized authors lift information from each other. They operate from within a common pool of information. In fact, the Internet is based on that concept. On the other hand, I know a book is special to me when I feel compelled to re-read it and underline different passages than I did the first time.

There are a few very special books that I have re-read as many as four or five times over the last twenty years.

To this day, in my consulting business, I love to take complex topics and make sense of them. I know others don't like to do this and they're willing to pay somebody who has the skills to integrate different kinds of information. That's what I do. I find that people often ask me for my book list. For example, they want to know the top ten books I've read. Apparently I deliver a powerful message to others when I talk about concepts I've read about or developed through integration from a variety of sources. In the last ten years, my reading pace has picked up considerably. I am able to integrate ideas at a much faster rate than before. All of this has helped me gravitate toward a passion of becoming a researcher. It has gotten to the point that the subject is irrelevant. The process of finding information, shaping thoughts and ideas from the content, classifying it, organizing it, and making recommendations based on the requestor's need has become very much the consulting business I am in today. I find it ironic that all of the information I work with is public, yet I have developed a passion and tolerance to spend hours researching to help my clients meet their needs. What is the lesson? Find your passion and trust the journey you begin.

Ed: That is an amazing story. And it all started when you were ten years old and discovered the Columbus library.

Jim: I think the older I get, the more balanced I become. Earlier in my life, I became absorbed in education and reading. I found myself reading books more than ever before. When I started out and received an associate degree in engineering, my interest shifted somewhat into psychology. I continued in that direction briefly and got about halfway through my master's degree in organizational psychology. One day I just stopped because education was getting in the way of my learning. It was slower than I wanted and my interest went beyond a disciplined field of study. I literally was trying to make sense of everything I did and wanted to do. It was extremely exciting and fulfilling to somehow balance all of these demands. In all respects, learning took over my life and still does to this day.

Skip Lindeman
My Journey to the Ministry

Skip: I've had many careers. I taught school a couple of years, went to seminary, had it with religion and school for a while, and worked as an airline ticket agent at San Francisco airport. I worked for Quantus, the Australian airlines. Then I got interested in broadcasting and worked in that medium for twenty-five years or so. In 2000, I felt called into the ministry.

Ed: What was that call like? What did it feel like? How did you know what you were supposed to be doing?

Skip: I was working part-time for a southern California CBS radio affiliate, KNX, in Los Angeles.

Ed: That was a pretty big-time job.

Skip: Sure. And the funny thing, Ed, was I hosted a TV show on a business channel in Los Angeles from 1988 until 2000. I used to think, "Boy, if I could work at CBS radio that would just be the neatest thing." Well, I got that chance.

Ed: It's like the old saying, be careful what you ask for, you might just get it.

Skip: Exactly. It's funny how timing is in your life. So, I did get a chance to work there. It wasn't that great. About that time, I was singing in church choirs. Occasionally I would tell the minister, "Look, if you have to go someplace, I have a seminary education. I'm not ordained yet, but I'd be glad to give the sermon." Occasionally I would preach the sermon.

One time I was preparing a sermon for a friend's church. He was a friend from seminary who had been on me saying, "Look, the ministry is a good place." He always thought I would be good as a minister. As I was giving this sermon, I just had this sense that I wanted to preach more. No lights went off in the sky or anything, like St. Paul on the road to Damascus. I just had this sense that I needed to preach more. I took steps to follow that up. I went to seminary under the care of the UCC (United Church of Christ). I am ordained now.

Ed: I can imagine you have some interesting titles to your sermons.

Skip: Thank you. Last week's scripture was out of Acts. Peter realized that all these Gentiles had felt the Holy Spirit. Peter said, "Well, it's obvious we can't withhold baptism from these people." My sermon was titled, "Welcome Ladies and Gentiles."

Ed: See. That's what I mean. I just had a thought about a book by Bruce Wilkinson, called *The Dream Giver*. It's a fable about a guy named Nobody who lives is a town called Nowhere. Nobody wants to pursue his dreams. As you read the fable, you realize that when we get to what we think our dream is, it's really only a stop along the way toward getting us to a bigger dream. Nobody goes through several phases, similar to the Hero's Journey that Campbell writes about in *A Hero of a Thousand Faces*. You face the adversity, you bust through the comfort zone, you finally get there, and it turns out the path is leading you somewhere else.

Each of those jobs in the media were things you were probably supposed to be doing at that time. Each one led you to another and your dream job didn't turn out to be such a dream job. Then you had opportunities to do some part-time ministering and preaching from the pulpit. Those opportunities led you to where you are now.

Skip: Right, Ed, and I agree. I've been the interim at my church for six and a half years.

Ed: Skip, if you'd only **do** something to try and impress them your title might change.

Skip: Yeah, thanks Ed. The neat thing is they are paying me as if I've had many years experience in the ministry. While I haven't had that, I've had lots of life experience. I'm grateful my church doesn't treat me like a guy just out of seminary. They pay me a really decent salary.

Ed: That's great. Skip, during that period of time that you had let your faith go, do you remember how you felt? Were you angry? Did you feel disillusioned? Did you feel like, "Oh my gosh, why did I ever think about wanting to enter the ministry?" Do you remember the kinds of feelings you had at that time?

Skip: Yeah, amazingly Ed, I don't remember being angry. During the time I was in seminary I just thought, "This is a good education, but I don't want to go into the ministry." I just didn't feel called into the ministry. And it's funny; some of the things I didn't like then, I still don't like. One example is meetings, but that's the democratic process and the meetings just go with the job.

Ed: And that's an especially strong point in the Congregational church.

Skip: Oh boy, aren't you right there! Yes. And it's funny, my dad who was in the insurance business hated meetings too. I got that from him. Every now and then you see courses in the church literature about how to conduct a good meeting.

The seminary people were very accepting and very just. They would ask, "How do you see your ministry?" I would say, "Well, I'm not going into the ministry." And they said, "No, no, no. Ministry could be working at a Boys Club." I recall hearing the words of Martin Luther in one of my college lectures, "A man can cobble shoes to the glory of God." Of course we get the Protestant work ethic out of that, or part of it. The seminary was a great experience with good teachers. It was a really loving community. However I thought, "You know, this isn't for me."

Cal Brand
My Professional Life

Cal: I got through my supervisory training in record time, eight months. These days, the process takes most folks three or four years. During my first three months I observed another supervisor-in-training, led a group, and supervised two students. During my second unit I supervised a group of four students independently, with a training supervisor observing me from time to time. In January, I was beginning my third unit with a group of five residents. My supervisor, Bernic Pennington, suggested I get my materials together to meet with the regional certification committee. I didn't have a clue what was going on. Getting my materials together turned out to be a much bigger job, once I got into it, than it looked on the surface.

In February, I met with the committee in Chicago. They voted to certify me as an acting supervisor. A year and a half later, I met the national committee and received my full certification.

After receiving the regional certification, I took a position at Swedish Covenant Hospital. The program at Swedish was in its heyday during the early '70s and was growing. We set up a two-year residency program and had enough students that we were able to put together what I believe was the first peer group that consisted of all female students. This was a wonderful thing to be a part of.

Swedish Covenant decided to build a two-hundred-bed, extended-care hospital and missed their market. Unable to fill the hospital, they began cutting the budget for our training programs. I could have stayed on as a chaplain, but didn't have any interest in doing that.

By this time, our son Chris was born. Donna started back to work. She and I were in our family therapy. I decided it was time to leave Swedish and began putting feelers out. St. Luke's Hospital in St. Louis was starting a training program and I was asked to accept a position there. It was the first time anybody came looking at me to do a job. It went right to my head; I accepted the position, and we moved to Webster Grove.

I was responsible for running the program, supervising students, and managing the administration for two three-hundred-fifty bed hospitals, one in downtown St. Louis and the other sixteen miles west, in Chesterfield. The management at the hospital had promised me I could hire another supervisor; however the screwball bishop we had in the Episcopal Church wouldn't approve anyone I brought in. Our administrator had launched a new professional office building fund campaign. He didn't want to alienate the Episcopalians and therefore didn't want to get crosswise with the bishop. I fought with the administrator like cats and dogs for about six months, until he had enough of that. My report was moved to a vice-president. That worked out all right, but didn't solve any of the problems.

Out of the blue, I received a phone call from a former student in Chicago, who had returned to Florida. Martha knew I was interested in having some parish experience. She knew of a little church in the town of McIntosh that was looking for a pastor. We moved to Florida so I could pastor this church of seventy-five, in a community of about four hundred people.

The congregation let me have one day off per week to do CPE and family therapy. I never carried more than three to five hours a week of family therapy. I also started a parish-based CPE program because there was absolutely no continuing education for ministers in Florida.

Eventually, I got crosswise in the church with some of the members. They kept saying they wanted the church to grow and wanted more young families to join. I was bringing people into the church. All of a sudden, we didn't have enough Sunday school rooms. Since my family wasn't living in the manse, some of the church leaders thought we could hold Sunday school there, giving us the room we needed.

Donna and I had moved out of the manse into a little cracker farmhouse that we renovated. We had seven and a half acres of ground and raised dairy goats, chicken, geese, and guinea hens. While our kids were in elementary school they each had their own dairy goat. They milked it each morning and evening, were there for the kidding, the shots, and all that kind of stuff. This experience took me back to the time I spent in Dudleytown as a youngster.

We had some folks in the church that didn't think the growth was going to last. They felt the church needed to hire a retired minister, part-time. Right about that time, I took a three week vacation, study leave at Princeton. When I returned to Florida, I learned the congregation had circulated a petition. Basically, the petition said if I was thinking about leaving, I needed to announce it and get on with it. I don't know where that came from. It was just church politics.

The Presbytery said as long as I was there, I was going to be the focus of the conflict, a conflict that really was within the congregation. If I agreed to a separation package, the Presbytery would work with the conflict that was in the congregation so whoever came in there next wouldn't have that problem. I got a nice separation package, enough to live on until I found another position, and I've never had any trouble finding another position.

Donna and I were looking for a place for the kids. They were getting old enough and the schools in Central Florida were poor enough, that we were getting concerned about the kids being prepared for college. I heard from a friend who'd been serving as a supervisor at The Mental Health Services of the Roanoke Valley, in Roanoke, Virginia. He was moving to New

York and would love to have me come up and take over for him. So we sold our little farm, found homes for all our critters, and moved to Roanoke.

Ed: Was that a good experience?

Cal: Yes and no. It had both good and bad points. Donna became director of a Methodist pre-school there. I loved my work at Roanoke. My programs were always full and there were a lot of good student experiences. My predecessor had been working three jobs that allowed them to keep his salary way lower than it should have been. By that time I had kids in braces, approaching college age, and I could not work at that price. They said they would get my salary raised to where it ought to be. A year and a half later, they had not gotten it done. I told my boss, "John, if this is not done by March, I'm going to send out resumes. I'm not in a place in my life where I can let this drag out."

March came and went; he couldn't get the raise through the community board, so I sent out resumes. We moved to Ft. Wayne, Indiana, where I became the associate director of pastoral education at a Lutheran hospital. That worked out pretty well for a while. It was a little difficult for me because of the fighting in the Lutheran Church between the conservatives and the not so conservatives. I had to advocate for my programs through my colleague, the department head. He was a great guy, but when someone else is speaking for me, I never feel like they're quite doing what needs to be done. I became increasingly restless in Fort Wayne.

I did a thirty day retreat with the Spiritual Exercise of St. Ignatius, the longest I'd ever been away from my family. The spiritual director allowed me a day of repose twice, so I could drive back to Ft. Wayne and see Donna. That was a very powerful experience – thirty days in prayer, with a quasi-fast going on. I got a lot of benefit from it.

Just prior to going on that retreat, I'd accepted an invitation to go to Albuquerque to begin a Clinical Pastoral Education Program out there. I admitted my first students in October, 1993. I was able to get a wonderful program going there, on the cutting edge of a couple of things. After five years there, they went through a workforce adjustment. They needed to save three million dollars for the next year's budget and got rid of about thirty senior department leaders. The theory was the department heads could be eliminated and the remaining directors could carry out the work, without reducing clinical services. That wasn't true in the pastoral department, but they didn't quite understand that and once the decision was made, it was made. I was given a nice severance package. I was madder than hell and hated to leave there. We loved Albuquerque and our neighbors in the South Valley, a Hispanic neighborhood.

Donna's mom died about a month before I was terminated. My parents were getting old and I'd never really been around home to provide them any care. I had an invitation to go back to Indianapolis and work at Clarion Health Partners. This opportunity would allow me to be close enough to Mom and Dad that I could be involved with them. So we moved and I stayed with Clarion for five years. My department director was getting tight with how much time I could take off to care for Mom and Dad. I wanted to go to a four day week, but they didn't want that, so I left and went up to St. Vincent. They were happy to have me four days a week. I stayed with them until two and a half years ago.

Donna and I bought a little old house here in Columbus and have been fixing it up. The First Presbyterian was in need of a pastor. I signed on with them and was their interim pastor and minister of pastoral care for a little more than a year and a half. I did some preaching and administration, but mostly I called on the people that were sick, shut-in, or just needed to be visited.

Now I'm working on going to Kenya. I feel like God's calling my bluff. I've been saying for so long that I want to do mission work and serve overseas, especially in developing areas.

Ed: That will be a great experience for you and Donna.

Cal: I hope it will be. As it gets closer, we're getting more and more excited.

I haven't said much about Donna and the important role she has played in all this. Her teaching got me out of seminary debt free. Once I got involved in being a supervisor, she was a good consultant for me around learning issues, as well as a proof reader for sermons and lectures. We've had our ups and downs, probably spent a third of our forty-five years together in one kind of therapy or another, but it has been good. This adventure to Kenya will be a new chapter for us.

Jim Battin
2005 to the Present: Giving Back to the Community

Jim: For the last ten years I've been working on workforce development, education, community development – what we call the regional learning system – while focusing on southeast Indiana. A year ago December, we were fortunate to receive a thirty-eight million dollar grant.

Ed: Oh, my gosh. That is an unbelievable accomplishment, as you work toward giving back to the community.

Jim: The grantors had worked with us on another project where we saw a lot of progress. They had a lot of confidence in us.

Ed: Do you work out of your home?

Jim: Yep. It's really funny. I was hiking this morning, thinking about our conversation, and another story came to mind. Of course, all we have to do is let the stories come out. In 2005, I became involved in a regional project that played well to my skill set and interest. The project involved collecting data on the regional workforce in ten counties of southeast Indiana, analyzing the data, and recommending solutions that would improve our regional economy. I was given complete access to labor information within the region and sought out additional studies that had been completed in the past. I was part of a small team that spent nine months collecting data through primary and secondary research methods. We conducted close to thirty focus groups, surveyed over two hundred employees, and interviewed forty business, education, and workforce development and community leaders. Based on our recommended solutions, over the next twelve months we received several grants to begin implementation. Over the last three years, we have implemented all the solutions and are beginning to see results that are impacting the region in positive ways. This consulting project has been very satisfying to me personally because of its complexity and the difference it is making in students, workers, and the economy of our region. We have many examples of people working together to make a difference in their communities and across the region. We are sharing practices and learning, so that we can sustain the effort and results for years to come. All of the years of learning to develop a compelling vision and then implementing that vision to meet the goals and objectives outlined are very rewarding. It's fitting that I was able to take the "aha" moment in 1953 at the Columbus Public Library and thread my way through life to be able to contribute in this manner.

Jack Hinkle

On My Way to Disability[4]

(Authors' Note) Some of you may remember Victor Frankl. He survived the Nazi concentration camps during World War II. During the Holocaust he lost his wife and his entire family to the Nazis. After he was freed, Frankl wrote the book *Man's Search for Meaning*, which has sold over nine million copies. In his book, Frankl wrote that all those who survived their experiences

---

4   From our perspective, "On My Way to Disability" is Jack's most important story. Its importance derives from the fact this story has changed Jack's life from the moment it began, through today, and into the future. The disability also dramatically altered the lives of his family and friends. You or someone you love may have a debilitating physical disability. Most likely, the disability is not identical to the one Jack shares with us. However, as you read this story, you will find the grace and acceptance that brought Jack to terms with his life as it is. Please have the patience to read and the wisdom to learn.

in the concentration camp at Auschwitz did so because of one common thread – they all felt they had unfinished business yet to do after their release. For example, Frankl pictured himself on the stage of a very large auditorium, sharing with the audience his experiences while in the concentration camps. Obviously, to accomplish this vision he had to survive the atrocities of the concentration camps. Frankl wrote, "The last of the human freedoms is to choose one's attitude in any given set of circumstances…It did not really matter what we expected from life, but rather what life expected from us… What matters, therefore, is not the meaning of life in general, but rather the specific meaning of a person's life at any given moment." Over a century ago William James wrote, "The greatest discovery of this generation is that a human being can alter their life by altering their attitudes."

Jack Hinkle has chosen his attitude – one of acceptance – and has the insight to know he has unfinished business yet to do.

Jack: My story begins in 1987. We used to play cards a lot, especially Euchre. My wife's family was Euchre players. I found that sitting in a card table chair was starting to bother my back. I started complaining about that. Early in 1988, I went to the doctor. He checked me over and said, "I think you might have a slipped disc." They took x-rays, which were awful. Because I was so large and overweight, the x-rays didn't clearly identify the problem. My body fat masked the spot on my body that was vital to see. Finally, I went back to the doctor and he referred me to a neurosurgeon.

I went to the emergency room at the community hospital in Indianapolis. The neurosurgeon said, "Those x-rays aren't any good. You have so much body fat that we can't tell anything. You probably need an MRI. While you're here, can you stand up on your tiptoes?" I couldn't do it. That was the first indication. One of my feet was a little numb at times. I could tell something was wrong. I could tell by the look on the doctor's face that I was in trouble. He proceeded to say I needed to get an MRI. "It looks like something's wrong and we need to take a look at it."

I was planning on starting a vacation that very day. It was a Thursday or Friday and we were going to San Diego. The doctor said, "Well, I can give you some Tylenol. We'll plan on your going to the hospital when you get back." He didn't try to hurry me or talk me out of the vacation. I had a miserable vacation because at that point I couldn't even lie down in bed. I had to sleep in a recliner.

When we got back, I reported to the Community North Hospital. I checked in and they were going to just check me over. That was on Sunday, the tenth of July. They put a tube down a blood vessel, to look through and try to find out where the trouble was. We spent about an hour and a half trying to get the thing inserted into my back. The doctor couldn't do it. He went all the way up to my neck and inserted the tube there. I was watching on a little, round TV set. I could see what he was doing because I was laying on my stomach. He said, "You've got a tumor there. We're going to have to get it out." It turns out that the tumor was where he was trying to insert the tube.

I remember waking up the next morning in the ICU, with the little button on the squeaker for pain. Every time I felt pain, I was supposed to squeeze the button and it dispensed some medicine to keep the pain down. I was playing a tune on that thing for most of that day. They finally got me back up to the room. The doctor came to me and said, "You had a tumor. We had to remove it. It was a big one. It's the largest tumor I've removed in my thirty-five years of surgery." I had six or eight staples in my back. The scar ran from the middle of my back all the way down to my butt crack. The doctor continued, "We think we got most of it but we may have a little more in the L2 area, which is the left butt area." Later that day, another doctor I was seeing came in and said, "It was benign." Those words were a shock. I was in so much pain, I didn't think about it being malignant or benign. I just thought it was an obstruction.

I went through an emotional adjustment period for the next couple of days. When Mom walked in the room I started crying. I had no idea why I would start crying. I decided it was the drugs I was under. Other than when my wife Linda would come to see me, Mom was there all the time. After she visited for a while, Mom went back to work. When she left, I started crying again. It took me two or three days before I got over that. Then it was a matter of just getting through the pain. I had a lot of pain in my back, because they had cut me. Since I had the surgery, my back hasn't bothered me.

Next, I had to learn how to walk. I could hardly move, even to turn over. The hospital staff had to help me get up. I could move around and with their help I could get into a wheelchair. The physical therapists took me to the rehab area to exercise. The therapists tried to get me to sit up, helped me stand up and do various other things. With their help, I was able to do most of that. To some degree I could feel my feet, but not completely. The professional staff stuck me with needles all the way up my leg. I could tell that some places were dull and others were not. The doctors were trying to zero in on where the problem was. The next day I went to the rehab section of the hospital, which was at Community Central in Indianapolis. I had to go by ambulance and that was a tough ride. Although somebody might say it'd be nice to ride in an ambulance, I didn't think so. I wouldn't recommend it.

During the surgery, the doctors had to cut through all kinds of stuff to get to the tumor. That was the source of pain for the next week and a half or so. The rehab lasted about six weeks. I was scheduled a couple of times in the morning and a couple in the afternoon. The physical therapists wanted to see what I could do – get up and walk, lift weights, and pull up things. The therapists took me through all that. I was progressing to the point where they figured I'd never be out of the wheelchair. I probably shot a hundred thousand dollars easily during that time.

Part of the tumor couldn't be removed because it was where all the nerves come out of the bottom and spread through your legs. The doctors couldn't remove it because they didn't want to damage the nerves. The tumor continued to grow. I had radiation treatments on that area every day. Just maneuvering to get in position on my stomach for the radiologist to do what he had to do was about an hour of agony. After about a week and a half, I finally got to the point where the pain was going away.

When I returned to rehab, the first thing I did was start lifting a dowel rod which was maybe the size of a yardstick. It was a little, bitty thing about as round as a dime. I couldn't lift that with both my arms, but I could with one arm. So, what it amounted to was when I lifted both arms in the air, the muscles in my back that work had been cut up a little bit. That was my problem. I couldn't lift my arms because the pain was so bad. The pain medicine was supposed to last four hours. I could guarantee it was only lasting for three and a half. The doctor said, "Well, you ought to go ahead and take that anyway. You need to get rid of the pain so you can get yourself back together."

For me, the oddity of rehab was that I was the only person that could move both arms. Most of the people there were stroke victims and had one arm they couldn't use. I could sit there and open my milk and drink it. The other people were waiting for the nurse to come by and open it and stick the straw in for them. I would think, "What am I doing here?" I felt like I was intruding on their party.

One day, the Oprah show was on. Oprah's guest was a kid that had killed his family. We watched shows like that for a week, the most depressing shows I've ever seen in my life. I was already depressed. Finally I said, "Don't ever let anybody put on anything but fun shows. There are people in here that don't appreciate depressing shows. It can't be helping them."

When I left rehab, I was able to walk on crutches – those forward hand ones where your arm goes through the stirrup rather than under your armpits. Steve, a guy in our graduating class, contracted polio when he was very young. Steve was still using that same kind of crutches when I saw him at our fortieth reunion. He really helped me. By working with a friend of

Steve's, I was able to get assistance from the state in modifying my van so I could get in and out of it while in my wheelchair.

I tried exercising in the neighborhood. I could get about a hundred yards down the street. My problem was, when you're walking on crutches, you don't want to fall. When I got a hundred yards away, I had to make sure I could make the hundred yards back. So, I didn't get too far away from the house. I never did make it around the block. I progressed to the point where I could finally walk without crutches, but it was a walk where I had to watch everything I did. I couldn't walk through the grass. I could stand up to take a shower, but I had to lean against the wall. I managed to do that for a while.

Towards the end of 1995, I was starting to go the other way. I went back to one crutch and then both crutches.

All during this time, I was still working. I worked in Connecticut and lived there by myself. Then I changed jobs and went out to Nevada for three and a half years. I was living in Nevada by myself. The people I worked with were more than helpful. We'd go out to eat and they'd come by to make sure I was able to get there. I was in an apartment which had a door about fifteen feet from the street. I was able to park, walk inside, and sit down. I managed it for a while. After a year and a half, I found I was having trouble doing that. I moved to a motel that had a handicapped unit. It had handles in the bathroom, and a parking spot right next to my room. For probably a year, I had hand controls in my car. After that, I couldn't even get up and into the car very easily. The last year I was there, I had to have a truck come and pick me up and cart me and my wheelchair to work. Then I started getting bedsores and I got to the point where I couldn't manage. I couldn't get up and go to the bathroom without help.

I called Linda and she came out. I drove all the way home. I had to drive because I couldn't get into the passenger side of the car. When I returned to Indianapolis, I got a job downtown and worked there part-time for another year. My son would take me back and forth to work. He would get me out of bed. We'd go out to the car and he'd help me stand up. I'd get in and drive to work. So even when he was taking me, I was driving. It felt really strange – a crippled guy driving himself to work with his son, not crippled, sitting in the passenger seat. After work, he'd come back and get me.

The first day I ever worked was November 30th, 1961. The last day I worked was November 30th, 2001, exactly forty years to the day. Since then I've been in bed.

That's probably the end of this story. I lay here in this bed. It's geared to keep me from getting bed sores. It's like a rubber boat, a life-saving boat. Inside the bed are beads. Air blows up through the beads. The bed does the stimulation to make my legs feel like there's something going on in there. The pressure points are relieved. I've been in this bed close to nine years. I turn over on my side to use the computer. I'm surprisingly mobile in the bed. It's been a drag, but I'm geared to it. I understand where I think I am. I'm willing to live this way, knowing I'd rather have something else, but I'm willing to hold it where I am. I read books, play on the computer, and my wife is nice enough to take care of me.

I recently underwent a sleep apnea test. The doctors determined I need to use a face mask breather to sleep at night. Normally I don't notice a treatment, but after a week of using it I am sure it's helping me. The mask is a little uncomfortable but the trade-off is amazing. I compare this to when I quit smoking. After a week or so I could really notice the change.

(Authors' Note) On February 9, 2009, Jack sent this email to The Columbus Crew. "Two out of the last three days, my special bed shut down. One night it was due to overheating. The next night, the electricity went off for an hour and a half. Both times it happened at about three o'clock in the morning. When the electricity goes off, it's like lying on wood, with my legs in a pile of sand. This situation has happened three times in eight years until this time, then twice in three days. Just life in the slow lane."

Dan FitzGibbon
Indianapolis after Harvard

Dan: I ended up spending the summer between my second and third years of law school at a firm in Indianapolis. I liked the people and the city a lot more than I thought I would. I decided I would come back after I graduated and I did. I joined a firm of forty-five lawyers. Now we have four hundred and fifty. It's really grown. The firm is Barnes and Thornburg. Our lawyers are in a total of seven different offices, including Chicago and Washington, D.C.

Ed: Have you been with that firm your entire career?

Dan: Yes. I'm still Of Counsel to them.

Ed: Were you a partner in that original group you joined?

Dan: Yes. I started out as an associate, which is essentially an employee who has a salary and is under the direction of partners in the law firm. After six and a half years, I was promoted to full partner. From that point on, I was given a vote and participated in a share of profits, which could vary depending upon how successful the firm was. I continued in that capacity until 2000, when I took early retirement. During my time with the firm, I spent thirteen years on the management committee. This committee service was right in the middle of the firm's growth period and there were a lot of decisions to be made and a lot of issues to be resolved. That was an opportunity to apply some of the teamwork skills and experiences I learned while in Vietnam, West Point, and while playing on our undefeated football team during our senior year in high school. I approached my legal work with that same spirit. Often I would be involved in working on a project with several other people. We always treated it as collaboration. Even those who were quite a bit younger than me were expected to disagree with me and tell me how they would do things. As a result, I think we ended up doing a better job for our client.

Ed: I'm sure it was partly because of the example you set. Were those younger attorneys fairly comfortable with being transparent and telling you like it was?

Dan: Yes. I thought so anyway. People certainly did tell me their candid views. I was always positive in receiving them, so I think that encouraged people to be open with me. Ed, I always had the philosophy that I wanted to hire people who were smarter than I was. I wasn't afraid of having people under me that were going to outsmart me. I wanted that and so I was fortunate in that I was able to hire some excellent people. They did a lot to make me look good.

Ed: Tell me about your law practice and why you left it.

Dan: I had a pretty good law practice. It was largely business consulting and transactional work of different sorts. My colleagues were good and I had excellent clients. After about twenty-five years or so, I just thought it got a little stale. I decided I wanted to try something different, something in the nature of public service that would give me a chance to draw on some of my experience, skills, and background. That's when I got involved in the international rule of law projects.

I was really doing something that was a continuation of what I had done before and was about to draw on my previous experiences, particularly on the assignment in Russia where I was doing commercial law that was consistent with my practice. When I attended West Point, I had two years of Russian language plus a couple of Russian history courses. I was always fascinated by the country and wanted to spend some time over there. Everything just came together and I had a chance to do all of those things. Since that time I've just built on it.

Ed: As I've been listening to your wonderful stories, a lot of it seems to go back to that '59 team and the confidence and determination all of you guys had. I know lots of people in Columbus never thought that team would go undefeated, but you did. We're back to the building blocks, the increase in your own concept of self and the things that you can do, that perhaps you never thought you could do. There's the teamwork piece that continued at West Point, then in West Berlin and Vietnam, and on into your legal career. There are some interesting and interconnected themes, themes that for me connect your stories together.

Dan: Well thanks, I think so too. Some people might look at my checkered career and think I've been bouncing all over the place, but I really do see a pattern there. It does seem that one thing was built upon another and, in turn, led to another. It all seems to sort itself out in my own view.

I consider myself semi-retired. As far as my law firm is concerned, I'm retired. Technically, I'm considered Of Counsel to the firm. I have an office. I go in a couple days a week, but I don't do any ongoing client work. The reason I say I'm semi-retired is that I'm very active in international legal reform projects. I do an awful lot of travel overseas on these things. In fact, I'm between a couple of trips right now. I just got back from the former Soviet Republic of Georgia. Next month, I'll be leaving for three weeks to go to Moldova.

Ed: I noticed the very first email you sent The Columbus Crew was sent from one of your locations and you were explaining a bit about some of the work you do. When you talk about law reform, what is your goal when you go into these countries?

Dan: It varies from project to project. By way of background, my historical practice with my law firm consisted of business planning and counseling, mergers and acquisitions, corporate tax planning, and commercial contracts. When I first got into international legal reform and spent a year in Russia during 1998 and 1999, I was in charge of a commercial law reform project. Since that time I've done some more commercial law, but I've also branched out and gotten involved in legal professional development, judicial reform and training, association building, and assessment of the status of the rule of law in various countries. What we try to do is bring legal reform to emerging democracies. Generally, this organization tries to help these emerging democracies get up to international standards in a whole range of areas – human rights, gender equity, anti-corruption, intellectual property protection, and many others. I want to point out that the international standards I look at aren't necessarily the conditions we see in the U.S. These international standards are based on United Nations principles related to the role of lawyers and various other international conventions and declarations that most countries have signed. In fact, there are some areas where our own system wouldn't measure up to the international standards.

Dan's Family

Dan: Ed, I've been incredibly lucky. I think no story about me would be complete without at least mentioning my family. My wife, Joan, is seven years younger than I am. I met Joan while I was at Harvard Law School, so she didn't know me during my army days. She was getting a masters degree in teaching at the Harvard graduate school of education. Joan became a math teacher. She is an absolutely wonderful person and a devoted wife and friend. I could not have asked for a better fellow traveler in this world.

Ed: That's wonderful. I know how wonderful it is just flat out to be able to say that.

Dan: Absolutely. After thirty-five years of marriage, I still feel the same way.

Ed: Do you have children?

Dan: We have two children. Kathy is thirty-two. She's a graduate of Princeton. Kathy got her master's degrees from Michigan. This past spring, she got a doctorate in musical arts from Boston University. She's out at Lewis and Clark College in Portland, Oregon. She's on the faculty, teaching music and conducting choirs. I haven't been there yet and am looking forward to spending a fair amount of time there. Joan and I are going out there in late June and we'll get a good look at Portland.

Our son, Tom, is thirty years old. He graduated from the University of Pennsylvania and then got a law degree from the University of Chicago. Tom worked for a major law firm in Chicago for three and a half years. He then decided, Ed, that he would much rather be a high school history teacher and coach. It's funny, that's something I always thought would be a neat thing to do, but I never had the guts to do it. Tom does. So, he quit his job and is getting his master's degree in education at Northwestern.

Skip Lindeman

Current Happenings with the Lindemans

Ed: It seems that right now you feel like you're doing what God wants you to be doing.

Skip: I really do. I'm not sorry for any of the time I spent in broadcasting. Part of me wonders, "Gee, why didn't I get into this church business a little sooner."

Ed: One explanation is you weren't ready. As I go through my own hero's journey on a daily basis, I think God has this wonderful ability of putting friends and gifts along my way just at the time I need them. Hopefully I receive those I'm supposed to and then continue on my journey.

Skip, when you're not busy with your work-a-day world, what do you do for fun? What brings you enjoyment out there in southern California?

Skip: My wife grew up in southern California and has a wonderful family. Every Saturday morning, we meet at a certain restaurant and have a mini family reunion. Obviously, not everybody can make it every Saturday, but I really enjoy that time.

Ed: What a wonderful tradition.

Skip: Yeah. It was started by her parents and her uncles and aunts. They've died, but the family carries it on.

During part of my broadcast career, I lived in Eugene, Oregon. The University of Oregon's got some pretty tough track teams. Eugene has a bunch of jogging trails. I ran my first ten kilometer race up there in 1980. I even did some half-marathons. I felt, "I'll never do a marathon." When I moved to Los Angeles, there was a group I heard about that would train you to do marathons. So, I've done a couple of marathons, I guess maybe six. My last one was in 2000. When I finished my first marathon I felt so good, Ed. I was doing it for myself, not for any world record time, but gosh, I trained. It was really neat. The group in L.A. runs near the beach and they start training six months ahead of time. Also, I continue to sing in my church's choir, even though I'm the minister. I've become addicted to crossword puzzles too.

Ed: Working crossword puzzles is supposed to be good for the dendrites in the brain and keeping the brain sharp.

Skip: When I came to L.A. I started going to this coffee shop, where I eventually met my wife. I would sit at a table with my male friends. The *Los Angeles Times* has a puzzle every day and we'd hand it around the table. Harlane came to that restaurant. She and her friends would sit at another table and do the puzzle. Sometimes people wouldn't show up, so the tables would merge. That's how we got together. I still kid her about a funny thing she did one time. The clue was "Daily Planet employee." She wrote in Superman and I thought, "No, this can't be right." The newspaper hired Clark Kent, not Superman. The answer was Lois Lane.

Larry Long
Forming My Own Company

Larry: After leaving Cummins and working with several companies, I was able to become what I considered a complete manager and president. With three other guys – their money and my brains – we founded a company in Greenville, South Carolina, in 1998. We've been in Greenville for eleven years. Telecom was still going wild. Within eighteen months, we had it up to eighteen million in revenue. We sold it for sixty million dollars. I thought, "I have finally retired." But we sold it to a company that moved in, sold it again, and put restrictions on the stock. We couldn't sell the stock for six months. The stock went from eighteen dollars a share to fifty-five cents a share before we could sell it. I just got hammered. That was in 2001. That's when I decided I had to hit another home run.

For the last four or five years, I've been searching for a cutting edge company in which I could get some good ownership. I happened to luck into Clean Fuel. We have three companies now. We make bio-diesel out of waste vegetable oil. We collect oil at restaurants or buy rendered fat from a chicken processing plant. We turn it into fuel that's so clean. It's eighty-seven percent cleaner on carbon emissions than regular diesel. You can drink it, which I have done, in order to show people how clean it is. It does give you the runs because it's waste vegetable oil. It tastes a lot like potato chips. I've been commuting from Greenville to Florida for eighteen months. I fly down every Monday, run the companies, and come back on Friday. Fortunately there's a direct flight from Greenville to Orlando.

Ed: Why did you decide to stay in Greenville as opposed to moving to Florida?

Larry: Two reasons. One, I wasn't sure the new venture would be successful. The second reason is, at age sixty-six I wasn't crazy about starting again in another new community. It was tough enough at fifty-six when we moved here. Mary Ann just doesn't want to go through it again. We like it here and Orlando is not someplace I want to retire.

Ed: How many companies are you competing with for the kind of product you have, Larry?

Larry: There are about twenty or thirty, but nobody's very good. We have the chance to be number one if we do it right and can raise enough money. Of course, now is not a good time to be raising money.

Ed: Don't I remember from one of our phone conversations that you recently got a big grant?

Larry: We got two and a half million from the state. We won that grant, but they haven't given us the money yet. We've put about twenty million of my partner's money into the company already. I didn't have any money to put in. We are hoping that we win a twenty million dollar federal grant, because we've got some natural gas guys that want to hedge their bets. They're looking at investing in us too. The Seminole Indians have some people who are interested. They own the Hard Rock Casinos. They have a lot of money and don't pay taxes, so the Seminoles are looking at investing. A group called the HoChunks out of Winnebago, Nebraska is also interested.

Ed: They have casinos, don't they?

Larry: Yes, they do, on the Missouri River and the borders of South Dakota and Nebraska. They have a quarter of a billion dollar fund. We're hoping to get the two Indian tribes and the natural gas group to invest, and then go forward.

We're Not Invincible

Larry: We always think we have perfect health throughout all the tensions and stress. I still play tennis with the thirty-year-olds and get beat regularly. A little over a year ago, I had my regular physical. The doctor said, "Larry, listen to your heart." For twenty-five years I've had a heart murmur, which is the politically correct way of saying the valve doesn't close. At the end of each beat there would be a little gurgle. As I'm listening, I said, "Bob, it never stops gurgling." He said, "You're right. It's not closing now." I asked, "What do you mean?" He said, "Well, it's gone from three or four percent backwash to fifty. It'd be a good idea to get it fixed."

If you get a replacement valve, you can take Coumadin and all those other neat things for the rest of your life. I found a guy down here that's one of the best at repairing heart valves. I put it off for five months because of the company, and on June 20, 2008 he put a titanium band around my mitral valve. I feel terrific, although I didn't feel real bad before. There are two parts to the story that are very interesting. One, I said I had to be back to work in twelve days. I couldn't take six weeks off. So the doctor said, "I'll do the minimally invasive procedure." That's where they don't crack your sternum; they just go through the ribs to the other side. I was back at work in twelve days and have done very well since then, until about a month ago. All of a sudden, I got this infection in the area where the incision was. I said, "Oh man, there must be some scar tissue that's a little messed up." Three weeks ago, I went to a clinic. By now the area's really swollen and I'm at least a "C-cup." The doctor said, "I can see you've had this surgery. I'm not doing anything until I can get a cat-scan on you." I went back and he asked, "Do you know why it's infected?" I said, "I have no idea." It turns out that during the previous procedure, the doctors had accidentally left in six inches of casing wire. An intern didn't pull it out. The wire went from my right armpit to my heart. The wire was still attached to the heart. It was getting banged around over by the pectoral area. I would feel it when I served, but I thought it was scar tissue.

So, guess what I did? I was back in Greenville for a week, and the next week I had to go back in and have the wire taken out. No big deal. Now I've got this nice, open incision. Because of the infection, the doctor wants to keep it open for ten days to make sure everything's better. We talk about thinking we're invincible and we're not. But the good news is, because of this and colonoscopies I may live forever.

Amidst All My Gifts, There are Still Those Wilderness Journeys

Larry: We have two daughters. Our older daughter was a very good runner and a neat kid, much more like her mother. My younger daughter was like me, taller and thinner. The younger one was a champion swimmer and an academic All American, even though she had scoliosis and couldn't lift weights. She lived twenty hours a day in this plastic body cast to keep her spine straight when she was in high school. I have no idea how she did it. She's now a mother and is expecting her second child. They live in Toledo.

Our older daughter will be thirty-eight this year. During her college days, she had a heavy drinking problem. It got worse and worse and worse. I remember one of the points you mentioned in one of your notes about your depression. I'm pretty sure she is clinically depressed. It's very hard because she won't be committed. We believe she has a borderline personality disorder, or bi-polar, and it just gets progressively worse. She can barely be around us anymore. She lives in Greenville somewhere; we're not exactly sure where. So, here was a very promising young lady who was married for a short time, and from about the age of thirty on has just regressed socially. My wife and I feel absolutely helpless. We tried "tough love" and several other approaches, but to no avail. When someone is an adult, unless they do something that threatens their own or someone else's security, you can't really get them committed, which is probably the most frustrating thing. Talk about the highs we've had. This is the absolute low.

Ed: I can't even imagine what that would be like, Larry.

Larry: It's much tougher on Mary Ann. I have three young ladies who have been a lot of fun. The one absolute joy is going to see our grandson, who at three already knows what an optical illusion is. I didn't know that until I was at least twenty.

Ed Poole
Following Those Paths Which Hold My Heart

In March, 2006, I resigned my last university teacher position and formed my own company, Lessons for Your Journey®. As I was working on my second book, I realized I wasn't doing justice to either my teaching or my writing. I was so blessed during my career in education and loved working with my graduate students in educational leadership. However, one day I decided to follow the advice Phil Jackson shares in his book *Sacred Hoops*, find those paths that hold your heart and follow them.

I always told my graduate students, "It's one thing to know when it's time to get into a job. It's probably more important to know when it's time to leave that job." It was my time to leave and I haven't regretted that decision for a single moment. I love my life as an entrepreneur – my writing, organizational consulting, professional coaching, and storytelling. I guess I'm still teaching, but in many different venues than before.

Unlike my father, I really would not want to go back and try to redo any part of my life, as if I could even if I wanted to. Being able to honestly share that thought with you gives me a great deal of comfort. I also make that statement with a great deal of confidence, because I believe – as Dan FitzGibbon shared in his story about the building blocks in his life – everything I've done has been for a reason. Each stop along my journey has prepared me for the next. My life would be much different today had I not made every single stop along the way, and I very much like my life today.

As We Age – Part of My Conversation with Larry Long

Ed: I go in for an annual physical. I have a colonoscopy every three to five years. I just had one a couple of months ago. Kathi and I are going to head over to the coast next year. One day about fifteen years ago, my body decided it was going to start producing too many red blood cells. The medical term for that is polycythemia vera. When the hematologist said, "Ed, it's something you'll die **with** and not **of**, "I thought, "Okay, I can deal with that." When I lived in Chicago, I'd go in every three to six months and have what's called a phlebotomy. They simply insert a needle and take out a unit of blood, as if I was at a Red Cross donation center. The procedure reduces the number of red blood cells. Over the next three to six months, the red blood cells would do their job of reproducing too many and I'd go in for another phlebotomy. I saw the hematologist once a year and everything was fine.

Larry: What's the down side of that, Ed?

Ed: I found out I had this condition on a fluke. A school district I was working for at the time provided administrators with a free physical. It was discovered during that physical and my internist there in Naperville wanted me to have it checked out. He said, "It's either an anomaly or something else." I did an overnight sleep study at Rush Presbyterian St. Luke's Hospital in Chicago. The results confirmed my body was producing too many red blood cells. The down side of that, Larry, is there are lots of people walking around today who have this same red blood cell disorder and don't know it. Over time, if you produce too many red blood cells, for one thing, it's going to contribute to a pretty healthy heart attack.

Larry: Like cholesterol, as far as the end result?

Ed: Yeah. In July, 2008, Kathi and I moved to a mountain-top cabin outside Boone, North Carolina. I found a hematologist here and have had more trouble with the red blood cells than at any other time. One time, I had a phlebotomy two weeks in a row. Now I'm having them every month instead of every three months. I had another overnight sleep study to make sure I don't have sleep apnea, which I don't. After considering every other reason for the more frequent increase in red blood cells, it finally came down to the altitude. Our cabin is at 3500 feet elevation.

Larry: Oh sure. The interesting point is for every thousand feet above one, you lose three percent of the oxygen. You're running at about nine or ten percent less oxygen where you live.

Ed: I'm putting that little, clear plastic tube of oxygen in my nose at night to supplement the oxygen. I told Kathi, "I'm not going to wear this tube in my nose for the rest of my life." So she and I are going to start looking around the coast of North Carolina this summer. We'd like to get close to Greenville, North Carolina so hopefully Kathi can get a job at East Carolina University. But, we just have to get to a lower elevation.

Larry: That's interesting. About a decade ago, I found out I have sleep apnea. I don't know if you ever tried one of those c-packs. I don't mind the claustrophobic thing on my face, but around three or four in the morning the machine wakes me up at about eighteen psi – blowing out my ears. It's so powerful. It wakes Mary Ann up too. I said, "Screw it. I can sleep on my face." If you sleep face down, what closes up your throat doesn't affect apnea. I said, "If they ever figure out a better solution than that c-pack, that's fine."

Rob Schafstall
Life as an Attorney, City Judge, Member of the Franklin College Board of Trustees – and Some Health Issues Along the Way

Rob: After I got through law school and passed the bar, they created a city court in Franklin. I'm the only guy that's ever been elected. There's never been another city judge in Franklin. As much as I might not like being the city judge, it's something I'm really proud of. Then, the most outlandish thing happened in 1993. I was elected to the Board of Trustees at Franklin College. I look back at my undergraduate days and say, "If we polled my class or all the people I was in school with and asked, 'Who's most likely to become a member of the board of trustees?' I wouldn't have had a mention." In the late eighties we had some very, very bad fires at Franklin College. One of the fires burned the main building quite extensively. My line is, "Due to the fires burning up my academic records and the death of the two presidents that were here when I was an undergraduate, I became eligible to be a member of the Board of Trustees." I have been serving for the last several years as treasurer of the Board of Trustees. More important than anything I've told you so far, is that since the early seventies, I have been the home team clock-keeper for Franklin College basketball games. In July of 1995 my first grandchild was born and on November 26th I had a very severe stroke. It put me on the shelf for five months with the rehab, hospital, and the in-patient and out-patient therapy. I've got some minor problems, but the stroke didn't affect my thinking which is most important to practice law. I came back well.

Ed: Did you have surgery?

Rob: No, physical and occupational therapy. If you ever have that misfortune, those therapists are magicians. They know what they're doing. I'm walking and there was a long, long time when I couldn't do that.

We're going through some adversity right now. My wife, who just turned sixty-five, is four months younger than I am. She's been in very good health, nursed me through the stroke, recovery, and all that. Last September, with no symptoms, no warning, she was diagnosed with ovarian and colon cancer. She's had two surgeries and is in her sixth round of chemotherapy.

The last three rounds have been in-patient. She's actually in the hospital right now. I get her out tomorrow.

My Children and Grandchildren

Rob: I've got three kids. Each of them has two children. My oldest son, who is forty-two years old now, has been practicing law with me for fourteen years. He's a fine lawyer and I'm proud to work with him. I've got two boys and a girl, the girl being the youngest. They were educated respectively at Wabash, Duke, and Emory University. Those are schools you're familiar with.

Ed: Three great schools.

Rob: My second son went to the University of Virginia to get his MBA. He's an engineer, doing real well in San Diego. He works for a company called Clark Construction, which has a project on just about every street in Washington, D.C. He went out there initially to build big, huge military residential developments. My little girl, who is thirty-four and the business graduate from Emory, is a CPA.

Ed: That is wonderful and speaks well for both you and your wife having encouraged their education.

Rob: Well, you know it's interesting you say that. I think you'll agree with me. That really speaks well for my wife, because I'm a lot like you. In my younger days, when I was trying to figure out what to do and how to make something out of myself, I was a lot more interested in myself and what was going to happen to me, than I was worrying about raising kids on a day-to-day basis.

Ed: That's true, Rob, for both of us.

Rob: My biggest accomplishment in life is that I have lived long enough that I now have two granddaughters wearing brassieres. I never thought I'd see that.

Ed: Now, **that's** what I call an accomplishment, Rob.

Rob: This is kind of a Jack Buck take-off line, but I always say I've got six grandchildren and they're all boys, except five.

I also want to mention the death of the guy I started practicing law with. He was also a Phi Delt at Franklin. He'd come to the alumni activities. He was an old man, but for some reason we had a real close friendship. I came into practice with him in '71. He had bypass surgery that same year. If you remember, there wasn't much of that going around in '71. He lived another nine years and died in 1980. I remember him being old and I wasn't really surprised that he would die, because he was old. He was sixty-six.

Ed: Wow, that's how old we are.

Rob: I know. One day I said to my son who's with me, "I practiced law with my other partner for nine years before he died. You know, we've almost practiced law for nine years together." My son said, "We've practiced law for twelve years together." That's how fast time goes by.

Ed: Rob, when we were growing up in Columbus I usually read *The Evening Republican*. Whenever a picture of a high school class having their fiftieth reunion showed up, I thought, "My god, those people are old." And here we are getting ready to have our fiftieth reunion a year from June.

Rob: I went to the forty-fifth reunion and I was shocked. I was taken aback by the people that were using canes and walkers, several carrying oxygen tanks. Poor Coach Andress was there. It was right before he died. Several faculty members were there. I kept thinking, I look at myself in the mirror every morning and I didn't think I looked that old.

Ed: I don't think I do either. I feel like I'm thirty.

Rob: I think I'm that young. Somebody asks, "How old are you?" "I'm thirty-five or forty." Later on that winter, I saw a picture from the reunion. I was standing with the college basketball team for a picture. The picture was from the side and I do look that old. I didn't think so.

Ed: Kathi's fourteen years younger than I am. It's funny when I talk about something from high school. She'll say one of two things, either I wasn't even born yet, or I was two years old, or three years old, or whatever.

Rob: When I got up to Franklin College, I got hooked up with a band that was there. It wasn't a college band; it was older guys. We got a lot of work. I could make twenty-five bucks a week. I had to join the union. Last year I got a letter from the union that said I had become a life member of the musicians union due to longevity.

Ed: Now that's something. I'd ask them if they didn't have a plaque or a certificate you could frame and put that up on your wall, buddy.

Rob: They did give me a billfold card. How could anybody live that long?

Charlie Schuette
After the Law Degree

Charlie: I got the law degree and went to the Bahamas. There was a guy I roomed with, another swimmer, who was from Miami. He invited me to the Bahamas for a debutante party. The women were extraordinary. I got down there, saw all the beautiful women, and thought "What the hell am I doing in Oklahoma City?" I was getting a divorce and he lined me up with a couple of job interviews. One law firm was general counsel to the group that started Freeport, Bahamas. The Bahamas group owned 255,000 acres on Grand Bahama Island in Freeport, an area known today as Lucaya. They also owned two casinos. In Freeport they owned the airport, the power company, and the water company. They had the right to license all businesses and the right to lease all businesses. Doctors paid a dollar a year for licenses, whereas other licenses cost a hell of a lot more. We had Bahamian lawyers, British lawyers, German lawyers, and Jamaican lawyers. There were fourteen of us. The attorneys got concerned about nationalization when a new government took control, so the Freeport Company moved me to Miami. I ran a large corporation for the Freeport group in Miami that handled all legal work for their assets outside of the Bahamas. I was single, so I was able to go to Europe every month for two weeks. I did that for five years.

Ed: When was that chronologically?

Charlie: Seventy-two to seventy-five. Then the senior partner in the law firm that I was associated with died. The firm started having problems. I took it over. They asked me to run it as president, which I did. I built up my own practice. Then I went to Akerman Senterfitt. They asked me to be chairman and I ran that firm. I took the firm from a hundred lawyers to three hundred and seventy lawyers. Akerman Senterfitt is the largest firm in Miami. There are a hundred and seventy lawyers in Miami alone. What I did was develop the firm throughout Florida – Jacksonville, Tallahassee, Tampa, West Palm Beach, and Fort Lauderdale. Today the firm is in New York, Washington, D.C., Dallas, Denver, and L.A. After eight years of running Akerman Senterfitt, I quit. They kept paying me just to keep me around. I was also on the board of a bank. They asked me to be chairman of the bank, which I didn't see myself doing. I don't know shit about banking. They kept pushing me, so I became chairman and built the hell out of that bank.

Ed: Are you still doing that?

Charlie: No. I got out a couple of months ago. It's a privately held bank, private family, 1926 bank – we're talking third generation owners. I was asked by the board to build the bank, which I did. The next thing we needed was capital. The shareholders weren't prepared to pay money for additional capital. They told me to fire these people I had hired, people that brought one hundred million dollars in assets to the bank in seven months, and close the bank's branches. I told them I wouldn't do it, so they said, "We're going to legally remove you." I said, "Fine, if you can get fifty percent of the shareholders to agree, then remove me." And they did, because they wanted to maintain control of the bank without the benefit of growth and profitability.

Ed: Are you still doing some consulting?

Charlie: I started a company with this lady. In the banking community, the banks are gone or they've got major federal support. The problems in banking are now filtering down to the small community banks, those of one and a half billion or less in assets. The small banks are now starting to have serious problems. They have loans to small shopping centers where employees have been fired, shops are closing, the landlord's not paying the bank, and the banks are going under. My partner and I – a friend of fifteen years – came up with this idea about going into these banks, taking over these defaulted properties, and managing the properties for them. We can manage. We can take care of the property and get the lawn mowed, collect the rent, take care of everything, and charge them a fee for that. We just started the company and the reaction has been phenomenal. A lot of people know me, know my name. Today my partner called after she had met with this banker. Given the fact that I was involved in this project, he absolutely wanted to get involved. We don't charge them much. We charge a monthly fee and a percentage for managing the places, collecting the rents, that sort of stuff.

Ed: Do you have more time to call your own these days or are you just as busy as ever?

Charlie: Oh no, I've got plenty of free time. I'm driving my wife nuts. I'm still with the law firm, Akerman Senterfitt. It's a big, big firm. They still pay me to come into the office, attend firm events, and occasionally advise on mergers and acquisitions. They can say, "This is the guy who grew this firm." So I show up, meet new associates, etc.

Ed: And they pay you for that? That sounds like a pretty good deal.

Charlie: Yeah, they pay me.

Ed: How did you meet your current wife?

Charlie: She made the horrible mistake of moving into the apartment above me when I lived in Freeport, Bahamas. I used to work out every day in the pool. I was still a competitive swimmer in Freeport. The Bahamian swimmers weren't competitive types. She mentioned to someone that she would like to meet me. We met and hit it off. We dated for quite a while and then we got married. She is a lovely, lovely woman. We get along very well. She's an artist and does very, very well. She sells her works at various art shows and galleries.

Jay Shumaker
Lady Luck Keeps Smiling on Me

Jay: Do you remember my earlier story about the St. Joe Paper Company?

Ed: I do. That company helped you a lot along your career.

Jay: It did. However, life started changing for St. Joe Paper Company in 1996. They decided that owning over a million acres of land in Florida might be a great way to redefine themselves. They owned more than seventy-five miles of virgin beach in the Panhandle of Florida. I owned quite a few shares of Joe stock, which exploded upward as they became real estate developers. Their stock, which changed from SJP to JOE stock, became a very valuable asset to own, especially if you sold out before the bust of 2008! A new and better career started with the selling of all eighteen box plants and one paper mill. I was able to write my own contract with St. Joe Paper Company before it sold to a new company called BOX USA. It sounds like a patriotic song, perfect by any American's standards. But it was pure luck for me. BOX USA had plants in areas where I had not been able to work. This helped me grow my own company, SJ Sales, Inc.

Ed: All of your professional jobs along the way helped prepare you for forming your own company. That's a great story.

Jay: Then a new and even better situation appeared before me. International Paper Co., which has plants all over the country and twelve or more foreign countries, purchased BOX USA! Bang! Again, good fortune came at the perfect time. Now, I represent the best and largest packaging maker in the world.

While companies were buying and creating new companies, another need for packaging was growing strongly. Bottled water was in demand and water plants all over the country needed packaging. Today I sell more packaging to water companies than I could have ever imagined. My career has blossomed three separate times. I now sell more packaging to more states than I could have thought possible. Success in selling is a matter of timing and being able to see the other person's point of view on a continuing basis. But working hard for your customer is the key to earning respect and having the satisfaction of creating business partnerships. However, being in the right place at the right time is most definitely luck.

Dave Steenbarger
Following the Plan God Has For My Life and the Gift of Family

Dave: God has a plan for each of our lives. That's exactly what happened in my life. Donna and I went together throughout our years at Purdue. Each year, my grades got better. I knew becoming a pharmacist was what I wanted to do because of what my mother gave me in guiding me to that job at Carpenter's Rexall Pharmacy. I had been able to spend some time in the pharmacy actually filling prescriptions, being watched by the pharmacist. There were others in the school of pharmacy that were a lot smarter than I, who dropped out because they weren't sure this was the path they wanted to follow. There again, my mother intervened. She was there at that time in my life and that was part of God's plan too.

As I said earlier, Donna and I married at the end of my fifth year at Purdue. It was a great time and a special time. We moved to Muncie. Donna was a speech and language pathologist and wanted to get her masters at Ball State. I worked at a local drugstore, Owl Drugs. The drugstore got its name because it was open until midnight. Two of us worked the store, putting in long hours. But I enjoyed it.

Although we didn't have children at the time, we knew Muncie wasn't conducive to raising a family, because of the long hours I worked. This period of time, when I was twenty-three, was a low point in that my mother, at the age of fifty-four, had a cerebral aneurism. They rushed her from Columbus to Methodist Hospital in Indianapolis. She didn't last twenty-four hours, which was a real shock to me because as I said, she and I were so close. She was more than a mother. She was a close friend and advisor. I get choked up now even thinking about it. I hope you can understand that.

Ed: I can understand that. Sure. That had to be a tremendous loss at such a young age, for both of you, really.

Dave: Having learned about God at an early age, He gave me a real peace about it all. I don't think I could have gotten through it without His help. That inner peace I had, it's just indescribable.

Donna's father worked for L.S. Ayers Department Stores. Her dad was getting ready to retire, so there was going to be an opening. That meant we could move to Indianapolis and I could manage the L.S. Ayers pharmacy at the Greenwood Park Mall. We would be close to Perry Township, where Donna got a job. I could work Monday through Friday, no nights and no holidays. The pay was less, but I would be home more. Putting the family first is one of the lessons I learned from Mom. Donna and I made the decision that in everything we do, we'd always put the family first. We've never regretted that decision.

As we were going along, it looked like we weren't going to have children. After five years of being married we did an infertility workshop, with no results. We decided to check out adopting. Of course forty years ago, before Roe vs. Wade, you could adopt and have a child in nine months. Sure enough, that's what happened. In 1971, we got our daughter. She was three months old. We adopted her and what a joyful day that was! Nine months from that period, our son was born, to us. We had two children, a year apart. There again, what a blessing! But now, you look back on God's hand. If we had our son first, or waited and had our son and didn't adopt, we'd never have been blessed with our daughter. She is grown now and lives close to us. She couldn't have children, so she has adopted. That's how we got our granddaughter, Abigail, who just turned six.

During this period of time, particularly when my mother passed away, working at Ayers, and adopting our daughter, having grown up in a church was such a gift.

Ed: What church did you attend?

Dave: First United Lutheran Church. My grandparents went there. In fact, all my relatives went there. I learned a lot in that church. I had a lot of head knowledge, but there comes a time in your life when you've got to make a personal commitment to Christ, to confess Him as Lord, and take Him personally as your savior. Doing so helped me to move from my head to my heart. Doing so really changed our lives.

I worked at L.S. Ayers for twenty years, while the kids were growing up. In 1987, Ayers was bought out. They made some changes and one change was eliminating the pharmacy. Even back then, there was a shortage of pharmacists so I knew I could get another job. But man, I really loved those hours. I could go to work for a chain, but if possible I really wanted the good hours.

One of the members of our church was president of a company called Health Care Prescriptions, here in Southport. The company serviced nursing homes. This was completely foreign to me because I was used to retail pharmacy. At this same time, the government passed a law stating a pharmacist must go into every nursing home and review every patient's chart. Up to this time pharmacists hadn't been doing that and pharmacies didn't have anybody on staff to make those visits. Nobody was trained to do this. Purdue set up three satellite programs – one in Fort Wayne, one in Evansville, and one in Indianapolis – to train people to become consultant pharmacists. I took the training. Even though I had been out of school now for twenty some years, these young kids just getting out of school didn't know any more than I did. They hadn't been trained either. Being trained together, all of a sudden I was in parity with them, caught up to their same level.

Our friend from church said, "We need a consultant pharmacist. You'd be a good one because it's a lot about personality and public relations. As you go into the nursing homes, you're representing a company. You just have to be flexible, adjust to each home. Each home has its own personality." So, that's what I do. I've been doing this for twenty-two years and just love it. There again, as I look back on it, God's hand was in that. It wasn't a coincidence, in 1987, when I lost my job and this opportunity just opened up.

Ed: In fact, Dave, most of the times in my own life as I've moved down a path and get stuck smack in the middle of a wilderness journey, I wonder how did I get in here and how am I going to get out? In March of 2006, I kept hearing this message that I should spend all my time writing, speaking, and consulting. Those feelings just kept coming at me day after day. I was trying to write in the evenings and teach my classes during the day. I discovered I was enjoying the writing more than the teaching and that says a lot, because I loved the teaching. I just felt that writing was what I was supposed to be doing. God led both Kathi and me to North Carolina, and that was not an accident.

To go back in time a bit, I grew up at East Columbus Church of Christ, out there on Indiana Avenue.

Dave: Exactly. I've been passed it a hundred times.

Ed: Dave, in that church, I learned how to fear, to be afraid of an angry God. It wasn't until I sang in the college choir at Hanover that I learned its okay to leave church with questions still in our heart and unresolved issues still on our mind. The little town of Hanover had a big Presbyterian church. The town didn't have enough people for a choir, so on Sunday mornings the college choir became the church choir. I spent four years in the choir loft at the Hanover Presbyterian Church. It was only at that point, beginning when I was eighteen years old, that I realized we're talking about a loving, caring, forgiving, unconditional God and not someone trying His best to grab me and catch me any way He can. It took me many years to get rid of that religious anger I took with me to Hanover.

Dave: I can imagine because you were at that church in Columbus for a long time.

Ed: When we grow up in a church, like you and I did, many of us are handed our religious beliefs before we're really able to understand them. As life goes on, we begin to understand our beliefs. In my own case, I've tended to adjust those beliefs so they make more sense to me now. I learned I needed to do my own searching, go through those periods of anxiety and frustration, and discover just what it is I really believe. Part of that searching was to find myself, stripped of all those fancy job titles I'd had in education. I'm admiring the fact that you were able to see that in your life, much earlier than I did.

Dave: I think all of us do that searching and reflecting at different times and ages. God's timing for us is so important.

Ed: Going into nursing homes on a regular basis must be difficult for you.

Dave: It makes me thankful for what I've got. Being in the nursing homes every day makes me so aware of what people are going through, many of them much younger than we are, through no fault of their own. How can I complain about anything? When I have those thoughts, I gain a real good perspective to have an attitude of gratitude.

Ed: Oh, I like that thought. I've often heard that said.

Dave: Whatever the circumstances that you're in, God is preparing you. So consider your present calling and circumstances. Starting back in high school when I was working at the Rexall Drug store, little did I know that God was preparing me for the mission field. In 1991, I took my first medical missionary trip to El Salvador. That was a life-changing experience. We had doctors and nurses on the trip and I set up a pharmacy. This summer, I'll be taking twenty-five people down there. This will be my twenty-second trip. It's always a life-changing experience for me, as well as for those I take. We take about ten teenagers. To watch their lives change during that week makes the trips worthwhile for me.

Ed: What do you mean, Dave, when you say those trips are life-changing for you?

Dave: First of all, you see what other people are going through. The teenagers down there don't have anything. Nothing. And yet, they're content. They've got a sense of peace that our teenagers don't have. We've got so much materialism here in America that it blinds our teenagers to what's really important in life. Through the experience of those trips, the blinders come off and our teenagers see what's really important in life. Our teenagers see things through a different perspective and return home more grateful for what they have and more concerned about others than themselves. It just gets into your system. You fall in love with the people down there.

We have a sister church there, so we live with families from that church. At the end of the week, you feel like a member of the family. They just love you and take care of you. The homes are very modest, as you can imagine. They have no hot water, but at the end of the week that doesn't seem to matter.

Each day, we take a bus out in the country, to a different location. We go to the very poor areas, where the people live in lean-tos. There's no water, no electricity, no healthcare. Nothing.

Ed: The days must be long.

Dave: Yeah, they are long days, but it's a good tired. We do some good, short-term care. Everybody's got parasites, worms, or upper respiratory infections that we treat. We can share the gospel of Christ with the people and give them hope for today and hope for tomorrow.

I want to be remembered as a person like Barnabas in the Bible. Barnabas was known as the son of encouragement. The Bible states he was full of spirit, full of faith, and he encouraged others. Because of that, he came to faith. That's what I want on my tombstone.

Ed: That's been a model for you.

Dave: That's me. We need to remember to look for God to providentially open doors. That's what He did for you and for me. I look back at the doors He opened for me. He opened the door to work at the Rexall Drug Store, to get into and complete pharmacy school, to get the job at L.S. Ayers and come back here, to have a job for the family. Now to be an elder in the church, be able to go on these mission trips, and still be effective in a job that I just truly love, it's not a coincidence. I call it a God-incidence.

Ed: We talked earlier about how everything is connected. As I get older and have time to look back, I begin to see the connections that I didn't always see when I was going through any particular time in my life. Every day I say the following to myself: "I am the place that God shines through. He and I are one, not two. He wants me where and as I am. I need not fret, nor will, nor plan. If I'll but be relaxed and free, He'll carry out his plan through me." In saying those words, I just feel this weight being lifted off my shoulders because I realize I don't have to do it myself. In fact, whenever I'm silly enough to try and do it by myself there have at times been some disastrous results.

Dave: Ed, most people haven't caught it yet. Most people are trying to do it on their own and you cannot.

Ed: You know, Dave, I wouldn't go back and change anything. First of all, I couldn't. It's all been a blessing and I'm in a much better place today. I know you are in the place that you've been in for a long time. I rejoice in that as well. I can hear the peace, comfort, solitude, joy, and love in your voice and the things you talk about. When it's all said and done what more should we ask for than that?

Dave: Exactly.

Tom Taylor
A Lesson about Moral Living

Tom: I've got real questions about the racism of my parents because growing up in Columbus there wasn't a lot of chance to show it. But, dad liked the white bands and not the black ones. While she was in college, my daughter was dating a Jewish boy from New York. My parents never said a thing about it, but one day Dad was talking about a new, big discount store in town that had put some local people out of business. In front of Pamela he started saying, "They're just a bunch of New York Je..Je..sharp dealers that come in here and take over." Again though, Dad was action not ideas. He supported the concrete finishers. There just weren't enough blacks in town for me to ever see a problem. At some point during college, Mother buried my Congress on Racial Equality pin, the one with the black and white hands shaking, in her geranium bed.

My parents were Christians. I started questioning my own faith while I was in the fifth grade. By the time I was a year out of high school, I was forever done with religion. The racial undertone in Columbus, the religious homogeneity, the political conservatism, all conflicted with the liberal, secular, government questioning '60s teenager I was quickly becoming. All these things led me to believe that I had no affiliation with Columbus anymore. I didn't go back there once we left. It was only after dad's heart attack that we began to rediscover those Columbus roots. The heart attack brought me back to town physically and started this realization about Dad's importance to me and who I am.

Linda and I consider ourselves to be secular humanists. Morally that means we're not responsible to anyone but ourselves for whether we're good or bad. There's not confession and forgiveness; we're either good or bad for ourselves. We believe that moral decisions are tested by their affect, not by whether they're in accordance with the law. I think that we are very moral people. We don't shoplift and if somebody drops a billfold, we run after them to give it back.

60 Days at Age 60 and Making Connections on Other Travel Adventures

Tom: I think I've mentioned to you, or maybe wrote about, my Yukon River trip. Sixty days by myself and my only worry was the "by myself part." I knew I had the skills and the equipment. My dermatologist said, "You could die out there." I said, "That's right. I understand. If I get appendicitis on a sandbar west of Eagle, Alaska, I'm going to die. If I get appendicitis at home, I'll be taken care of. I understand that. If I'm at home, a hurricane can drop a tree on my bedroom or a pick-up truck driver can hit me as I drive into town." He says, "Yeah, you're right. I can live with that," and gave me the medicine I wanted. But the thing I was afraid of was being by myself. Will I go crazy on a sandbar with nobody to talk to? I love to talk to people. I had a coronet with me, so I could play my horn. Being by myself turned out not to be a problem.

Ed: Is that where you took the picture of you in that dilapidated open house?

Tom: Yep. That's a roadhouse where the winter trail used to cross the Yukon between Dawson and White Horse. The river would be frozen in the winter and people could cross there. If the ice wasn't good, they could hang out at the roadhouse until it was.

Ed: I wrote most of my second book by taking personal retreats in lots of different places around the country. The retreats were usually a couple weeks long. The first retreat I took was at Brown County State Park, about fifteen miles from Columbus. I stayed in one of their log cabins. What scared me was I didn't know if I could stand to be with **me** for two weeks.

Tom: That was it. That was my fear.

Tommy "brings down the house" with his trumpet playing at the Yukon Roadhouse

Ed: Then I came to the conclusion that there's a difference between being alone and being lonely. I love my alone time; however my perspective says we are by nature communal creatures and there is a time when in savoring our aloneness we also want to be around people. So I'd sit and write in my log cabin. Every once in a while, maybe each day or maybe every other day, I'd get this urge to go into Nashville, Indiana, and be around some of the people I met there. I started out thinking, my god, I don't know if I can stand Ed Poole for two weeks. I learned to love my alone time. I think it's good for all of us to have that time.

Tom: After I went to the Yukon for two months, Linda made a hiking and camping trip in Australia and New Zealand for two months. She saw what the time alone had done for me and needed the same recharging. I agree with you. I like your expression about the difference between being alone and being lonely. Of course I wasn't lonely, because I knew my family and friends were still back home, even though they were not with me. I don't know where that came from. I don't think my father would like to be alone. I think one of his great fears after my mother died was that he would die alone, or that he would be alone. I don't seem to have that thought anymore and I really don't know when and where I began to enjoy being alone. But one of the great things is getting on my motorcycle and doing a two thousand mile solo ride over to North Carolina, riding some of the twisty roads, and then returning back home.

Ed: Well, the next time you take a bike trip to North Carolina, you've got to come to Boone.

All You Have to Do is Give Yourself Permission

Tom: Shortly before my father died, I had a partner at Ropes and Gray, a lawyer who had a degree from Harvard and an MBA from Wharton School. His name is Don Glaser. Donny was a specialist in mutual funds and highly valued at Ropes and Gray. When he was a young boy, he wanted to be a rabbi. It just didn't turn out; he didn't go that way. Donny was always academically gifted and was pushed in academic directions. He became an extremely successful lawyer. In fact, enough so that he left our firm and became president of one of our client's small businesses. He did very well for himself.

Several years later, one of my partner's sons was killed in an automobile accident and a memorial was held for him. Linda and I happened to be in Boston at the time, so I went to the funeral. A younger woman, who was a former associate at the firm, was there. A very moving final eulogy was made and we went outside. The woman and I and a couple of other lawyers and Don were there. She was crying. Donny was the one who spoke up and asked if she was okay. She said, "Yeah. This hit particularly hard." Her mother was dying. Her mother lived in the Maryland suburbs of Washington, D.C. This woman would like to go spend time with her mother, but she had responsibilities. She had two kids and they were busy with piano lessons, skating lessons, and school. Her husband was busy working. She volunteered on the library committee. She just didn't know how much time she was going to get to spend with her mother. Donny said, "You know, my father died last year. It took three months. But for those three months, I was with him every day. I simply left what I do here in Boston and went down and stayed at his bedside. I read to him. I talked to him. He slept a lot of the time, but I was there. When he died, I was in the room. That's one of the best things I've ever done." Then Donny put it in context and said, "Mary, all you have to do is give yourself permission to go. What I did was give myself permission to leave all this business that isn't supposed to be going on without me, put aside the social life I have here in Boston, and gave myself permission to give my father three months." Mary quit crying and said, "I can do that." Then she walked away. Donny walked away and I yelled, "Donny." He turned around. I said, "I remember once you said you wanted to be a rabbi. I think today you were one."

Six months later when I got the call from my sister and she said, "Dad's decided that he's going to die," I remembered what Donny had said. I was out at Chaco. We had promised Chaco that we'd be there for six weeks doing astronomy programs. We had friends who lived in Albuquerque who were going to come out and visit us. I thought about that, but for Linda there was no question. Linda's a little more "family" than I am. She said we had to go. I said,

"Donny said to give yourself permission and I can do that." That's how I got back to my father.

Ed: My dad died after about a twenty year struggle with emphysema. It was heart failure that finally caused his death. At the time, I was a hot-shot high school principal in suburban Chicago. I thought the sun rose and set on my ass. I thought the damn school was going to fall apart if I left. I wish I had heard Donny's statement twenty years ago because I would have picked up and said, "Hey, I've hired good people. This place is going to run just fine without me." I should have taken a couple of weeks off and gone down there.

...Savoring Your Memories...

1. What do you most enjoy about your life right now?

2. What do you wish you could change?

3. If you're retired, what do you remember about that transition?

4. What's the most fun thing you've done in the past fifteen years?

5. Who are some of your friends? What is it about them that tells you they're a friend for a lifetime?

Chapter 8   Our 1959 Undefeated Season[5]

These next two chapters focus on the CHS Bull Dogs, their undefeated season and 50th Football Reunion. At first glance, you may be wondering what these chapters have to do with Baby Boomer Memories. Sure, we included these stories to show you what a special time we seniors had in the fall of 1959. However, and much more importantly, we share these stories to help you understand the special group of young men who represented their school and community. The commitment, hard work, love, caring, and selfless character come through loud and clear.

As you read about these players, remember your high school years. Do you remember classmates and former athletes who exhibited similar personal attributes as did the 1959 players for Columbus High School? Do you remember events from your high school days that generated this type of excitement and school spirit?

The first day of practice for sixty hopeful football candidates was on Saturday, August 15, 1959. Practice began at eight o'clock in the morning. According to Coach Max Andress, the practice was a good one, considering it was the first day out. We were run through all types of drills except hard body contact, which would be saved until we got the kinks out and re-learned our assignments.

---

5   The Columbus Crew is greatly indebted to George Abel for the content of this section of the book. George spent countless hours researching and compiling the information about this undefeated season – 50 years ago and still remembered today. George chronicled the entire season, game by game and incorporated comments from some of the players – sharing their memories about several of the games. In writing the complete history, George researched articles in the Columbus paper, *The Evening Republican, The Louisville Courier-Journal,* and the *Indianapolis Star*. Initially, George prepared this story as a memory to give to all the players who returned to the 50th Reunion of the 1959 Bull Dogs – what a wonderful gift. Kathi and I have excerpted parts of George's work to include in this book.

Last year's squad finished 6-3-1, fourth in the South Central Conference (SCC), but of course it was too early to tell what this team would do. The coach thought there would be lots of competition for positions and that "the boys" were in pretty good shape. Twelve lettermen returned from last year's squad. Linemen were: Dan Mobley, senior end; Al Betz and Gene Critzer, senior tackles; John Gentry, senior guard; and Jack Hinkle, senior center. Backfield was: Skip Lindeman, senior quarterback; Bill Spicer, senior fullback; Paul Pringle, junior fullback; and halfbacks John Moore and Graham Updike, seniors and Jim Rapp and Tony Patterson, juniors.

Monday would be the first of many two-a-day practices. The first week was hot, but it always is when you're doing two-a-days in August. The second week we were greeted by the worst heat wave to hit the Midwest in seven years. It lasted all week. By eleven o'clock on Monday the 24th, the temperature had reached ninety-one degrees and was expected to get close to one hundred. Evening practice was switched from six o'clock to seven-fifteen. Part of the practice would be under the lights, which was good because all our games would be played at night. We all remember the pain and agony, and in some cases lost lunches, caused by these workouts. The weather finally broke around the first of September.

Bull Dog Memories

Bill Spicer: First of all, I want to say, I had the privilege of playing on three undefeated teams in my life – one football and two basketball teams. The highlight was of course the Columbus football team, but all three of those teams had something in common. There were no individuals on those teams. As they say, "There's no 'I' in team." They were guys you enjoyed being around. They were generally smarter than the average bunch of athletes I was associated with. I also will say that at the beginning of the season, I believe Coach Andress had decided we would be lucky to win six games. Let me backtrack a bit.

At the end of junior year, it was after the prom, a group of guys and gals had a big party at Lake Lemon. I wasn't there. There was beer at this party and of course in Columbus that was a taboo. As you know, I would drink the odd beer here or there.

Ed: Yes, once in a while.

Bill: But I always tried to do it with some sense of responsibility and I didn't drink when I was out for a team sport. One day, I was visiting my cousins, Frank Runge and his wife. We'd been bailing hay that day. We were sitting at a picnic table in the front yard and drinking beer. Evidently somebody went by and saw me sitting out there drinking beer, either the daughter of a school board member or some concerned citizen. This person reported it to someone of authority. About a week later I was out somewhere. I can't remember who was with me. We'd also picked up Little Blickenstaff.

Ed: Mel's son?

Bill: Yes, the trainer's son, Little Blick. I don't know how we came to pick him up, but we were giving him a ride someplace and we'd been drinking a couple of beers. Little Blick wanted to stop somewhere. He had a girlfriend or something. So we stopped. Evidently he told her that we were drinking beer and of course, it was the same girl.

When I got back to school, I heard that after the prom a bunch of guys, and I don't remember who all these guys were, went somewhere and had this wild drinking party in a state park. I didn't think anything about it. I didn't even know Hinkle was with them. So, I'm sitting in class one day and here comes Coach Andress and Coach Stearman. They dragged me down to the office. They said, "We heard you did this and this and this." I said, "No, I didn't." They were saying I was with these guys in the state park. I said, "I don't know anything about it." Then Coach Andress said, "And we also heard you were sitting out on Country Road #7 at a picnic table, drinking beer." I said, "Yes, I was." Coach goes, "I don't believe it. I don't believe it." I said, "Well, I did."

Ed: I remember Max could have a temper.

Bill: I said, "I don't see the big deal." Of course Stearman was pretty quiet about it. Andress asked, "What do you mean you don't think it's a big deal?" I said, "Well, I was on private property. I'd been working out there all day long. I wasn't on any school teams at the time. I wasn't representing the school. I wasn't on school property. How can you be so upset? If anything, my parents should be the ones to be upset." My parents were not big drinkers, but they knew I did things like that. As long as alcohol was not abused they thought nothing of it. The coaches sent me back to class and that was it. The next thing I know, I get this letter. I believe it was signed by Judson S. Erne, the principal. The letter stated I wasn't going to be able to be in sports. Later they decided I could play, but I couldn't be recognized. I couldn't win a letter. My name couldn't appear in the paper. Nothing.

It wasn't any of these peoples' business. I had gotten lumped in with these other guys. As it turned out, the other guys got the same letter. I showed the letter to my cousin and she got really pissed about it. She showed the letter to Scott Alexander, the sport's writer. Scott had to worry about his job, but he thought about the arrogance of the fact that the school had overstepped their bounds, by a quantum amount as far as he was concerned. Scott agreed with me and my family. For me, that became a motivator and it was a motivator for Hinkle. Hinkle and I talked about this to a couple of our best friend teammates, Graham Updike and John Moore. We hung around together a lot. This was right before summer practice. I said, "I wouldn't normally drink or smoke or anything like that during the season. But this season, I'm not drinking. I'm not smoking. I'm not dating. From Wednesday on, I ain't even talking to people that aren't my teammates. I'm going to give it all I can give. For years, I've heard a coach say, 'Give me a hundred percent on every play and if you fall over, I'll run somebody in and replace you'. I'm going to do that. And I'm going to see how long it takes me to fall over." It turned out I never did. But I decided I was going to give one hundred percent on every play.

Ed: Did your decision have the same effect on the other guys?

Bill: I know it did for Hinkle and John Moore. John didn't date that much anyway, but Graham did. Graham said, "I'll go along with everything else, but I'm going to date." Of course John Moore was a real character. We were kind of like the Four Musketeers. I think word got out to the rest of the team about the way we felt. Everybody felt the same. I never thought about winning games or winning the next game or anything. I really thought about the next play and then all of a sudden, the game was over.

I don't remember a lot of details about the undefeated season. At the twenty-five-year reunion, I believe Skip Lindeman gave a play-by-play of every game.

Ed: The difficult conditions under which you started out that season were almost a gift, in terms of the impact you four guys had on your teammates, and may well have been one of the contributing factors to that undefeated season.

Bill: I think in some small way it probably was. For instance, there wasn't anybody that could tell you who scored the most touchdowns, or who carried for the most yards, or who made the most tackles. We all got in there and did it. But I think the fact that we led by example, by the way we felt, was somewhat infectious. Everybody got with the program.

Ed: Was Max Andress able to get past his anger, enabling you and he to have a good season together?

Bill: Oh yes. I think he counted on me quite a bit. He would have conversations with me before the game or in preparation during the week, asking me how I felt about this or that. The one thing he knew was that I wasn't going to lie to him

Ed: That's true, because you didn't when you had the chance to. You stood there in the eye of the storm and took the heat on that one.

Bill: Having said that about my teammates, that year was one of those marvelous moments in time that don't happen very often and you'll never get it back.

Ed: No, you never do.

Bill: I remember, when we started the season everyone started calling the defensive team the Blue Bandits. At that time, LSU had the really good defense and they were called the Chinese Bandits. Scott Alexander started calling us the Blue Bandits. Only one team ever scored twice on us and that was in the last game, when the coach put the underclassmen in toward the end. The coach I really admired was Barrows. Barrows was a factor. I think if you looked at the scores and statistics you would find that Columbus got tougher as the ball game went on.

Ed: Was Barrows the defensive coach?

Bill: No, he was the line coach. We were conditioned much better than any of our opponents. We knew we had them in the fourth quarter because you'd see them start blowing and putting their hands on their hips. We'd be getting wound up. We'd joke and say, "Okay, it's time to take it to 'em now and really put it on 'em."

Tuesdays were not heavy knock days. We did a lot of scrimmage. After that, Barrows would drag our asses over to the track and make us run a mile. And, he would tell you how fast you had to run it. If you didn't make it, you'd have to run an extra lap. That right there gave us more endurance than most teams because we would have done everything else including wind-sprints and all this bull and then we still, with all of our crap on, had to run this mile. Coach Barrows was a good human being.

I remember it was very hot that August, even for Indiana. I think we literally beat the hell out of each other in the intra-squad game. I took a late hit, a real cheap shot in that game. I started to take the guy on when Barrows stepped in to break it up. I ended up with a badly bruised hip. When I went to get out of bed the next day, I had to slide out on the floor on my hands and knees to get into a standing position. I was so banged up, I didn't dress for the

Jamboree. I remember before the Jamboree the coaches thought we might be lucky to go five and five for the season. After the Jamboree, they thought that was being optimistic.

Jack Hinkle: One day before practice, the coaches were checking our weight and height. As we went through, they asked us our age. As it turned out, some of the seniors were not yet seventeen years old. Andress and Barrows said we were not going to scare anyone with our sizes or ages. I was one of the heaviest on the team, weighing 190.

Ron Galloway: During two-a-days, I remember we were instructed to take salt tablets prior to each practice! It's a wonder none of us died from dehydration. Coach announced that he was going to use a two platoon system, which means there were going to be twenty-two positions available to start and an additional twenty-two slots on the second team. Everyone was excited about the ability to get in some playing time and letter. Most of us juniors had been on the JV squad and dressed for home games in '58, so we were all excited about the opportunity. I think this was one of the reasons for our success, knowing that we were being counted on. It also made the two-a-days very aggressive. I was one of those guys that swore off dating for the season. My steady girlfriend was the beautiful Bonnie Reynolds – class officer, honor roll, etc. – who for the last forty-five years, to my amazement, has shared my name and bed. Bonnie dated other guys that fall, including several football players! Boy was I clueless.

Jack Hinkle: Bill Spicer, Graham Updike and I hung together the whole year. On the evenings of home games, the three of us went to Graham's house and prepped for the game. We had the same meal each time—meat, potatoes, and salad. We took turns with the food supply, but Graham's dad always prepared the meal. I remember the 45rpm record we played, "Woman Love" which was the flip side of "Be Bop a Loo La."

Jeff Crump: My take on the season is that we worked hard, and we were faster and smarter. Plus, we had an outstanding staff of coaches that had us doing the right things at the right times. I can't forget to mention desire and hustle on the players' parts. Larry Long and I were subs. I remember after a lot of hard practices, everyone on the first string was tired. Then Coach had us run a mile after practice. Larry and I would beat everybody else because we had relatively fresh legs.

George Abel: I had three reasons for not dating during the season. I didn't have any money, I wanted to focus on the football season, and I couldn't get a girlfriend.

Larry Long: One of the things I remember is the opposition always had a star or two and we didn't. The opposition couldn't key on anybody on our team. If you shut down Spicer or Wiley, Pringle or Patterson would get you, or Johnny Moore. There was no way to shut us down. The second thing was we were in better shape than anybody. I don't know if you've seen the numbers, but in the first half we scored fifty-two points and the opposition scored like twenty or something. I think in the second half we outscored our opponents two hundred to thirteen.

Ed: Everyone who's talked about that team has talked about the conditioning. You have all lauded the talents of Duane Barrows in that category. I remember Spice and some others saying that somewhere in the third quarter you could look at the other team and see they were dragging ass.

Larry: I thought we were in better shape than any other team. I'm sure you've been told that everybody gave up dating. I looked at it as a cost reduction because I never scored or had much success. I had a lot of nice, cute girlfriends but as I remember it was a very frustrating experience. Pringle and I double-dated a lot. He said, "Not dating is a great idea." So we didn't date during the season. Any of the guys that did drink, quit. I didn't start drinking until after my senior year season.

Ed: Everybody pretty much stuck by that agreement, no dating and no drinking.

Larry: No dating, no drinking. The other thing that helped us was that three stars got hurt before the year started. Fred Yentz was one of them. He only played the first game. His shoulder was so bad he couldn't play anymore. Bobby Hamilton was a great sprinter. I don't think he came out his senior year. And there was somebody else that was good that didn't get to play either. Basically, three of the better guys we counted on didn't play. We really had to grind because everybody was small.

The other two points, and I don't have the exact data, but I believe there were nineteen seniors on the team. I think all but one or two earned their college degree. Thirteen or fourteen of those earned graduate degrees, which is staggering when you think about it. It was amazing how well everyone did. Separate from everything else, we had a bunch of smart guys, smart enough to outsmart our opponents in the second half.

Ed: I want to go back to the chemistry of that '59 team. The season probably would have turned out differently had it not been for the chemistry. You know this from teams you've worked with during your professional career or other groups you've been in. If those three people had been on that team, the chemistry would have been entirely different.

Larry: Yes. Absolutely, and it's not that they were bad people. They were just different. Bobby was by far the fastest guy. I remember Graham went to the Culver Military Academy and he'd come late for the start of fall practices. Andress would always go through this thing about, "Come on Graham. You've got to be here for all the practices." Graham just couldn't do it. I think he had to beg to get to play.

George Abel: I wasn't fortunate enough to play sports. I finally got to play my senior year. In hindsight, I'm amazed they let me play, with no experience. And I'm amazed I was able to get a letter after that. It didn't mean much to me as it was happening because we just never lost a game. I didn't realize how hard and unusual that is. I just knew that everybody was into it and I always wondered why. How could an undersized bunch of kids get together in one particular year and do something nobody expected or suspected they'd come close to doing?

Ed: That's what made it even more fun because nobody expected you to go unbeaten, so you felt like the underdog and were going to show them.

George: If we had a five and five year, it would have been what you would call a decent year. It just turned into something quite memorable. As I read the different comments from the guys on the team, I began to get a feeling there was something there that silently said, "We're just not going to lose." We focused on each individual game. It all started building around the Seymour game. The desire and buy-in that you hear so much about today, buying into the system, everyone of us just believed everything the coaches told us. It's amazing how some of the things they would go over in practice – "and this is what we're going to do in this situation" and "be ready for this" – would work. Most coaches of the opposing teams thought they matched up well with us and should win. Afterwards, they were really impressed with us. Even they wanted to see us do well.

Ed: Were you on offense or defense?

George: Mostly defense. I did play end a little, behind Dan Mobley.

Ed: So you were a member of the Blue Bandits.

George: No, because I wasn't a starter. The Blue Bandits were the starters. Trust me, though, when you were in there, you **were** a Blue Bandit.

Steve Everroad: I remember one time in class some kid just smarted off to Coach Barrows and he just put him up against the wall, slammed him up high. Another time, when I was a senior, we were in a circle. I was leading calisthenics at practice and Barrows said, "Let's do the…" I forget what they're called, but each guy would have another guy jump on his back and you'd do deep-knee bends, with the guy on your back. Everybody paired up, but I was odd man out. There was nobody to jump on my back.

Ed: So you got Barrows?

Steve: Yeah. Barrows yelled, "Everroad, where's your partner?" With a little bit of a smile I said, "I'm not sure there's anybody left." He said, "Oh yes there is. Here I come." I thought, "Oh no!" I had to brace myself. Barrows came running at me, hit me on the dead run, jumped on my back, and hit me in the helmet with his hand.

I remember another time, when I was quarterbacking, Andress said, "No Everroad. Let me show you how to do that." He pushed me out of the way and took the hike. He told Pringle to come through. Andress was going to give him the ball. Pringle brought his arm up and just smashed Andress right in the nose. I think he broke it. Andress was bleeding all over the place and I thought, "Yeah, there you go coach." It's always embarrassing when the coach does that in front of the whole team. But that's the way we learned and we learned a lot on that team. It was a special, special, special experience.

The Season Begins, Game 1, September 2, 1959: Columbus 25 – Franklin 6

Bull Dog Memories

George Abel: This is the only game I did not play in. As a matter of fact, I did not get to go to the game. I had not played football prior to my senior year and didn't have enough experience to make the smaller traveling squad. Coach Andress told me not to worry; I'd get to play some football this year.

Paul Pringle: I think Jack Hinkle may be the only one who remembers my brief, one game career as a place kicker in 1959. I was 1 for 3 and Jack quite properly took over in our second game at home against Martinsville. I have no idea why Jack didn't do kick-offs. His extra points went further than Al Betz's and mine ever did!

Jack Hinkle: I think I have the answer as to why I didn't handle the kick-offs. After some serious thought about this question, I think it was speed and coverage. I wasn't very speedy and coach wanted eleven men covering the kick-offs, not ten.

Gene Critzer: I remember in the Franklin game Al Betz telling me he had overheard the opposing tackle telling his teammates to gang up on Al, so they could take him out in the next play (who knows what Al did to whack him off). Knowing this, when they ganged up on Betz, I was able to slip behind the line and nail the quarterback for a huge loss.

Ron Galloway: I got to be on the traveling squad and was really pumped up, so I didn't listen to the coach when he announced the starters. As the teams lined up for the kickoff, Max counted out ten players on the field for the Bull Dogs and hollered at me to go in. What a thrill. After the kickoff, I started to run off the field and Coach yelled for me to stay in. That is the moment I realized I was a starter. We were using a spilt wide receiver in our formation. I had hands of stone but could throw a pretty good cross-body block with my 165 pounds. Nobody that knows me today believes I was ever that light.

Columbus (*The Evening Republican*): "Dogs to Host Artesian in Home Opener"
Pleasantly surprised at his team's showing in their gridiron debut at Franklin last week, Columbus Coach Max Andress unhesitantly predicted a victory over Martinsville in the home opener here Friday night. "I don't usually like to be that optimistic, but then I don't believe in fooling the boys either," said Andress in making the victory prediction. "Since it's the home opener – rain or no rain – we're hoping for a good turnout," said Andress. The weatherman is promising ideal football weather conditions. Even Gail Davis, star of the TV series "Annie Oakley" will be on hand at halftime. She will be presented a key to the city by Mayor Fred C. Owens.

Game 2, Home Opener – September 11, 1959: Columbus 22 – Martinsville 7

Columbus (*The Evening Republican*): Scott Alexander's "Sports Stuff"

Every now and then (not often) we sports scribblers get a little lucky with our predictions. Last week Lady Luck apparently hopped on our bandwagon since our prognostications of SCC grid activity were one hundred percent accurate. And that's a mighty unusual friend. We predicted a 2-TD win for the Bull Dogs over Martinsville. The Canines won by such a margin, but added a safety just for good measure.

Bull Dog Memories

Ron Galloway: As I recall most of the Martinsville starters were guys we faced on JV in '58, so we knew we were the more talented team. I was surprised at how long it took us to put them away.

Paul Pringle: Here's what happened in our game against Martinsville. We fumbled at the Martinsville six-yard-line on the opening drive. On Martinsville's third down, Al Betz hit halfback Dick Cramer in the end zone for a safety, 2-0. In the second quarter, Wiley scored and Jack converted, 9-0 at the half. In the third quarter Martinsville scored on a sixty-eight yard run, 9-7. Updike scored and then a high pass from center on PAT, 15-7. John Moore scored and Jack converted, 22-7. Second team offense played most of the fourth quarter.

Columbus (*The Evening Republican*) Thursday, September 17, 1959:
"Bull Dogs Prepare for Heated Battle – Both Teams are Undefeated"

Game 3, September 18, 1959: Columbus 28 – Seymour 0

At 9:22 p.m. Friday night, Columbus football coach Max Andress and longtime assistant Duane Barrows, were hoisted atop the shoulders of several weary but jubilant Bull Dog footballers and hustled off Seymour's Emerson Field to a waiting bus. The Columbus coach waved helplessly to Seymour's disheartened Dave Shaw, while being scooped up and taken away by his boisterous gladiators. No doubt the CHS coach would like to have passed out a few consoling words to his vanquished competitor. But then what can you say to a coach who just watched his ball club surrender a 28-0 gridiron decision?

Particularly outstanding was the Columbus defensive unit…These eleven "Blue Bandits" literally demolished any semblance of an offensive pattern the Owls may have had. They "stole the show."

Bull Dog Memories

Paul Pringle: Alexander's article after the Seymour game was the first mention of our defense as the "Blue Bandits."

Ron Galloway: We all wanted to beat the Owls. Once again, the offensive line did wide splits, trap blocked, and watched the holes open for Wiley and Updike to have a great game. After that game, it seemed that everyone wanted to become a part of the "Blue Bandits."

George Abel: That reminded me that Alexander was honoring our defense by giving us this moniker referring to the vaunted LSU Tiger's defense of 1958 and 1959. Paul Dietzal began to refer to his defensive units as the "Chinese Bandits." These "Chinese Bandits" of 1959 helped LSU win a national championship. The defense held opponents to an average of 143 yards; no LSU defense has since done better. The bandits earned their nickname due to their size, style of play, and number of turnovers they created. They were small, quick, fearless, and they only had two players that weighed more than two hundred pounds. I remember thinking, "Gosh, this makes all that heat and those practices worthwhile."

Skip Lindeman: I thought we would beat Franklin and Martinsville and we did. What I was really aiming for was Seymour, but as the time got close I wasn't sure we were mentally ready. I was worried. As we dressed for the game in our locker room, I remember telling Bill Spicer that I just didn't think we were ready to go out and beat Seymour. We pounded them. Sometime in the fourth quarter, when we were ahead 21-0 or 28-0, Bill came up to me on the sidelines and said, "I think we're ready to beat Seymour." I said something like, "What? Oh yeah! Right!" I also remember the trip home from Seymour. We were so happy and so "up" after that great victory. At that time, the Coasters had a song called "Poison Ivy." Many of us were singing at the top of our lungs (Jock Itch) to the tune of "Poison Ivy." It was funny.

Bill Spicer: We used to rotate who the captain was. I think John Gentry and I were the honorary captains for this game. Seymour had a guy that was a star player, Hill. We went out for the coin toss and the referee was standing there with his arm around Mark Hill. The referee said, "Mark, this is so and so." He's calling him by his first name. I thought, "Well this is great." By the way, we put Mark Hill out of the game. I think we either broke his leg or sprained his ankle. We shut him down. We got him out of there the first quarter. We had to punt and Hill caught the ball. We had three guys going down the field real fast. I believe one of them was Tony Patterson and maybe George Abel. The third guy was John Moore. John was the first guy to hit Hill and leveled him. The other two guys were right on top of Moore. They jumped up right away and started walking away. Moore's laying there pummeling the hell out of this guy. The referee threw the flag and said, "You, thirty-one, unnecessary roughness, fifteen yards." He turned to me and said, "You, forty-one, you're the captain. You get control of your players." So I said to Moore, "Damn it, John. What do you think you're doing?" Old John gave me that rye, shit eatin' grin he always had and said, "I was just roughin' him up a little."

Wednesday, September 23, 1959: *Indianapolis Star* poll has Columbus ranked 22nd in the state. This is the first time we show up in the rankings.

Columbus (*The Evening Republican*): "Dogs Host Bloomington in Dad's Night – To Be Battle of Unbeatens"

Bloomington, a non-conference gridiron opponent that already claims three decisive wins and the esteem of most southern Indiana scribes, will invade the Columbus Bull Dog domain Friday night in hopes of spoiling Dad's Night festivities by handing the Andressmen their first setback in four outings.

Reports have it that Coach Fred Huff's small but highly-trained club expects an easy time of it here. They've whipped the Canines the past three years by scores of 7-2, 34-7, and 20-0, and figure on accomplishing a similar feat Friday night. And they've got horses to do it, provided the Canines lay down low and play dead, which isn't likely.

Game 4, September 25, 1959: Columbus 21 – Bloomington 6

Columbus (*The Evening Republican*): Proving pre-game prognosticators poorly prepared, the mighty maulers of Monsieur Max Andress pleased an enthusiastic Dad's Night crowd at jam-packed Memorial Field Friday night by pulverizing Bloomington's previously unbeaten Panther eleven by a surprising 21-6 spread. It was a great ballgame and certainly one most fans who attended will long remember.

Bull Dog Memories

George Abel: As we all remember, this was Dad's Night. I had to beg my dad to go. He had never been to any kind of football game in his life and never went again, but he was impressed with the experience. His greatest memory was going to the locker room at halftime and hearing the coaches talk. He has talked about it for many years. We just grew up in a time and place where sports were considered play and we didn't have time for it. After three years of high school, my dad finally let me play sports, but I had to walk or hitch-hike about eight miles to get home after school. I think there may have been a few others on the team in a similar situation.

Bill Spicer: I knew this would be a tough game and it was, for the first half. Their quarterback was a wise-ass and all of us in the middle had words with him. I remember recovering a fumble that Jack Hinkle caused and he has bitched for nearly fifty years about me getting a milk shake and not him. Larry Trueblood, a Bloomington end, who was later a teammate at Franklin, hit me with the most perfect cross-body I ever saw or felt. One minute I was running full-speed after the ball carrier and the next instant I was literally upside-down on my head. It didn't hurt that much but it must have looked spectacular. I remember getting up and saying to him, "Nice block. I think that was the most perfect cross-body block ever." He just smiled and said, "Thanks."

Skip Lindeman: Bloomington had beaten us five times in a row, including 7-2 in 1958 when their halfback caught a ball while lying on his back in the end zone, on the next to the last play of the game. Our defense had batted the ball down. This guy caught it simply because he was in the right place at the right time. Okay, now the Bloomington game at home in 1959. We were tied 0-0 with less than a minute to go in the half. I had just thrown an incomplete pass to Dan Mobley. I threw slightly behind him. But as I let the pass go, I saw Graham Updike standing alone in the end zone. We called a timeout and I ran over to Coach Andress on the sidelines. I said, "Let me try that play again," because Graham had gotten free in the end zone. Coach said, "Okay." We ran the play, I lofted a pass, Graham caught it and ran for a 7-0 lead at halftime. At halftime, I remember Andress saying, "Boys, you and I both know it's too soon to be talking about an undefeated season. But, you and I both know that if we can beat these guys, we can go all the way!" I remember a huge ROAR and tide of emotion that swept us back out on the field as we left the dressing room. We went out and did it! I still get chills thinking about some of those times.

Ron Galloway: As we reviewed the game films from '58, I'll bet Coach ran the "miracle last second reception" at least twenty times. He didn't have to say a word. We all wanted revenge. I got to play some defense in that game. Coach Wally Page had taught me that when I saw a play was going wide to spin and pivot on my inside foot rather than push through the blocker, so I could get free to make the tackle. As Boruff juked wide, I made the pivot, ran down the line of scrimmage, and hit him full speed, driving Boruff out of bounds for a loss. What fun! We really had great coaches that trained us in techniques that would compensate for our lack of power.

Steve Everroad: I got knocked out cold in the Bloomington game. I remember Mike Brock was fullback. He was supposed to go out on a screen pass, out to the left. I looked up and when I turned to throw the ball to him, I saw he had fallen down. I thought, "I'll run back a few more yards and by that time he'll be back on his feet and back on his route. I'll throw it over his head out of bounds." I turned around, ran a few more yards back, turned and looked at Brock. He'd gotten up sure enough, but rather than running towards the out of bounds line, he was running back towards me. Later, he said, "I was going to come help block for you." I said, "Oh yeah, Brock." He was in between all of these defenders, so I just had to pull down the ball and eat it. This guy grabbed me on the shoulder pads and flipped me down, right on my head. I remember going down to the ground. The hit knocked me out cold. I was laying there when I woke up. I had cradled the ball. I never lost the ball. They got me to the sideline and one of the coaches said, "Everroad!" I said, "Let me back in. I can go back in." One of the coaches asked, "Who are we playing?" I said, "Who are we playing? Good question." Then he asked, "What's the score?" I'm looking for the scoreboard, trying to see the score. What a headache I had that night!

Columbus (*The Evening Republican*): "Golden Bears Seek Upset Over Dogs Friday – Getting Better Says CHS Coach"
"Mental Attitude" a predominant ingredient in the four Columbus wins to date "will be a very important factor" in Friday night's SCC tilt here with Shelbyville's puzzling Golden Bears, Dog Coach Max Andress predicts today. Coach Andress knows full well that he has the kind of ball club that can't rest on its heels. "We can't afford to coast – or rest – in any ball game, no matter who the opponent is," he said.

Game 5, October 2, 1959: Columbus 27 – Shelbyville 0

After honing their offensive machinery to a razor sharp edge during the halftime rest period, Coach Max Andress' undefeated Columbus High School gridmen tore into Shelby's Golden Bears with revived vengeance during the final twenty-four minutes of action here Friday night to gain a 27-0 win.

Columbus (*The Evening Republican*): Scott Alexander's "Sports Stuff"
Shelbyville's 27-0 loss here Friday night was "the worst handed a Shelby team in three seasons of play," reports scribe Jim McKinney. "The Bull Dogs were rated twelfth best in Hoosierland in the latest prep poll and the club lived up to all expectations and then some," says McKinney. "The Canines are a go-go bunch that might have the stuff to go all the way in the league this time," he adds graciously.

Jack Hinkle practices kicking field goals with his favorite holder Dan "The Finger" FitzGibbon

Lou Groza (1924-2000) was a placekicker who played his entire professional career with the Cleveland Browns. Groza's accuracy as a placekicker was so outstanding, former Cleveland sportswriter Robert Yonkers dubbed him Lou "The Toe" Groza. On our 1959 undefeated football team, Jack kicked field goals as well as points-after-touchdown. Scott Alexander also gave the nickname "The Toe" to Jack. Later on in the season, as Jack's accuracy continued to improve, Alexander changed the nickname to "Mr. Automatic." Even to this day, after fifty years, our classmates will often refer to Jack by one of these two nicknames. What a wonderful legacy Jack left as part of that undefeated team.

Bull Dog Memories

Ron Galloway: The Bears were the first team to consistently put eight men in the box against our offense. Our trap blocking was not getting our usual open holes. At half time the coaches switched us over to no spilts, wedge blocking, and the belly series. That did the trick. We cruised after that.

Jeff Crump: From my vantage point on the sidelines, I do remember the brain trust (Coach Barrows and Coach Marston) coming up with suggestions to Coach Andress of plays to call and personnel to substitute. I think during a lot of the early games, Coach Marston was out scouting our opponents.

Game 6: October 9, 1959: Columbus – 31 – Greensburg 0

Columbus (*The Evening Republican*): "Homecoming is a Success—Bull Dogs Win 31-0" Eager to please a host of returning Bull Dog alumni (which they did) the undefeated, versatile charges of Max Andress completely overwhelmed an outclassed Greensburg club here Friday night by a score of 31-0. And the win – the sixth of the season and the fifth in SCC play for the Bull Dogs – was just about as easy as the score might indicate.

Bull Dog Memories

Jack Hinkle: The day before the bonfire we had a pep rally. I was asked to say something. I remember saying we would play hard and I would try to keep my string of extra points going. It was a rainy, wet night and although we won 31-0, I was only 1 for 5 kicking extra points.

Ron Galloway: The only thing I remember about this game was that Bonnie went to the Homecoming Dance with someone else.

Larry Long: In the Greensburg game, and any easy game, the coaches let me start. I'm playing across from a guy named Dave Rickey. I'm one-sixty as a tackle and this is the fifth game of the year. Rickey was two-forty. He was really good. The second play of the game I went to Skip Lindeman and said, "Skip, do not run a dive over me. This guy is great. I can barely keep him out of the backfield. If you do a pitch to my side, have a step back, because he's coming over me and you don't want to get hurt." It was one of these, "Are you serious?" I said, "I'm doing everything I can just to keep him from getting in the backfield." At the end of the first half, it's twenty-eight to nothing. We were a much better team, but Rickey was way better than me. I came out for the second half and Max says, "Larry, it appears you can't block Dave Rickey." I should have said, "You're right coach," or "I was doing my best." Instead I said, "No shit coach. He's killing me." Coach asked, "Well do you not want to play this second half?" I said, "I'd love to play the second half, but I'm not going to be able to block him in the second half any better than I did in the first." So, he sat me down and put Critzer in, who obviously did a better job against Rickey than I did. But that was an experience with a really good player.

Game 7, October 16, 1959: Columbus 21 – Jeffersonville 7

Bull Dog Memories

Bill Spicer: They had a guy that was some kind of a Joe Studley, supposed to be real fast. He was a big halfback and a state sprint champion. I remember we were able to catch him from behind a couple times in the game. We had a battle royal there. The thing I remember about that game was that we had two goal line stands. They had the ball inside our five-yard line on two occasions. We held them out both times. Those two stands took the steam out of those guys for the rest of the night.

George Abel: I was in on the kick-off which went to Bob Welsh. I was told to get down the field as quickly as I could. I did, but as I zeroed in on him, he side-stepped me and I barely got a hand on him. Thankfully, Moore, Critzer, or another good tackler made the play. As I went off the field Coach Barrows reminded me that I not only needed to get down the field, I needed to make the tackle. I was a sprinter and ran track against Welsh in the sectional. He won the 100, the 220, and the broad jump. He was a man against boys. At that track meet, I remember thinking what an accomplishment for the Blue Bandits to hold this guy in check the way they did in this game. You had to see what an athlete this guy was to appreciate what our team had done.

Jack Hinkle: They had roughed us up in the Jamboree, but we returned the favor at Jeffersonville. I kicked one of the extra points out of the stadium, but Henry Blessing (the bus driver who drove the team to all away games) found it and brought it back.

Columbus (*The Evening Republican*): "Top Rated Football Teams Win With Ease"
Indiana's winningest high school football teams did it again Friday night as eight out of twelve unbeatens won, and the top rated squads made victory look like no trouble at all. Columbus, No. 10, and Southport, the South Central Conference's two unbeaten teams made it seven straight for the year. Columbus beat Jeffersonville, 21-7, while Southport traveled to Seymour for a 42-13 win.

Columbus (*The Evening Republican*): "Dogs, Cards Play Dream Game Here on Wednesday"
The "Dream Game" most Southport and Columbus fans have been anticipating for the past couple of weeks will materialize at Memorial Field here Wednesday night under anticipated ideal weather conditions. Principals involved will be the Columbus High School Bull Dogs and Southport's Marion County Cardinals, who both claim perfect 7-0 gridiron records. At stake will be the South Central Conference football championship and visions of a spotless seasonal gridiron record.

Although Coach Andress didn't make too much of it, Cards Coach Morgan has a belt the CHS coach would like to retrieve after Wednesday night's game. Coach Andress forfeited the belt and Morgan's red cap (claimed by the CHS coach after the Dog victory two years ago) last year when the Canines were beat by the Cards. A win Wednesday night would cost Coach Morgan not only the belt, but his cap as well. Latest reports from both camps indicate that the two arch-rivals will enter action Wednesday night at full strength.

Game 8, October 21, 1959: Columbus 13 – Southport 6

Columbus (*The Evening Republican*): Front Page, Thursday, October 22, 1959
Cheering their 13-6 victory over Southport after collecting the traditional belt and cap, Columbus Bull Dogs hoist Coach Max Andress to their shoulders as they join a gala crowd of fans estimated at 5,000, the largest ever to attend a football game here. From left players are Larry West (75), Ron Galloway (51), George Abel (53), Charles Wells, (55), and John Moore (31).

Bull Dog Memories

Bill Spicer: This was our toughest game against our best opponent. These guys were well coached and well trained. I was pretty sure it would boil down to who made the least mistakes and who hit the hardest. I believe one of the keys to our success was the conditioning Barrows put us through. Southport felt the pressure in the fourth quarter and eventually made a mistake on a pitchout and Rapp recovered. I was playing across from their left guard who made all-state as a junior. We had a battle royal all evening, but when that happened, I could tell by the look on his face it was over. Three games in ten days, or something like that. It's something to go undefeated, but to have to do it by playing three games in ten days was unheard of. I think a lot of people overlook the significance of that.

Ron Galloway: It seemed like an advantage that there were only two days to prepare for the Southport game. The fact that coach was rotating teams, two deep, and Southport was playing its starters all the way made a difference.

Game 9, October 24, 1959: Columbus 26 – North Vernon 0

Columbus (*The Evening Republican*): "Bull Dogs Turn 'Mudders', Whip Panthers 26-0"
Proving their adaptability as real top-rated "mudders", Columbus' eighth-ranked high school grid team slipped, slid, and sloshed to a 26-0 non-conference win on North Vernon's slickened football field Saturday night.

It marked only the second time in five years that the canines have upended their Jennings County foes and provided the gladiators of Coach Max Andress with a sparkling 9-0 seasonal record.

Bull Dog Memories

Skip Lindeman: It was cold and rainy, and there was water standing on the North Vernon field. Scott Alexander wrote that our "mudders" would be proud of us, or some such pun. Anyway, in the ooze and mud we played in that night, I pitched the ball out to somebody, probably Graham Updike. The flow of the play took us toward our bench where Coach Andress was sitting. After I pitched the ball, I was sort of trotting and not very fast. (I was not anxious to hit the ground any more than I absolutely had to!) Andress yelled at me in his most sarcastic tone – and boy, could he be sarcastic – "Lindeman, if you are not going to throw a block, you might as well at least get out of the way!" Also, one time during the game, Jack Hinkle noted that my jersey wasn't very dirty. So in the huddle, he wiped mud from his uniform onto mine. Mrs. Crump, Jeff's mother, loved telling me that story.

Jack Hinkle: RAIN, RAIN, RAIN. I got the first tackle on a run up the middle. The North Vernon player had momentum and I brought him down on top of me. I created a large ditch on the field. It was fun after that. We were ahead 7-0 at halftime and Coach wasn't happy. Coach Barrows was blasting and lecturing. Some of us noticed a "rubber" hanging down from the light bulb. Everyone was looking at that and trying not to laugh. We rode back to Columbus and took showers with our uniforms on. I don't know who had to clean the bus.

Bill Spicer: RAIN, the field was a pig pen and smelled of wild onions. Someone had put a condom on a light bulb in our locker room and we all caught hell for laughing about it. Coach Andress sent Mike Wiley in the game for me. I went up to the coach to see what was wrong. He said, "Aw nothing, I just wanted to see if you were still out there." I went back in a few plays later; I was out just long enough for poor Mike to get all muddy. We rode home in that dripping, muddy equipment and had to shower with all our equipment on. John Moore and I got yelled at because we were the last guys out of the shower. John kept going around unclogging the mud out of the shower drain and I was trying to help. When the coach yelled at us John said, "Well hell with it Coach. You can unclog the damn drain." I think John got to run a few extra laps on Monday.

George Abel: I was in on the kick-off. As I stood on the field looking down at my shoes, I couldn't believe there was water covering my high-tops. I slipped and slid down the field as quickly as I could and reached the receiver about the same time as a teammate. A collision among the three of us sent me sprawling face first in the muck and mud. The reward for my effort was getting to stand on the side-line, cold and dripping wet, until late in the third quarter. Fortunately I got some playing time in, before climbing onto the bus. We were all muddy, chilled, and wet as we took a seat. Many thoughts ran through my mind, one being that maybe two-a-days in August weren't that bad after all.

Columbus (*The Evening Republican*): "Bull Dogs Seek 10-0 Season at Connersville"
This is it. The really big game Bull Dog gridmen have been pointing for since the season opened back in September – the game that could make or break Columbus' quest for the first undefeated season since back in 1907. "Winning the conference was fine," said Canine Coach Max Andress, "but I think our kids have been pointing for Friday night's game at Connersville since mid-season when it first occurred to them that they could go all the way without suffering a defeat. We've been hoping to be in this position all year – and I don't think the kids will be satisfied unless they finish 10-0." But finishing 10-0 won't be quite so easy.

Game 10, October 30, 1959

Columbus (*The Evening Republican*): "Bull Dogs Whip C'ville 40-13 for a Perfect Season – 1ˢᵗ Undefeated Season Since 1907" – Scott Alexander
They were dirty. They were wet. They were tired and battered. But man, were they happy. "It was almost like a dream or something," said lineman Max Ziegler as he rested along the sideline on bended knee. He was happy – real happy. So were his teammates, the coaching staff and approximately 800 loyal fans that made the trip to Connersville Friday night. And well they

should have been. But as little Max pondered the dream, the lazy old clock slowly ticked away – 8-7-6-5-4-3-2-1. Then it was over

The Dogs had conquered Connersville by the surprising score of 40-13 to become the first CHS team since 1907 to rack up an unblemished gridiron record. "And I want you to know it feels great – just great," said Andress. "They're a great bunch – in fact, the greatest," he repeated over and over again as he tried to keep his balance atop the shoulders of his gladiators. And in all probability anyone who has been following the Bull Dog gridiron fortunes the past two months would have to go along with Andress. Racking up ten consecutive victories in the pigskin sport just doesn't come easy. It takes weeks of hard scrimmage sessions, desire, good coaching, and last but not least, support of the student body and community. Obviously this year's CHS club had everything it takes. And they may have set a precedent which won't be overlooked by next year's club or future Canine gridiron elevens. At least Coach Andress and his competent staff hope so anyway.

Bull Dog Memories

George Abel: This is my memory of the halftime talk of our final game. I remember it well, I expect all the seniors will also. For a few minutes, the coaches were going over good play, bad play, missed assignments, etc. when Coach Andress addressed everybody. He said, "In a few minutes the underclassmen and coaches will go back out onto the field to get ready for the second half. I'll be leaving you seniors here. This may be your one and only chance to accomplish something that you will remember for a lifetime, an undefeated season. The rest of us will be back, hungry to do the same thing again next year, but you will be gone. I will play seniors in every position I can. This season belongs to you—win or lose, I'm proud to have been your coach. You have about five minutes to think about how you want this season to end. I'll be out on the field."

We sat there for about a minute, total silence. I wish I could know what everyone was thinking. For me, cold chills ran down my stiff spine. I think for the first time ever I realized how special this was, how close we really were. Then Bill Spicer looked at every one of us, trying to make eye contact, and said, "I don't know about you guys, but I didn't go through all this hell to lose this last game." Everyone started shouting and yelling. We expressed many forms of the same opinion. We had come a long way in a short time. Two and a half months ago, we were a bunch of kids wondering what we were doing out there in one-hundred-degree heat following a few old, crazed men's every demand. But we did, we believed, we listened, we learned, we followed, we endured; we would go undefeated. When we went back on the field, there was no doubt that we would finish what we had started.

Bill Spicer: This was the last game. This was the first time, I think, some of the guys really thought about the fact that if we win this we're undefeated. Of course, I think that was the natural thing to do. Connersville got the ball first and scored quickly by using a trick play. They had a man run in late to the huddle as if he were replacing someone and the guy that ran out of the huddle was actually the eleventh man. He ran to the sideline, but didn't leave the field of play. We assumed there had been a substitution and didn't pay attention. When they snapped the ball, the player who had stopped at the sideline ran down the field. They threw the pass to him and he scored. We had come all this way, undefeated, and just gave up six easy points.

To my knowledge, no one had talked about how important this game was to us, but I know in our hearts we were concerned about losing. This is one of my strongest memories. As we were gathering ourselves after the ref's whistle, the first thing I noticed was the look on my teammates' faces. Connersville was up six to nothing. We were all down there on the goal line, getting ready to line up for the extra point. The first guy I noticed looking at me was Hinkle, then Gentry, then Moore. As I scanned around, it appeared to me that every one of my teammates was staring right at me. They looked like deer caught in the headlights. It's like, oh god, we've come this far and now we're going to blow it. I remember I smiled, looked at them, and said, "All right you son-of-a-bitches, I'll give them seven points on a trick play, but they won't score another point. Not one F-ing point." The referee came over and said, "Watch your language." But when I said that, my teammates' expressions seemed to change as if to say, "Okay. Okay. It's all right." Then we went ahead and really put it to them.

I remember when we were in the locker room at halftime, finally realizing what we could accomplish. I told the seniors left in the locker room that I hadn't gone through all this hell to lose our last game. I didn't think about it again until we got back into the locker room at the end of the game. I was sitting on the bench. I just started crying. I couldn't stop. It was just raw emotion coming out. Next thing I know, Barrows was standing in front of me. He said, "What's the matter?" I said, "It won't ever happen again." He asked, "What do you mean?" I said, "Most of us will never play anymore and this will probably never happen again for any of us." I remember he put his arm around me and said, "You're probably right." Well for Columbus, it hasn't happened again.

Columbus (*The Evening Republican*): "Thousands Cheer Bull Dogs After Perfect Season – Bonfire, Parade Staged"

Over 1,000 cheering fans gathered at Memorial Field late Friday night to welcome home their champs, Columbus high school footballers who won 40-13 over Connersville and came home with the first unblemished record in 52 years. Coach Max Andress was thanking everyone connected with the grid sport this year, summed up the "dream" season by saying that his kids "just wouldn't be beat." Students riding in school buses that made the trip to Connersville and adult fans returned to Columbus to wait at the junction of Roads 46 and 31 for their team. Upon arrival, the gridders boarded fire trucks and paraded down Twenty-Fifth Street to Washington Street, down Washington Street through the downtown area, and back to the football field.

Do the smiles on our faces tell you what a great once-in-a lifetime experience this fire truck ride was for us?

Many fans went directly to the football field to await the team after the noisy jaunt through downtown Columbus. During the wait, the entire season was played dozens of times in small and large conversation groups.

Overwhelmed with happiness, Coach Andress and his coaching staff, Ted Marston, Walter Page, and Duane Barrows, simply smiled and shook the seemingly thousands of hands thrust at them. Team members milled around accepting congratulations from friends, fans, and parents while others talked over the performance put on by the Canines at Connersville to gain the final win. Robert Weber, of the Chamber of Commerce, took the microphone to emcee the short celebration. Coach Andress was introduced to the cheering supporters and was presented a large placard labeled, "Mr. Football." Coach Andress' speech was short, but in a few words he expressed appreciation to coaches, students, administration, fans, and to "his boys" who did him, themselves, and their community proud. Columbus pep band played the school song and cheerleaders led several cheers. Mr. Andress set the match to the victory bonfire and the activities then flagged to informal conversations and congratulations.

Bull Dog Memories

Ron Galloway: I remember the ride on the fire engine. I would not have guessed that we had accomplished a feat that has yet to be repeated at Columbus North. I know the lessons I learned from high school sports gave me the experience to understand and appreciate that teamwork and determination are valuable and rare commodities.

Bill Spicer: My final memory about the season was the bus ride home. We had a state police escort and must have been doing eighty. And of course, the fire truck ride downtown and back to the football field.

Columbus (*The Evening Republican*): November, 1959

Coach Andress was unanimous choice for South Central Conference "Coach of the Year" and two CHS linemen and three backs were named to the All-Star Team.

For the record, we can't and won't single out any individual player for extra plaudits. But to simply say they compiled a 10-0 seasonal record on unified team effort alone isn't sufficient. They tackled low and hard. They blocked victoriously both at the line of scrimmage and downfield. They trained with diligence and worked just about as hard in scrimmage sessions as during a ball game. They were willing to sacrifice almost everything for two months to compile a perfect gridiron record. And they listened and practiced what their coaches "preached." They were their own worst critics. If a teammate made a miscue, he heard about it from the fellow next to him. And compliments came just as easy.

Mix all these ingredients up with tremendous school and community spirit and you can't help but wind up with a winner. Personally we think this year's team set a precedent, not only from the standpoint of their record but team, school, and community spirit as well. Truly they've been a great group – a credit to their school, community, coaches, and most of all, **themselves**.

Max Andress

Max was head football coach at Columbus High School from 1951 to 1972. During those twenty-one years, his team won 188 games. As one example that Max was a beloved member of the Columbus community, in 1971 he was elected to two consecutive four-year terms as Mayor of the city. He took a very active role in his community. During his tenure as mayor, Max was a very active supporter of the city's Parks and Recreation Department. He also played a major role in helping bring major sporting events to Columbus and helped the Columbus sports scene grow. After his second term as mayor, Max joined Cummins Engine Company as community-relations director.

Max Andress died on March 20, 2007, at the age of 84. In 2004, Memorial Field at Columbus High School was renamed Andress Field. After his death, former players and friends shared memories about Max. What follows are a few of the comments shared.

"In your life, your path crosses with a lot of people, and a lot of them have a tremendous impact on who you are. He certainly had a positive impact on me; I'm grateful that happened," said Mike Phipps, the 1966 Columbus High School quarterback who went on to play at Purdue and the NFL.

"You always knew where he stood," said another former player, Steve Hollenbeck. "He was willing to make a decision and stand by that decision. I think that's a good lesson for all of us."

Bill McCaa, who became the Bull Dog coach after Max was elected mayor said, "After I had been head football coach for fifteen, sixteen years, I was still saying 'Yes sir, coach,' 'No sir, coach'." (to Andress).

Chapter 9   A Dream Remembered: the 50th Reunion of the Undefeated Bull Dogs —August 21, 2009

Columbus (*The Republic*): " '59 Legacy Still Felt on Fields Today" – Harry McCawley

Let's be honest…football linemen get no respect. It's always been that way. The quarterbacks and running backs get the headlines. If they get any mention, football linemen are usually lumped in the next to last paragraph beginning with, "Also playing were…"

The quarterbacks usually end the game with the same jersey they wore at the beginning… still pure white. Linemen are coated with mud, dirt, grass stains, and footprints – even on clear sunny days.

But bless their souls, those quarterbacks and running backs love their linemen. They'd better. If those usually hefty fellows weren't clearing the paths for them, they'd spend most of the game under a pile of other players wearing different uniforms.

Friday night, Columbus' Max Ziegler, a former football lineman, and his compatriots on the 1959 Columbus High School football team will get their just recognition. Heck, they're even letting the running backs and quarterbacks and anybody else associated with the 1959 team join in the respect-a-thon. The 1959 team will be honored at halftime of Friday night's season opening game between Columbus North and Seymour. Ironically, they'll stand in the middle of the same field they played on 50 years ago when there was only one high school in Columbus.

The field is named for the coach who led them to their greatest achievement as a team – the late Max Andress. This is the 50th anniversary of the 1959 season and the Bull Dog team that raced through the entire 10-game schedule without a defeat.

"It was the biggest thrill of my high school career," said Max, who now works for the ColumBus system. It was also a thrill for his teammates, but on a larger scale, it was a thrill for the Columbus community.

Like linemen, the sport of football never really did get its measure of respect in a town where basketball ruled. "Basketball paid the bills," Max observed. "I imagine that after all the expenses were factored out, football was a money loser." The Bull Dog gridders drew decent crowds, but nothing that could match the sell-out crowds which turned out for the basketball games. Except for that magical season of 1959.

"I especially remember the Southport game," Max Ziegler said. "The stands were completely filled long before the game got started and fans began standing on the cinders around the field. The whole track was full of people." Southport was the eighth game of the season and by that time the Dogs had raced through seven opponents in convincing fashion. The possibility of going undefeated was on everybody's mind, but wasn't something that the players and coaches dwelled upon. "I don't think we ever realized what it would mean until we saw the size of the crowd for the Southport game," Max said. "They were the toughest team we faced." When it was over, Columbus had claimed a hard fought 13-6 victory and the thought of an undefeated season was inescapable.

That was reached two weeks later at Connersville. "It was an awful night," Max recalled. "Cold, rainy, lots of mist and muddy. We didn't mind though. We won." Convincingly. The Bull Dogs posted a 40-13 victory. There was a sizable Columbus contingent at Connersville for that final game. Several buses had brought hundreds of local fans to the game.

It was when the team and their fans got home that the significance really hit home. "There was a fire engine waiting for us," Max said. "We all hopped on and got a ride to the downtown. There were hundreds of people lined up Washington Street and that was really late at night."

Unlike a lot of teams that are often associated with a star player like Mike Phipps or Blair Kiel, the 1959 team was a pretty Democratic bunch. "If there was a star, I suppose it would be Graham Updike," Max said. "He was a little fellow but he could run and slip out of tackles." The quarterback was Skip Lindeman, a signal caller Max described as "very smart." He lived up to the name. He was listed in the 1960 CHS *Log* at the head of the class in academics.

To a large degree, the linemen were equal stars. Max at right guard, was among the smaller of the front group in the 230-pound range. John Gentry was 220 and Jack Hinkle tipped the scales at 170. In today's world of 300-plus pound linemen such an array would have been underweight. In 1959 they were earthmovers.

For a football team that lacked in "name" players, the 1959 squad turned out pretty well. Some can argue that they earned football a whole new respect, one that continues today in the fields of both Columbus high schools.

Our 50th Reunion…According to Jack

I didn't sleep much last night because today is the day. Breakfast in bed as usual – Cracklin' Oat Bran, Cran Grape juice, one mushy banana, one Prozac, one cholesterol pill, brushed teeth… ready for action.

At thirty-five minutes past two in the afternoon, my driver son, Jon, pulled in with my sporty NASCAR-labeled van. Clown shoes on, the rhino man was properly lifted from my bed to the power chair, for loading me into the van. Since I planned to stay in a motel for the first time in over ten years, my life was loaded up – medical supplies, change of outfit, shirt only. Jon, Linda, and I were ready to go.

The trip around Indianapolis I-465 and south on I-65 is a little over fifty-five miles. We arrived outside Andress Field, not sure how to get to the school cafeteria where we were all going to meet. After a little heated discussion with my driver, he proceeded to go past a "Road Closed" sign at my encouragement. We circled the gym and at thirty-five minutes past four found the picnic area, just outside the cafeteria.

We mingled and introduced ourselves, mostly to the wives. Some of the guys were easily recognized, others weren't. All appeared to have been eating regularly. From five o'clock until shortly before seven, we were entertained by the North cheerleaders. They have more good-looking girls cheerleading than we had in the whole high school! There were comments made by various people – Mrs. Andress, Coach Marston, and some of the players. We took a group picture and then it was game time.

The group proceeded to Andress Field and sat in the bleachers at the south end which was a nice situation, except for the guy with the 55MM Howitzer that kept going off after every Columbus score. Columbus scored forty points.

At halftime, the band put on an excellent show. They told me to head down the hash mark to the fifty-yard-line. The announcer introduced the players. It was a great few minutes.

We all wandered back to the south end. As I got to the ten yard line, I almost turned and went over to line up for an extra point, but I couldn't find Dan FitzGibbon, and anyway, my feet don't work anymore.

Near the end of the third quarter, many of us thought about leaving and slowly made our way out. It was back to the van and the trip to the motel. After securing some bibles from other rooms, we were able to elevate my bed high enough to allow my son to unload me. I was dumped into bed, propped up on pillows, and ready for action.

Soon after I was settled, five of my best friends and former classmates managed to find my room. For the next few hours, this small group covered some great memories to finish the day.

Saturday proved to be even better than Friday was, because we had more time to unwind and enjoy. One of my special girlfriends from high school, Melinda Engleking along with her family and friends, hosted a picnic at her residence. It was a real thrill for me. I had not been there for more than thirty years. Tragically, some years ago the big house burned down, but the place is still magnificent.

The event started at noon. For the next six plus hours we mingled, looked at scrapbooks, looked at pictures, and took group pictures. About seventy-four people attended.

I arrived home at little past seven-thirty Saturday night and passed out about thirty minutes later. As a final comment, I want to thank everyone for showing up and supporting us, as well as the wives who had to take a back seat for the weekend. I think there were twenty-nine of the '59 Bull Dogs in attendance.

For Oprah's benefit, this is a true story.

Each player who attended the reunion signed the football. The team members gave the football to the athletic department to be displayed in one of the glass trophy cases in the field house, so all passing by can remember that amazing season.

Steve Everroad holds the football signed by all who attended the reunion

On August 23, 2009, the emails once again began flying in machine-gun like fashion.

"Jack, you guys did something no one else in Columbus High School history has ever done and in my opinion never will. Dad always spoke so highly of you guys and how the '59 team was a "special" group of guys. After observing the very sincere camaraderie and learning more about each of you, I now understand what he meant. Dad always said that the "cream always rises to the top". No doubt, the 1959 football team was all about that cream, not only in the game of football, but also in the game of life." Dave (Coach Max Andress' son)

"I hope all of you had a great reunion, recognition at the game, and fun at Melinda's party. I listened to Sam Simmermaker's talk about the game and heard that so many of you were in attendance. That's great! I hope the weekend was everything you hoped it would be, and more." Ed Poole

"I'm so glad you were able to pull your guys together and enjoy the memories of your accomplishment. Congratulations from all of us that did not play football, but remember with pride how great your season was and how everyone remembers the incredible defense and explosive offense. Go Bull Dogs!!!" Jay Shumaker

"Although I am an outsider, I thoroughly enjoyed visiting with all the guys. It was great to hear all of you share so many wonderful memories. These guys are a classy group and it is no wonder they were so successful in high school and have done so well as adults." Larry Bray

"We had such a wonderful time this weekend. The game Friday night was fun…although I think I have also lost a little bit of my hearing! On Saturday, I loved watching everyone smile and share memories." Melinda Engleking

"Dear Hink, Congrats on a job well done. You pulled it off and I think all involved had a great time. If the truth were known, I don't think they could thank you enough. I was as proud as anything when you led us on the field at halftime…" Spice

"I echo Jack's comments…it was absolutely great! Thanks to all who put it together. I was not on the football team, but it was a proud moment to see the team go out on the field at halftime. I watched the stands and it was amazing how many fans were engaged in showing their gratitude." Jim Battin

Chapter 10 Fond Memories, Good Thoughts, and a Little Humor

Each of us holds memories of days gone by. Sometimes we need a little help to rekindle those memories. Some of the memories we're about to share you may have seen posted on the World Wide Web or shared through emails, things we never had access to while growing up. Ironically, the Internet is the very thing that brought The Columbus Crew back together.

It's time to sit back, kick up your feet, and begin your own stroll down memory lane, remembering your years of growing up in the best of times. As the song goes, "Those were the days my friend, we thought they'd never end." Enjoy!

Let's go back in time to 1955. It's a warm, summer evening and the neighbors are gathering on the porch, discussing what's going on in the world today. Listen to what our parents are saying.

- "I'll tell you one thing, if things keep going the way they are, it's going to be impossible to buy a week's worth of groceries for $20.00.
- "Have you seen the new cars coming out next year? It won't be long before $2000.00 will only buy a good used one."
- "If cigarettes keep going up in price, I'm going to quit. A quarter a pack is ridiculous."
- "Did you hear the post office is thinking about charging a dime just to mail a letter?"
- "When I first started driving, who would have thought that gas would someday cost 29 cents a gallon? Guess we'd be better off leaving the car in the garage."
- "Kids today are impossible. Those duck tail haircuts make it impossible to stay groomed. Next thing you know, boys will be wearing their hair as long as girls."

- "I never thought I'd see the day all our kitchen appliances would be electric. They're even making electric typewriters now!"
- "I'm afraid to send my kids to the movies anymore. Ever since they let Clark Gable get by with saying damn in "Gone With the Wind," it seems every new movie has either hell or damn in it."
- "It's too bad things are so tough nowadays. I see where a few married women have to work to make ends meet."
- "There is no sense going away for the weekend. It costs nearly $15.00 a night to stay in a hotel."
- "If they think I'll pay fifty cents for a haircut, forget it!"
- "No one can afford to be sick anymore. At $35.00 a day in the hospital, it's too rich for my blood."

It sounds like the cost of living was going up. How about those exorbitant prices we were paying back in 1954?

- Milk – 92 cents/gallon
- Loaf of bread – 17 cents
- Swiss cheese – 69 cents/pound
- T-Bone steak – 95 cents/pound
- Post Grape Nuts – 19 cents/10 oz. package
- Clorox Bleach – 19 cents/half gallon
- Postage stamp – 3 cents
- Gas – 21 cents/gallon
- Ford Car - $1548 - $2415

Jack Hinkle is a number's guy. Over the years, he has seen changes in all sorts of numbers. Jack shares his "expense history."

Jack: When I was young, I would walk about a mile and a half from my house to downtown Columbus to go to a movie. At that time there were three movie theaters downtown, all within three blocks of each other.

The Rio Theater was my favorite; it was there I saw all of the old cowboy movies. In the early fifties, I paid seventeen cents to get into the theater. This price included a luxury tax, whatever that meant. It cost a nickel for a coke and ten cents for popcorn. A box of Milk Duds and I was good to go! In those days, the show consisted of a newsreel, cartoon, serial feature, and the movie itself – all for seventeen cents! Do you remember those days? The last time I went to a movie I drove four miles, got a thirty-two ounce coke, a bucket of popcorn, watched the coming attractions, and the movie itself – all for the small sum of twenty dollars and some change.

During my life, I have purchased several cars. My first car was a 1962 Volkswagen bug. The sticker price was $1,181.26. A few years later, I went on a car buying spree. I bought a 1965 Pontiac Catalina for $3,500. Next I purchased a 1966 Pontiac Catalina for $3,600. In July of 1966, I was told there were good deals at the Oldsmobile dealership. I proceeded to purchase a 1966 Delta 88 Olds convertible for a cool $4,200.

In 1968, I got married and buying new cars took a back burner for a few years. We purchased a 1973 Buick Century station wagon for $6,500. That car was nice to drive but bad for the pocketbook. I think the catalytic converter allowed me to get nine miles per gallon in town, as well as on the highway. We went from the station wagon to a Buick Apollo to get better gas mileage. When the tires wore out, we decided to go with more size. In 1978, we bought a Buick with a six-cylinder aluminum engine for $7,800. Some people said the engine wouldn't last more than 50,000 miles. We traded the car in fifteen years later with 215,000 miles on that engine.

In 1985, we bought a Mini Astro Van with some fancy customizing. That van cost us a little over $22,000. It was an excellent family vehicle. The only problem was the front tires didn't last long, due to the engine weight. The last new car we bought was another van, which had to be modified to install a lift for the wheelchair transport. We purchased it for $31,000 in 1999. It was another nicely customized car. Unfortunately, we messed it up when we converted it for the lift. Over almost forty years of buying cars, the prices went from $2000 to $31,000.

I purchased my first house in 1971 for $16,000. It had three bedrooms and a two-car garage. In 1973, we stepped up to a $28,000 home with three bedrooms and a one-car garage. A change of jobs took us to Olathe, Kansas. There we purchased a four bedroom, split-level home with a basement and a two-car garage for $70,000. Our final stop, in 1985, was back within two miles of the $28,000 house. This house has three bedrooms and a two-car garage and cost $70,000.

Oldies but goodies...

Do you remember "Doo-Wop"? Several cities claimed to originate this musical style – Chicago, New York, Baltimore, and Los Angeles. Many early Doo-Wop groups were made up of teenagers who couldn't afford musical instruments. Instead, they sang a cappella. By 1958, Doo-Wop was the most popular style of music being played on the airwaves. Doo-Wop was the closest to rock, lasting from the mid-1950s through the British invasion of 1964.

The music of our day caused our parents and teachers grief. How do you rate as a true 'Oldies Fan'? Write down your answers and check them against the correct answers found at the end of the quiz. Don't cheat, now!

1. When did 'Little Suzie' finally wake up?
    a) 2 o'clock   b) 3 o'clock   c) 4 o'clock

2. 'Rock Around the Clock' can be heard in what movie?
    a) Rebel Without a Cause   b) Blackboard Jungle   c) The Wild Ones

3. What's missing from a Rock & Roll standpoint? Earth _____
    a) Angel   b) Mother   c) Worm

4. 'I found my thrill...' where?
    a) Heartbreak Hotel   b) Kansas City   c) Blueberry Hill

5. 'Please turn on your magic beam, _____ _____ bring me a dream,'
    a) Mr. Sandman   b) Earth Angel   c) Dream Lover

6. Elvis Presley first recorded on which label?
    a) Atlantic   b) RCA   c) Sun

7. Who asked, 'Why's everybody always pickin' on me?'
    a) Buster Brown   b) Charlie Brown   c) Bad, Bad Leroy Brown

8. Who was the one with the knife in Bobby Darin's 'Mack the Knife'?
    a) Mac Heath   b) Mac Cloud   c) Mac Namara

9. Name the song with 'A-wop bop a-loo bop a-lop bam boom.'
    a) Tutti Fruitti   b) Be-Bop-A-Lula   c) Good Golly, Miss Molly

10. Who is generally given credit for originating the term 'Rock and Roll'?
    a) Dick Clark   b) Wolfman Jack   c) Alan Freed

11. In 1957, he left the music business to become a preacher.
    a) Little Richard   b)Frankie Lymon   c) Tony Orlando

12. Paul Anka's 'Puppy Love' is written to what star?
    a) Brenda Lee   b) Connie Francis   c) Annette Funicello

13. The Everly Brothers are:
    a) Pete and Dick   b) Don and Phil   c) Bob and Bill

14. In 1959, Berry Gordy, Jr. started a small record company called...
    a)Decca   b) Cameo   c) Motown

15. Edd Brynes had a hit with 'Kookie, Kookie, Lend Me Your Comb.'
    What TV show was he on?
    a) 77 Sunset Strip   b) Hawaiian Eye   c) Surfside Six

16. In 1960 Bobby Darin married:
    a) Carol Lynley   b) Sandra Dee   c) Natalie Wood

17. They were a one hit wonder with 'The Book of Love'
    a) The Penguins   b) The Monotones   c) The Moonglows

18. The Everly Brothers sang a song called 'Till I _____ You."
    a) Loved   b) Kissed   c) Met

19. Chuck Berry sang 'Oh, _____, why can't you be true?'
    a) Suzie Q   b) Peggy Sue   c) Maybelline

20. 'Wooly _____'
    a) Mammouth   b) Bully   c) Pully

21. 'They often call me Speedo, but my real name is...'
    a) Mr. Earl   b) Jackie Pearl   c) Milton Berle

22. 'You're my Fanny and nobody else's _____'
    a) girl   b) butt   c) love

23. 'I want you to play with my...
    a) heart   b) dreams   c) ding a ling

24. 'Be Bop A Lula...'
    a) she's got the rabies b) she's my baby   c) she loves me, maybe

25. 'Fine Love, Fine Kissing...'
    a) right here   b) fifty cents   c) just for you

26. 'He wore black denim trousers and...'
    a) a pink carnation   b) pink leotards   c) motorcycle boots

27. 'I got a gal named...'
    a) Jenny Zamboni   b) Gerri Mahoney   c) Boney Maroney

Answers: 1(c) it's 4 o'clock; 2(b) Blackboard Jungle; 3(a) Angel; 4(c) Blueberry Hill; 5(a) Mr. Sandman; 6(c) Sun; 7(b) Charlie Brown; 8(a) Mac Heath; 9(a) Tutti Fruitti; 10(c) Alan Freed; 11(a) Little Richard; 12(c) Annette Funicello; 13(b) Don and Phil; 14(c) Motown; 15(a) 77 Sunset Strip; 16(b) Sandra Dee; 17(b) The Monotones; 18(b) Kissed; 19(c) Maybelline; 20(b) Bully; 21(a) Mr. Earl; 22(b) butt; 23(c) ding a ling; 24(b) she's my baby; 25(a) right here; 26(c) motorcycle boots; 27(c) Boney Maroney.

Do you remember what was happening in the country and world during the 40s, 50s, and 60s?

National Events:
- Walt Disney releases the movie *Bambi* – 1942
- President Roosevelt is elected for the 4th term – 1944
- Vice-President Harry Truman becomes president after Roosevelt's death – 1945
- A U.S. plane is first to break the supersonic barrier – 1947
- Jackie Robinson becomes the first black major league baseball player – 1947
- Assassination attempt against Truman by Puerto Rican nationalists fails – 1950
- Rosenbergs found guilty of espionage – 1951. Executed in 1953
- General Douglas McArthur fired for insubordination – 1951
- Dwight Eisenhower becomes President of the U.S. – 1953

- Landmark Supreme Court Decision bans school segregation – 1954
- Senator Joseph McCarthy's televised hearings into alleged Communist influence in the army backfire. He is condemned by the Senate – 1954
- Refusal of Rosa Parks to move to the back of the bus leads to Montgomery bus boycott – 1955
- Rise of Dr. Martin Luther King, Jr. to national prominence – 1955
- Eisenhower uses federal troops to desegregate schools in Little Rock, Arkansas – 1957
- Explorer I, first U.S. Satellite is launched – 1958
- Alaska and Hawaii are admitted as the 49th and 50th states of the United States of America – 1959
- Sit-ins against segregation when black college students demonstrated at the Woolworth lunch counter in Greensboro, North Carolina – 1960
- Massachusetts Senator John F. Kennedy defeats Vice President Richard Nixon to become president – 1960
- Commander Alan B. Shepherd rode the first U.S. suborbital spacecraft – 1961
- Lt. Col. John Glenn became the first American to orbit the earth – 1962
- Governor George Wallace was forced to step aside and the University of Alabama was integrated – 1963
- 200,000 people marched on Washington to demand civil rights for all. Dr. Martin Luther King, Jr. delivered his famous "I Have a Dream" speech – 1963
- President Kennedy was assassinated in Dallas and Lyndon Johnson becomes president - 1963
- Malcolm X is murdered – 1965
- Long, hot summer begins with rioting in the Watts area of Los Angeles – 1965
- Thurgood Marshall becomes first black justice of the U.S. Supreme Court – 1967
- Dr. Martin Luther King, Jr. is assassinated in Memphis – 1968
- Presidential candidate Robert F. Kennedy is assassinated in Los Angeles - 1968
- Riots erupt at the Democratic National Convention in Chicago – 1968
- Former Vice-President Richard Nixon defeats Vice-President Hubert Humphrey and Alabama Governor George Wallace in the presidential election – 1968
- U.S. Astronaut Neil Armstrong becomes the first human to walk on the moon – 1969
- First Woodstock Festival draws 500,000-plus people to small New York town – 1969
- 250,000 march on Washington to protest the Vietnam conflict – 1969

International:

- Nazi Germany invades Norway, Denmark, Holland, Belgium, and Luxembourg – 1940
- Winston Churchill becomes Prime Minister of Great Britain – 1940
- Japanese bomb Pearl Harbor. Germany and Italy declare war on the United States – 1941
- The Holocaust begins – 1942
- Mahatma Ghandi is arrested in India for demanding independence from England – 1942
- Enrico Fermi splits an atom for the first time – 1942
- Penicillin goes into common use for chronic disease and streptomycin is invented – 1942
- D-Day invasion of France launched on June 6, 1944
- League of Nations holds final meeting and the United Nations is formed – 1945
- Mussolini is killed. Hitler commits suicide – 1945
- Atomic bomb is dropped on Japan, Japan surrenders, and WWII ends – 1945
- Nuremberg trials sentence twelve Nazi leaders to death – 1946
- Ghandi is assassinated – 1948
- Communist China is formed as Chaing Kai-shek takes forces to Formosa – 1949
- North Korean forces invade South Korea, precipitating war – 1950
- First hydrogen bomb test at Eniwetok Atoll in the South Pacific – 1952
- Soviet dictator Josef Stalin dies – 1953
- Korean War ends in truce – 1953
- The U.S. agrees to train South Vietnamese army – 1955
- Soviet satellite Sputnik circles the Earth – 1957
- Soviet leader Nikita Khrushchev tours the U.S. – 1959
- Fidel Castro comes to power in Cuba – 1959
- Tensions between the U.S. and Soviet Union grew, following the shooting down of an American U-2 spy plane – 1960
- An invasion of Cuba by anti-Castro forces ends in disaster at the Bay of Pigs – 1961
- Congress passed the Tonkin Gulf Resolution authorizing presidential action in Vietnam – 1964
- President Johnson orders continuous bombing of North Vietnam – 1965
- Over 385,000 U.S. military personnel stationed in Vietnam and full-scale bombing of Hanoi is underway – 1966
- Israel defeats combined forces of Egypt, Jordan, and Syria in Six Day War – 1967
- Tet Offensive by Communists stuns American forces in Vietnam – 1958

- Peace talks on Vietnam War open in Paris – 1968
- U.S. forces in Vietnam peak at 543,000 in April -1969
- Withdrawal from Vietnam began in July – 1969

Memories of Growing up in the '40s, '50s, and '60s…..to think we survived our youth!

- As babies, we slept on our tummies in cribs covered in bright colored lead-based paints.
- There were no childproof lids on medicine bottles, locks on doors or cabinets, and we didn't ride in car seats.
- We didn't wear helmets when riding our bikes. We fell out of trees, got cut, broke bones and teeth, and there were no lawsuits as a result of these accidents.
- We drank water from the garden hose, shared a soft drink with friends (all drinking from the same bottle), and ate worms and mud pies.
- We ate cupcakes made with real butter and drank Kool-Aid made with real sugar. And we weren't overweight because we spent our time outside playing!
- We didn't have Nintendo, Playstation, and X-boxes. We survived without Cable TV, videos and DVDs, CDs, cell phones, computers and the Internet. We had friends to spend the day with.
- We spent our days building go-carts out of scraps we found. We shot BB guns and didn't put too many eyes out. We tried out for Little League and not everyone made the team. Those who didn't learned how to deal with the disappointment.
- If we got into trouble in the neighborhood or at school, our parents actually sided with the law and our teachers.
- We whispered the "F" word and our parents knew about it within the hour.
- We could never buy cigarettes because the clerks at the store knew how old we were. Even if we were old enough, the clerks would tell our parents if we bought them.
- We went to the 'Five and Dime' where we could actually buy things for five and ten cents.
- Our teachers remembered when they taught our parents.
- Most people went by a nickname.
- We could charge at the local store or write checks without an ID.
- There were no McDonalds, Burger Kings, or Wendys.
- We listened to the Big Bands on our radios.
- We experienced freedom, success, failure, and responsibility. We learned how to deal with whatever came our way.

Hoosier Memories…

Since I'm a native-born Hoosier, I just had to include stories about my home state. Cut me a little slack!

We Hoosiers have always been able to poke fun at ourselves. Many "barbs" have come our way over the years. The most frequently asked question by non-native-born Hoosiers has always been, "Okay, **exactly** what does the term Hoosier mean?"

Do you remember earlier when I shared the basketball story about the first four weeks of a Hoosier baby's life? Well, I purposely saved the story about the fifth week until now. During the fifth week of life, Hoosier babies are told **the one official** meaning of the term "Hoosier." However, they are sworn to secrecy about that meaning. If anyone has to ask a Hoosier about the meaning of that term, we know they're not from Indiana. Heck, my wife Kathi is an Illini. She doesn't even know **the one official** meaning of Hoosier. Now **that's** being sworn to secrecy.

FRIENDS vs. INDIANA FRIENDS

Friends never ask for food. Indiana friends always bring the food.

Friends will say 'hello." Indiana friends will give you a big hug and kiss.

Friends call your parents Mr. and Mrs. Indiana friends call your parents Mom and Dad.

Friends have never seen you cry. Indiana friends cry with you.

Friends will eat at your dinner table and leave. Indiana friends will spend hours there talking, laughing, and just being together.

Friends know a few things about you. Indiana friends could write a book with direct quotes from you.

Friends will leave you behind if that's what the crowd is doing. Indiana friends will kick the whole crowds' back-ends that left you.

Friends will knock on your door. Indiana friends walk right in and say 'I'm home!'

Friends will visit you in jail. Indiana friends will spend the night in jail with you.

Friends will visit you in the hospital when you're sick. Indiana friends will cut your grass, clean your house, come spend the night with you in the hospital, and cook for you when you come home.

Friends will have you on speed dial. Indiana friends have your number memorized.

Friends are for a while. Indiana friends are for a life-time. (author unknown)

A friend and fellow 1960 CHS graduate, Doug Emig, shared with me the following story about "The Hoosier Culture." If you're not from Indiana, just slide out the word Hoosier and slip in the nickname for your own state – that'll work for you. As we've shared earlier, "the story of any one of us is, in part, the story of all of us."

Know the Hoosier casserole: The state casserole consists of canned green beans, Campbell's cream of mushroom soup, and dried onions. You can safely take this casserole to any social event and know you'll be accepted.

The Indiana General Assembly, in an effort to grow bigger athletes, passed legislation years ago requiring every incorporated community to have at least one festival per year dedicated to high-fat food. It is your duty as a Hoosier to attend these festivals and eat at least one elephant ear.

You know you're a Hoosier when…

- You think the state bird is Larry.
- Your feelings get hurt whenever someone points out the acronym for Purdue University is PU.
- You know several people who have hit a deer.
- Down south to you means Kentucky.
- You know what the phrase "knee-high by the Fourth of July" means.
- You've heard of Euchre; you know how to play Euchre; and you are a master of Euchre.
- You say things like catty-wampus and catty-corner and know what they mean.
- You install security lights on your home and garage and then leave both unlocked.
- You know that baling wire was the predecessor to duct tape.
- High school basketball games draw bigger crowds on the weekend than movie theaters, if you even have a movie theater in town.
- Driving in the winter is better because the potholes are packed with snow.
- You know that strangers are the only ones who come to your front door.
- Everyone knows who the town cops are, where they live, and whether they're at home or on duty.
- You've been to the Covered Bridge Festival.
- To you, tenderloin is not an expensive cut of beef but a big, salty, breaded and fried piece of pork served on a bun with a pickle.

There, now you have the official cultural meaning of the word Hoosier – not **the one official** meaning, but the "cultural" meaning.

A man in Topeka, Kansas, decided to write a book about churches across the country. He started by flying to San Francisco and working east from there.

Going to a very large church, he began taking photographs and making notes. He spotted a golden telephone on the vestibule wall and was intrigued with a sign which read, "Calls: $10,000 a minute."

Seeking out the pastor he asked about the phone and the sign. The pastor answered that the golden phone is, in fact, a direct line to heaven and if he pays the price he can talk directly to God. The man thanked the pastor and continued on his way. As he visited churches in Seattle, Dallas, St. Louis, Chicago, Milwaukee, and around the United States, he found more golden phones with the same sign, and received the same answer from each and every pastor he spoke with.

Finally he arrived in Indiana. Upon entering a church in Columbus, Indiana, behold – he saw the usual golden phone. This time the sign read, "Calls: 35 cents each." Fascinated, he asked to talk to the pastor. "Reverend, I have been in cities all across the country and in each church I have found this golden telephone. I've been told it's a direct line to heaven and that I could talk to God. In the other churches, the cost was $10,000 a minute. Your sign reads only thirty-five cents."

The pastor, smiling benignly, replied. "Son, you're in Indiana now. You're in God's country. It's a local call." American by birth…Hoosier by the grace of God.

...Savoring Your Memories...

1. What memories did the Oldies Quiz bring to mind?

2. Looking back from your current place in your life, what are some experiences you had that you feel you couldn't have today? Why not?

3. You remember my dad would only have changed one part of his life if he could—getting an education. What parts of your journey would you like to change, if you could?

4. If you could release some of your worries while still here, what would they be, and how could you go about that?

5. Have you shared with your family and friends the stories about your life? What was easy and what was difficult about sharing your stories? If you haven't shared your life with others, why have you chosen not to?

6. What have you done, or what do you now have to do, so you can slide in sideways and shout "WOO HOO, what a ride it's been?"

Epilogue

As Walter Cronkite said at the end of every one of his newscasts, "That's the way it is"… in this instance with sixteen guys who grew up together in Columbus, went our separate ways after high school, and then came back full cycle, forty-nine years later to share our stories with each other and with you.

Above all else, Kathi and I, as well as The Columbus Crew, hope you've enjoyed your trip through the seasons of your life in that '57 Chevy ragtop. We're all very sure that – just as with our own trip through the seasons of our lives – your memories have not all been good ones. We hope you have chosen to include those not-so-happy memories as you have begun to fill in the blank spaces at the end of some chapters. You know what? The memories that haven't been positive are **the** very ones we need to spend more time reflecting on and learning lessons from.

The Columbus Crew has realized that many of our lessons have come from those times we've made decisions that haven't resulted in pleasant remembrances. While our "life has been good to me" experiences have taught us many lessons, our "life has thrown me a curveball" experiences have resulted in many more. Do you remember the thought we shared from Richard Bode's book *First You Have to Learn to Row a Little Boat*? Bode was savoring **all** his memories. Without savoring all memories, we do not have all the information we need to learn how we lived our life and how that living brought us to where we are today.

The Columbus Crew hopes our memories have been a catalyst for you to continue – or begin – that inner journey toward self-understanding and self-growth. Please remember, it's a journey you **cannot** avoid taking, no matter how much you resist doing so. We hope you have laughed and cried as you have remembered! Above all, we hope you have begun to share your stories with those near to you, so they too can always remember.

Kathi and I have chosen to end this part of the journey with a thought she and I wish for ourselves, The Columbus Crew, and each and every one of you.

Life should not be a journey to the grave with the intention of arriving safely in an attractive and well preserved body, but rather to skid in sideways, body thoroughly used up, worn out, screaming "WOO HOO What a Ride!"

Life is an unending, wonderful journey. It would be great if all of us could say, "I've lived my life to the fullest. I've done most of what I've wished to do. I've made my mistakes; I've learned from them, and now I can honestly slide in sideways screaming WOO HOO! What a ride!" What more could we possibly ask than that?

As my favorite cowboy – and maybe yours – Roy Rogers said, "Happy trails."

THE COLUMBUS CREW

George Abel: After graduating from Columbus High School, George attended Purdue University, Chapman College, and the University of California at Riverside. He took additional course work at Indiana University/Purdue University in Columbus. From 1963-1965 George served in the United States Air Force and was an Honor Graduate from Technical Training School in Inventory Management. He did his basic training in San Antonio, Texas and was stationed at both Norton AFB and March AFB in California. In December, 2006, George retired after thirty-eight years working at Arvin Industries, Inc./Arvin Meritor in Columbus, Indiana. He and his wife Debby have two daughters and a son. Additionally they have four grandchildren and four step-grandchildren, ranging in age from twenty-three to three.

Jim Battin: Jim and his wife, Charlotte, live in Columbus, Indiana. They have two daughters, Samantha and Steffany, and four grandchildren, Jacob, Taylor, Luke, and Emma. His children and their families also live in Columbus. Jim retired from Cummins Engine Company in 1998 after a twenty-five year career in Human Resources. Currently, Jim is President of Strategic Consulting Group, Inc., and is working with several regional stakeholders to improve collaboration among education, workforce development, community and business leaders to improve economic opportunities in southeast Indiana.

Cal Brand: Cal lives in Columbus, Indiana, with his wife Donna. He received his Bachelor of Arts degree from Hanover College, Hanover, Indiana. He attended Princeton Theological

Seminary where he was awarded the Master of Divinity degree. Cal earned his Doctor of Ministry from the Graduate Theological Foundation in Donaldson, Indiana. Cal is an ordained minister, Presbyterian Church (U.S.A.) and has served as senior and assistant pastor in Presbyterian churches in McIntosh, Florida, and Newtown, Pennsylvania. He has had Interim Pastoral Assignments in Willow Springs, Illinois; Peotone, Illinois; Glenview, Illinois; and Fincastle, Virginia. Currently Cal is the Regional Director, East Central Region for the Association for Clinical Pastoral Education (ACPE). He has worked in several healthcare facilities throughout the United States, serving in a variety of positions. Cal is a Licensed Mental Health Counselor, a Certified Family Therapist, and a Full Supervisor with ACPE.

Jeff Crump: After graduating from Columbus High School, Jeff attended Virginia Military Institute where he played basketball all four years. Jeff then went to Indiana University and received his Doctor of Jurisprudence in 1967. He was in the U.S. Army (Air Defense Artillery), serving in Ft. Bliss, Texas and Seoul, Korea. Since 1970 Jeff has been an attorney in Columbus, Indiana, in the firm of Jewell, Crump, Angermeier & Prall. Jeff and his wife, Nancy, have three children and five grandchildren, including one set of triplets. For relaxation, Jeff plays on various traveling softball teams.

Steve Everroad: Steve was born in Seymour, Indiana, and has one brother, Richard Everroad, a retired middle school principal. He has a Bachelor of Arts degree from Milligan College and a Masters of Divinity in Christian Education from Emmanuel School of Religion in Johnson City, Tennessee. Steve also took coursework at several other institutions: Purdue University, Christopher-Newport College, Anderson University Seminary, and the Rio Grande Bible Institute in Edinburg, Texas graduating from their Spanish Language School. Steve was ordained into the ministry of the Gospel of Jesus Christ in 1966 at the First Christian Church in Columbus, Indiana. He has served churches in Columbus and Anderson, Indiana; Knoxville, Kingsport, Blountville, and Johnson City, Tennessee; Altoona, Pennsylvania; and Los Angeles, California—either as a youth or senior minister. Steve has been an Administrator of Northside Christian School (grades K4-9) in Newport News, Virginia; a Chaplain of Asbury Retirement Center in Johnson City, Tennessee; and a Cross-Cultural Missionary with C.M.F. in Mexico City, Mexico. Presently Steve is the Executive Director of East Tennessee Christian Home and Academy in Elizabethton, Tennessee. Steve and his wife Paulette have four grown children: Tina, Heath, Bambi, and Heidi, along with four grandchildren: Haven, Declan, Levi, and Hared, all residing in northeast Tennessee, *"Where Tennessee Began!"*

Dan FitzGibbon: Dan is a native of Columbus, Indiana, and a 1964 graduate of West Point. He was commissioned in the Infantry, and earned his Ranger and Special Forces tabs and Airborne wings. Dan served in West Berlin, Germany for three years before volunteering for Vietnam, where he served for nineteen months as an Army Special Forces captain during 1968 and 1969. The Indiana Historical Society recently published a book of Dan's letters home from Vietnam, *To Bear any Burden: A Hoosier Green Beret's Letters from Vietnam.* After Vietnam, Dan left the army to attend Harvard Law School, graduating with honors in 1972. Since then, he has been an attorney with Barnes & Thornburg, Indiana's largest law firm, based in Indianapolis. Dan served for thirteen years as a member of the firm's management committee. While his law practice has traditionally concentrated on business counseling, tax planning, and transactional work, for the past eleven years he has spent most of his time on international legal reform projects in the former Soviet Union, the Balkans, North Africa, and the Middle East. As of mid-2009, Dan had carried out a total of eighteen projects in fourteen different countries.

Jack Hinkle: After spending his first year after graduating from Columbus High School with a full-ride football scholarship at Indiana University, Jack found his calling in the relatively new invention called computers. Beginning on November 30, 1961, Jack was employed as a proof operator at Irwin Union Bank and Trust Company in Columbus, Indiana. He worked as a teller, programmer, and analyst operator. In 1973 Jack joined Computer Accounting, Inc. This company performed data processing services for three Indiana banks and forty-two credit unions in six states. In 1976 Anacom purchased Computer Accounting and Jack began working on the development of major hospital processing systems in the financial area. He then worked for a federally funded Child Support System. Jack continued working as a consultant for Child Support Systems, with his last day of work being exactly forty years to the date of his first: November 30, 2001. At that time, Jack became too disabled to work and has not worked since. He and his wife Linda live in Carmel, Indiana.

Skip Lindeman: Skip is a 1960 graduate of Columbus High School and a 1964 graduate of Wabash College in Crawfordsville, Indiana. After teaching in a private school for two years in Colorado Springs, Colorado, Skip enrolled in the theological seminary at Pacific School of Religion in Berkeley, California, graduating with a Master of Divinity degree in 1970. At that time, Skip did not go into church work. Instead he became a broadcaster, working first as a radio announcer in West Palm Beach, Florida and San Jose, California. Skip then moved into television and worked in smaller markets in Pocatello, Idaho; Aberdeen, South Dakota; and

Eugene, Oregon. Following a stint in Reno, Nevada as a TV weatherman and news anchor, Skip became an interviewer on a business television station in San Jose. Moving to Los Angeles, he did business interviews for a Los Angeles business channel and later worked as a radio newsman for KNX 1070 Newsradio, the CBS affiliate in L.A. About ten years ago, Skip felt called into the Christian ministry, and is currently the Interim Minister at a Congregational Church in La Canada, California. He is married to Harlane Loeff Lindeman, who is a psychologist with Kaiser Permanente in southern California.

Larry Long: Currently, Larry is CEO and twenty-two percent owner of Innovative Odor Solutions and Principal, Long & Associates, LLC. After graduating from Purdue University, Larry spent fifteen years with Cummins Engine Company in Columbus, Indiana, as General Manager of Construction/Industrial in both the United States and the United Kingdom. During that time, Larry received his MBA with a finance concentration from Harvard University. He then worked as vice-president of Marketing with The Reece Corporation, and from there became president and COO of Nebraska Engineering and CEO of Phoenix Engineering. Larry served as president of the Personal Communications Group at American Express. From there he became president and COO of MFS Internet and then president, COO, board member, and minority owner of Tie Communications. He was also CEO, board member, and minority owner of Omnicall, Inc. Prior to his current position, Larry was president and board member with Comm South Companies. Larry and his wife, Mary Ann, live in Greenville, South Carolina.

Ed Poole: Ed majored in history and minored in sociology while obtaining his Bachelor's Degree at Hanover College. In 1964, he began his professional career in education as a high school social studies teacher. During that time, he obtained his Master of Arts degree at the University of Northern Colorado, in Greeley, Colorado. Ed taught one more year and then resigned to pursue his doctorate at Indiana University. He was awarded the Doctorate in Education Degree in 1971. In addition to teaching social studies, Ed served as a middle school principal, high school assistant principal and principal, associate superintendent for instruction, and superintendent of schools. He also taught in the Colleges of Education at The University of Georgia, Indiana University, Northern Illinois University, and Aurora University. In 2006, Ed resigned his last university teaching position to found his own company, Lessons for Your Journey®. Within his company, Ed has had three books published, with a fourth to be released in April, 2010. He is also an organizational consultant, workshop facilitator, professional success coach, and storyteller. Ed and his wife, Kathi, live in North Carolina. Ed has two children Eric and Tracie and four granddaughters Allie, Aimee, and twins Emma and Kate.

Rob Schafstall: After high school graduation, Rob attended and graduated with a Bachelor of Arts degree from Franklin College in Franklin, Indiana. Rob received his Doctor of Jurisprudence from Indiana University. He has resided in Franklin since beginning his college career there. He and his wife, Janet, have two sons Robert and Joseph, a daughter Sarah, five granddaughters and one grandson. Since 1972 and continuing to today, Rob serves as Judge of the Franklin City Court, and is an attorney with Cutsinger and Schafstall. Rob is a member of the American Bar Association, the Indiana State Bar Association, the Johnson County Bar Association, the Indiana Cities and Towns Judges Association, and a life member of the Indianapolis Musicians Local No. 3. Rob is the Treasurer and member of Franklin College's Board of Trustees and a member of the Board of Directors for Mutual Savings Bank in Franklin.

Charlie Schuette: Charlie was a member of two straight undefeated state championship swimming teams at Columbus High School—his junior and senior years. He received a full athletic scholarship to the University of Oklahoma where he was a two-time All American. After receiving his bachelor's degree at Oklahoma, Charlie stayed there and received his Doctor of Jurisprudence Degree from the College of Law. After receiving his law degree, he served in several legal capacities with a variety of organizations throughout the world. He became Chairman and CEO of Akerman Senterfitt Law Firm in Miami, Florida and remains there today as Of Counsel and Chairman Emeritus to the firm. He is also former Chairman of the Coconut Grove Bank. His Court Admissions include the U.S. District Court, Southern District of Florida; U.S. District Court, Middle District of Florida; and the United States Supreme Court. Under Charlie's leadership, Akerman Senterfitt became the fastest growing law firm in the United States.

Jay Shumaker: After Jay graduated from Ball State University in Muncie, Indiana, he landed his first job with a corrugated box company headquartered in Columbus, Ohio. As he gained sales knowledge and experience, Jay got two big accounts in Anderson and Muncie, Indiana. He then went with a different company, but remained in the corrugated box industry. This company was St. Joe Paper Company, a manufacturing company started in the 1930's by Alfred I. duPont. In 1996 St. Joe Paper Company was purchased by BOX USA. Eventually Jay formed his own company, S J Sales, Inc.

Bill Spicer: Bill graduated with the class of 1960 at Columbus High School. He was born in Columbus in 1942. After his father was killed in WWII, his mother remarried and the family moved to Phoenix, Arizona. In 1950 Bill returned to Indiana and lived in Indianapolis until 1958 when the family returned to Columbus. He was a member of the undefeated 1959 championship football team at Columbus High School, playing fullback and linebacker. After graduating in May, 1960, Bill attended the University of Louisville and Franklin College for one year each. In August 1962, Bill enlisted in the United States Marine Corps. He received a commission as 2/lt in December, 1965, was designated a Naval Aviator in 1967, and returned to combat duty in Vietnam in 1968. He returned from Vietnam a decorated Marine, being awarded the Air Medal twenty-eight times and the Navy Commendation with combat V for Valor. Bill was one of the early AV8A Harrier pilots in the Marine Corps and went on to command Marine Attack Squadron 231, "The Aces of Spades," and an Aviation Combat Element. Bill has been married to his wife Marguerite for forth-three years. Upon his retirement from the Marine Corps in 1983, Bill, wife Marguerite, daughter Katie, and son Rob moved to Florida and had a successful citrus and hay business until they sold both and retired in 2003. In 2008 Bill and Marguerite road a motorcycle to Alaska and back. Currently, they are writing a book about their adventures.

Dave Steenbarger: After graduating from Columbus High School, Dave attended Purdue University's School of Pharmacy. While attending Purdue, Dave met Donna Daubenspeck and they were married in 1965. They moved to Muncie, Indiana, where Donna got her Masters Degree in Speech and Language Pathology. Dave worked in a local drug store chain. The Steenbargers moved to the south side of Indianapolis in 1968. Dave managed the L.S. Ayers pharmacy for twenty years, and Donna stayed home for eight years with their two children—Joy, who is now thirty-seven, and Mark, who is thirty-six. Later Donna taught for thirty-four years in one of the suburban Indianapolis school systems. She retired in May, 2008. For the past twenty years, Dave has worked as a consultant pharmacist for a long-term care pharmacy. He travels to nursing homes in central Indiana, making sure patients are on proper medication therapy. Dave is active in sports—basketball, racquetball, a player-manager for his church's softball team, and golf. Donna and Dave bowl in a church league during the winter. He is an elder at their church—Stones Crossing Community Church in Greenwood, Indiana. In the summer of 2009, Dave took his twenty-second medical mission trip to El Salvador. He has also been to Haiti, The Dominican, Paraguay, and Ecuador. Since Donna's retirement, she and Dave enjoy traveling. Their granddaughter, Abigail, is the joy of their lives—living only five minutes away.

Tom Taylor: In 1966, Tom received his Bachelor of Arts degree at Indiana University, with Departmental Honors. He then attended Harvard Law School, graduating *cum laude* in 1968. At that time Tom began his career in law as Associate, Partner, and Of Counsel with Ropes & Gray law firm in Boston, Massachusetts. He retired from active practice in 1998. Tom is the Founding Fellow of American College Bond Counsel. He was a lecturer, panelist, and program chairman for the National Association of Bond Lawyers from 1973-1998. Tom was an advisor to President Carter's White House concerning refinancing of public utilities. He was also an advisor to President Ford's White House concerning the $1.2 billion financial assistance package for New York City. From 1999 to 2006 Tom was a snowboard instructor and snowboard staff trainer at the Nashoba Valley Ski Area. Tom played a wicked trumpet in high school and continues to perform many concerts every year. He loves mountaineering and has volunteered in trail maintenance, alpine stewardship, and as a shelter/tent site caretaker with the Appalachian Mountain Club in the White Mountain National Forest. From 2000-2006 Tom volunteered as an Archeo-Astronomer at Chaco Culture National Historical Park. Presently, Tom is a self-described swamp rat and ski bum.

BUY A SHARE OF THE FUTURE IN YOUR COMMUNITY

These certificates make great holiday, graduation and birthday gifts that can be personalized with the recipient's name. The cost of one S.H.A.R.E. or one square foot is $54.17. The personalized certificate is suitable for framing and will state the number of shares purchased and the amount of each share, as well as the recipient's name. The home that you participate in "building" will last for many years and will continue to grow in value.

Here is a sample SHARE certificate:

HABITAT FOR HUMANITY

THIS CERTIFIES THAT

__YOUR NAME HERE__

HAS INVESTED IN A HOME FOR A DESERVING FAMILY

1985-2005

TWENTY YEARS OF BUILDING FUTURES IN OUR
COMMUNITY ONE HOME AT A TIME

1200 SQUARE FOOT HOUSE @ $65,000 = $54.17 PER SQUARE FOOT
This certificate represents a tax deductible donation. It has no cash value.

YES, I WOULD LIKE TO HELP!

*I support the work that Habitat for Humanity does and I want to be part of the excitement! As a donor, I will receive periodic updates on your construction activities but, more importantly, I know my gift will help a family in our community realize the dream of homeownership. **I would like to SHARE in your efforts against substandard housing in my community!** (Please print below)*

PLEASE SEND ME _____ SHARES at $54.17 EACH = $ $_____

In Honor Of: _____

Occasion: (Circle One) HOLIDAY BIRTHDAY ANNIVERSARY

      OTHER: _____

Address of Recipient: _____

Gift From: _____ *Donor Address:* _____

Donor Email: _____

I AM ENCLOSING A CHECK FOR $ $_____ PAYABLE TO HABITAT FOR HUMANITY <u>OR</u> PLEASE CHARGE MY VISA OR MASTERCARD *(CIRCLE ONE)*

Card Number _____ Expiration Date: _____

Name as it appears on Credit Card _____ Charge Amount $ _____

Signature _____

Billing Address _____

Telephone # Day _____ Eve _____

PLEASE NOTE: Your contribution is tax-deductible to the fullest extent allowed by law.
Habitat for Humanity • P.O. Box 1443 • Newport News, VA 23601 • 757-596-5553
www.HelpHabitatforHumanity.org

9 781600 377389